Music Theory for Computer Musicians

Michael Hewitt

Course Technology PTR
A part of Cengage Learning

COURSE TECHNOLOGY
CENGAGE Learning

Australia • Brazil • Japan · Millennium Centre · Inited Kingdom • United States

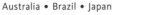

COURSE TECHNOLOGY
CENGAGE Learning

Music Theory for Computer Musicians
Michael Hewitt

Publisher and General Manager, Course Technology PTR: Stacy L. Hiquet

Associate Director of Marketing: Sarah Panella

Manager of Editorial Services: Heather Talbot

Marketing Manager: Mark Hughes

Executive Editor: Mark Garvey

Development Editor: Fran Vincent

Project Editor/Copy Editor: Cathleen D. Small

PTR Editorial Services Coordinator: Erin Johnson

Interior Layout Tech: ICC Macmillan Inc.

Cover Designer: Mike Tanamachi

CD-ROM Producer: Brandon Penticuff

Indexer: Katherine Stimson

Proofreader: Melba Hopper

For product information and technology assistance, contact us at
Cengage Learning Customer & Sales Support, 1-800-354-9706

For permission to use material from this text or product, submit all requests online at **cengage.com/permissions**
Further permissions questions can be emailed to
permissionrequest@cengage.com

All trademarks are the property of their respective owners.

Library of Congress Control Number: 2007941722

ISBN-13: 978-1-59863-503-4

ISBN-10: 1-59863-503-4

Course Technology
25 Thomson Place
Boston, MA 02210
USA

Cengage Learning is a leading provider of customized learning solutions with office locations around the globe, including Singapore, the United Kingdom, Australia, Mexico, Brazil, and Japan. Locate your local office at:
international.cengage.com/region

Cengage Learning products are represented in Canada by Nelson Education, Ltd.

For your lifelong learning solutions, visit **courseptr.com**

Visit our corporate website at **cengage.com**

Printed in the United States of America
6 7 8 9 12 11

This book is dedicated to Coleg Harlech, N. Wales—may it long continue to provide vital adult education.

Acknowledgments

Thanks are due to Mark Garvey for his foresight in seeing the necessity for such a book; Fran Vincent for her intelligent suggestions for the book's further progress; Cathleen Small for her patient, meticulous, and detailed editing; and last but not least, my son, Ashley—a computer musician whose need inspired the writing of this book.

About the Author

Dr. Mike Hewitt was born in South Wales in the United Kingdom. He earned his bachelor of music degree at London University and a master's degree and doctorate at the University of North Wales, Bangor, where he specialized in musical composition. He is a classically trained musician, composer, lecturer, and author on musical subjects. Working to commission, he writes classical scores as well as soundtracks for various television productions both at home and abroad. He is currently working as a music technology tutor at Coleg Harlech in North Wales, whose full-time residential adult education courses are run against the backdrop of the beautiful mountains of Snowdonia.

Contents

Chapter 4
Rhythm, Tempo, and Note Lengths   39

Chapter 5
Score Editing   53

Chapter 6
Intervals   63

Chapter 7
Meter   71

Chapter 8
Chords   87

Chapter 9
The Natural Minor Scale   111

Chapter 10
Melody and Motives   123

Chapter 11
The Harmonic and Melodic Minor Scales 131

Chapter 12
Augmented and Diminished Intervals and Interval Inversions 145

Chapter 13
Chordal Inversions, Octave Doubling, and Spacing 157

Chapter 14
Additive Rhythms 167

Chapter 15
Expanding Your Knowledge of Keys 173

Chapter 16
The Pentatonic Scale 181

Chapter 21
Chords of the Seventh   229

Chapter 22
Exotic Scales   243

Chapter 23
Complex Harmony   253

Chapter 24
Arpeggiation

Chapter 25
Intonation

Chapter 26
Conclusion

Appendix A
Scales

Appendix B
Audio CD and Accompanying Text Sidebars   291

Introduction

With the advancing development of digital technology, today's aspiring electronic music producers enjoy a significant degree of creative freedom. For a cost that seemed unimaginable 10 years ago, electronic music producers now can set up studios in their own homes and produce highly accomplished soundtracks. So professional are some of these tracks that they can literally be sent straight to the record company for final mastering.

This facility has led to a boom of both interest and creativity in the areas of music production. Many independent artists are now producing their own unique music independent of market-led forces. The development of the World Wide Web further enables them to upload their tracks to a potential audience of millions. The degree of freedom such producers now enjoy is clearly unparalleled.

One of the downsides to this freedom is a glut of available music with sometimes dubious quality. Previously, music had to attract the attention of a record label or a radio station to get heard. To do so, it probably had to be music of a high standard in terms of both its originality and its salability. Now anybody can post music online, even if they are just starting out. In some ways this can be useful, because feedback obtained from listeners enables a musician to make improvements. But it also means that there is a lot of bad music out there.

One of the biggest mistakes would-be producers make is believing that by carefully listening to and studying their genre, they can acquire all of the knowledge necessary to be a successful producer. This knowledge can certainly get them a long way toward that point. But sometimes it simply is not enough.

Producers need other kinds of knowledge, such as knowledge of how music works as a language. It is no good writing an effective bass line, lead, and pads, for example, if they are all in different keys. The result is chaotic and unpleasant to listen to. Yet this is a common mistake I hear over and over again. The student's knowledge of the genre is unsurpassed, but the final result falls down because, in purely musical terms, the producer doesn't really know what he is doing.

Beneath all of the enormously different styles of modern electronic music lie certain fundamentals of the musical language that are exactly the same no matter what kind of music you write. It is very important to acquire an understanding of these fundamentals if you are to develop as a music producer. Put simply, you need to know what you are doing with regard to the music that you are writing.

This book aims to explain these fundamentals in as simple and accessible a way as possible. By reading this book and following the exercises contained within it, you, the aspiring music producer/ computer musician, will find yourself making great progress toward understanding and using these fundamentals of the musical language. The result will be a great improvement in your ability to write and produce your own original music.

To help you along your path, this book includes an audio CD with numerous music examples that demonstrate the fundamentals covered in the text. In addition, each chapter ends with a set of chapter exercises. The answers to these exercises can be downloaded from courseptr.com/ downloads.

1 Musical Sound

Whatever your own particular studio setup, it is likely that you will be using a particular music production program as the heart of that setup. Within your program of choice, you will have access to numerous sound-producing devices, such as synthesizers and drum machines. In the end, no matter what kinds of devices you ultimately use, your desired result is the same—a finished musical track. So to begin, I want to take a look at the various characteristics of the sounds you'll be using to create those finished tracks.

Music versus Noise

First, we need to distinguish between noises and musical sounds. Realistically, you can use any sound whatsoever in a track, such as the sound of waves crashing on the shore, excerpts of speeches, samples of animal noises, the noises made by machines, and so on. Samplers, of course, are ideal for importing, manipulating, and sequencing such sounds into compositions.

Percussive noises are also important in electronic music. Whether these result from shaking, scratching, scraping, or banging, they are interpreted by the ear as being musical, provided that they are used within an intelligible rhythmic framework.

However, noises are only a part of the picture. If music used nothing but noises, its appeal to an audience would be much more limited. What makes music so special are sounds that are specifically thought of as being musical. So what makes a sound musical, rather than just being a noise?

The sounds we hear in music result from a vibratory disturbance of the atmosphere and objects in the environment around us—sound waves, in other words. When those sound waves are chaotic, jumbled, and confused, we call the result a *noise*. The pleasure we get from noise is limited. However, some sound sources—particularly musical instruments—produce regular, ordered, and patterned sound waves. These sound sources create music, rather than just noise.

Perhaps you have heard of the experiments of the scientist and acoustician Ernst Chladni, who, by placing sand on metallic plates, discovered that when the plates are bowed with a violin bow, the sand forms into regular geometric patterns. Due to the various harmonic modes of vibration of the metal plate, this regular geometrical patterning is more akin to what we would call music than noise. And, like the crystalline patterns formed by snowflakes, such regular geometric designs have a deep appeal for us.

Compare the waveforms in Figure 1.1. The first one depicts the waveform produced by a random noise, while the second depicts the waveform of a musical sound. Comparing the two, you will see that the first is quite erratic. There is no order or pattern in the waveform. This, in fact, is what we would normally expect from the waveform produced by a noise. Looking now at the second, you will see that the waveform is much more regular and ordered. The peaks and troughs are regular, and the distances between successive phases of the sound wave are more or less uniform. In simple terms, this waveform is ordered, patterned, and, above all, periodic. Here it is no coincidence to see that the second waveform comes from a musical note. Track 1 of the audio CD helps to illustrate this point because it presents what would normally classified as being a noise, as well as a very musical sound.

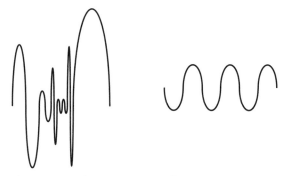

Figure 1.1 The erratic waveform of noise contrasted with the regular periodic vibration of musical sound.

Most musical instruments—including synthesizers—are designed to produce sounds that have regular, harmonic properties. Because of these properties, such sounds have a deep aesthetic appeal that is attractive to the human ear. Musical instruments produce and communicate vibrations through the surrounding atmosphere in the form of sound waves that are regular and periodic, which we call *tones*. Consequently, it is the presence of tone that generally distinguishes music from noise.

A large part of our music is built up from combinations of tones (such as melody and harmony), so to best understand the materials and language of music, you should become familiar with the various parameters of musical tone. These parameters are pitch, intensity, and tone quality, as shown in Figure 1.2.

Before studying these parameters in more detail, you might like to listen to Track 2 on the CD, which presents a single chord that is then transformed in three ways—in terms of its pitch, its intensity, and then its timbre. This example will help you to understand more clearly the parameters discussed later in this chapter.

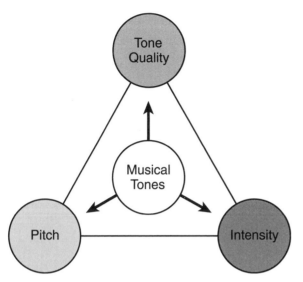

Figure 1.2   The three major parameters of musical tone.

Pitch (Frequency)

Musical tones all have certain pitches. Pitched tones are also called *musical notes*. The pitch of a musical note refers to how high or low the note is in the overall pitch register. Bass notes are lower in the pitch register than treble sounds are. A soprano sings higher notes than a bass does. Pitch is the ear's perception of the wavelengths of the sounds being produced (see Figure 1.3). Lower-pitched sounds have relatively long wavelengths, while higher-pitched sounds have relatively short wavelengths.

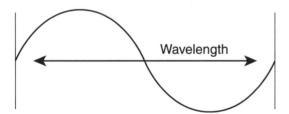

Figure 1.3   Wavelength.

Pitch is also referred to as *frequency*. Frequency is usually measured in Hertz, which is a measurement of the number of sound waves per second. Hertz is often abbreviated as Hz; measurements of frequency in thousands of Hertz are abbreviated as kHz (kilohertz).

The general range of human hearing extends from about 20 Hz to 20 kHz, although this can vary depending upon the sensitivity of the individual ear. Beyond this range are sounds too low to be heard (sub-audible sounds) or those too high to be heard by humans (the super-audible sound register). Even though we cannot hear them, there are other creatures that can. Elephants communicate to each other using sub-audible sounds, as do male alligators seeking a mate. Similarly, operating in the super-audible register, there is the dog whistle, which we cannot hear, as well as the sonic pulses emitted by bats. In both of these cases, the frequencies are so high that we do not register them.

The range of frequencies generally used in music covers a little more than seven octaves of sound, which is the general range covered by a concert grand piano. The ranges of most other instruments tend to be mapped out within that generalized limit. The range is referred to as the *characteristic register* of that instrument (see Figure 1.4).

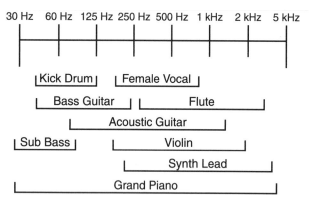

Figure 1.4 General pitch ranges of various instruments.

The notes produced by such instruments are typically stable in terms of their frequency, meaning the ear hears them as notes of a definite pitch. In order for different instruments to work together, they must be tuned. This means that note A on one instrument should ideally be the same note A heard on another instrument. General adjustments in the tuning of instruments are often made to ensure this consistency. So that all instruments sound in tune with each other, there is a generalized pitch standard in which note A (above Middle C) is taken to be 440 Hz. This is the master tuning universally adopted for both standard and electronic musical instruments. I am sure you have heard a symphony orchestra tuning up. Each of the players is ensuring that his instrument produces the correct A. Without this process of tuning, those slight discrepancies of tuning between different instruments would severely mar the performance. Of course, for some instruments, this discrepancy is actually required. A good example is the honky-tonk piano, which produces the kind of sound you get from an old, neglected upright piano that has gradually fallen out of tune.

Another very important pitch standard is note Middle C, which is universally recognized as the central point of the pitch register. Middle C is the note that lies to the left of the two black keys nearest the lock on a piano. Within music software programs that offer a score or notation editor (such as Cubase, Logic, SONAR, Digital Performer, Sibelius, or Finale), Middle C is used as the reference point to decide whether a note goes on the bass or the treble clef. Middle C and all of the notes above it go on the treble clef, while those below it go on the bass clef (see Figure 1.5).

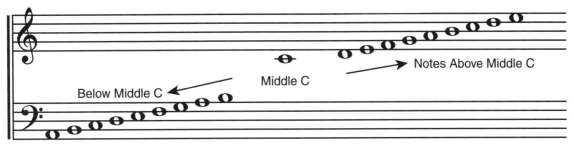

Figure 1.5   Middle C as the midway point between the treble and bass clefs.

Those of you who don't use notation editors will probably be more familiar with the piano roll view, in which a vertical keyboard is placed at the side of a grid. The grid is composed of horizontal bars that represent the pitches of the notes, while the vertical bars represent the length of the notes. In this case, Middle C is the note at the general midpoint of the keyboard, as shown in Figure 1.6.

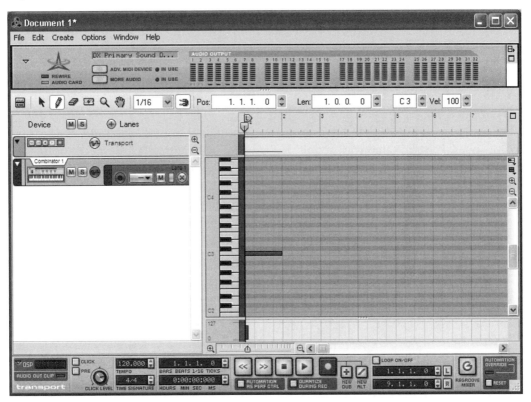

Figure 1.6   Piano roll view of Middle C. (Reason 4.0 software by Propellerhead.)

In Figure 1.6, Middle C is drawn in as a note lasting one bar in length. Notice the number given with each appearance of the note C on the keyboard. This has to do with MIDI (*Musical Instrument Digital Interface*) conventions of pitch, in which each note in the register is identified by a note letter and a number. The number denotes the octave, with Middle C usually recognized as the beginning of the third octave (see Figure 1.7).

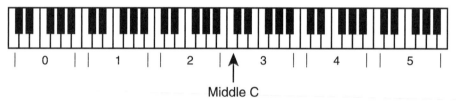

Figure 1.7   Middle C as note C3.

Learning Note Names

It is important for every computer musician to learn the names of the various notes in the pitch register as early as possible. If you don't know these names, it is more difficult to understand, retain, and utilize the complex information about scales, chords, keys, modes, and so on that will follow. The information in Chapter 2, "The Notes," will help you learn these note names.

Intensity (Amplitude)

Another important property of musical tone is the intensity—also known as the *volume,* or how loud or soft the sound is. While the frequency is governed by the length of the sound waves, the intensity is governed by their height. The wave height can also be referred to as the *wave amplitude.* To understand this, think of the waves in the sea. Huge, high waves carry more energy than small, shallow ones. It is the same with sound. High-amplitude sound waves produce sounds of loud volume, compared to low-amplitude sounds, which produce sounds of a softer volume. Consequently, an increase of amplitude will register to the ear as an increase in volume, and vice versa. So Figure 1.8 denotes a musical note that is getting louder.

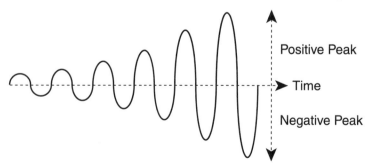

Figure 1.8   Increasing amplitude in a sound wave of a constant wavelength.

Generally, levels of volume are measured in decibels (dB), with 0 dB being considered the quietest possible level of sound that the human ear can pick up. The average conversation takes place at a level of 70 dB, while a jet taking off from a distance of about 200 feet will produce a volume of about 120 dB.

A computer musician will encounter volume in a variety of ways. The master volume of the track is defined through the fader on the main outputs of the mixer. The faders on the separate mixer channels identify the relative volume of each track within the overall mix (see Figure 1.9).

Figure 1.9 Fader levels in a software mixer (Logic).

The volume or intensity of each note (or beat, in the case of drums) used within each of those tracks is called the *velocity*. Velocity is ordinarily represented on a scale from 0 to 127, with 0 being no velocity, 64 being a moderate velocity, and 127 being the maximum velocity (see Figure 1.10).

Variations in the velocity of events, as seen in Figure 1.10, give individual parts a distinct sense of realism in a MIDI environment. You can hear clear differences in velocity in Track 3 on the CD, where you can hear the conga pattern whose velocity graph is given in Figure 1.10.

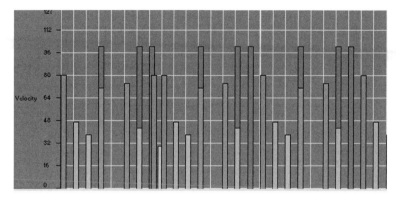

Figure 1.10 Velocity graph of a conga pattern.

Tone Quality (Waveform)

Tone quality—also called *tone color* or *timbre*—is the property that enables the ear to distinguish between the sound of, say, a flute and a violin playing the same note. The tone of the violin has a richness and a warmth compared to the tone of the flute, which is smooth and less complex.

To explain why these sounds have a different timbral quality, you must consider something that is vitally important to both music and our perception of it—the complex makeup of a single musical tone. When you hear a musical tone, you hear it as a readily recognizable singular event. Closer scientific examination of musical tones, however, shows that this is very much an illusion. Each musical tone that you hear is in fact a highly complex blend of vibrations.

This can be understood through reference to the musical tones produced by, say, a guitar. When a string on a guitar is plucked, it vibrates to and fro at a particular rate or speed. As you know from our discussion of frequency, that speed determines the frequency (in cycles per second), and therefore the pitch of the note heard.

However, the guitar string does not just vibrate along its whole length. It also vibrates along the regular fractional lengths of the string, which are the various halves, thirds, quarters, fifths, and so on from which the string as a whole is comprised. These fractional lengths are called *modes of vibration,* and each mode of vibration produces its own characteristic frequency. Figure 1.11 shows a diagram of the first four modes of vibration of the guitar string.

The first mode is called the *fundamental frequency.* Another term for it is the *first partial,* or alternatively the *first harmonic.* The fundamental frequency is of vital importance because it determines the pitch of the note that we hear. But in addition to the fundamental, there are the frequencies produced by the other modes of vibration. These accompany the fundamental, although they are not so distinct. The second mode, for example, corresponding to the vibrations of the halves of the string, produces a frequency double that of the first. Consequently, it is called

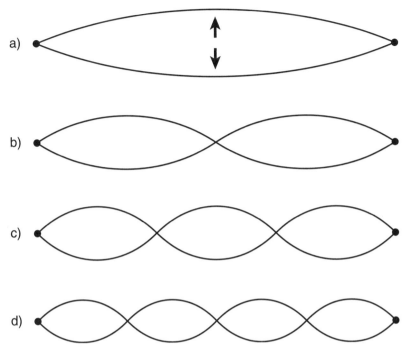

Figure 1.11 The first four modes of vibration of a guitar string.

the *second partial*. The third mode, produced by the various thirds of the string, produces a frequency three times that of the first harmonic. So it is called the *third partial*, and so on.

Theoretically, this extends to infinity, with each fractional part of the string contributing its own frequency to the mix of frequencies that we call a *musical tone*. A musical tone is thus very complex, composed as it is of a whole galaxy of vibrations.

The study of the way in which we hear and perceive these vibrations is called *psychoacoustics*. It is important to realize that after the fundamental, subsequent partials are much fainter to the ear. They do, however, contribute to our perception of the particular tone quality or timbre of that tone. This is rather like the way our eyes blend thousands of separate pixels of different colors on a computer image into an overall visual image. The ear does the same with a musical tone. It blends a huge number of separate vibrations present in a musical tone into a musical note with its own characteristic tone color or quality.

Another good analogy is an atom composed of a nucleus surrounded by a whirling vortex of vibration called the *electron cloud*. The comparative solidity of the nucleus is like the fundamental; the electron cloud is like the harmonics.

Most musical instruments produce musical tones that are rich in such partials. Partials whose frequencies represent whole-number multiples of the fundamental frequency are called *harmonics*.

A succession of such partials—such as 100 Hz, 200 Hz, 300 Hz, 400 Hz, 500 Hz, and so on—is called a *harmonic series*. Most of the instruments we are familiar with produce harmonic partials. This is due to the characteristic nature of the vibrating mechanisms that produce the tone. Pipes, strings, and tubes produce mathematically regular modes of vibration arising from their fractional lengths.

The spectrum of harmonic partials that can be present within a given tone is theoretically infinite. This spectrum is called the harmonic series. In Table 1.1, you can see the first eight harmonics of note A1, frequency of 110 Hz. The table has three columns. In the first column, you will find the harmonic, while the second column gives the note produced by that harmonic. Recall that A2 is an octave higher than A1. A3 is similarly an octave higher than A2, and so on. In the third column, you will see that precise frequency of the harmonic. The final column yields the frequency ratios between harmonics. The ratio between the first and second harmonics is thus 1:2, while the ratio between the third and fifth harmonics is 3:5. The importance of these is that they show the simple mathematical relationships between harmonics.

If you would like to hear these harmonics they are presented in direct succession in audio Track 5. Just remember that the harmonic series as shown in Table 1.1 goes on *ad infinitum*.

Some instruments, such as gongs, bells, and other percussion instruments, produce partials that are not whole-number multiples of the frequency of the fundamental. These are called *inharmonic partials,* and they give rise to sounds of more indefinite pitch.

It has often been said that there is a strong connection between mathematics and music. The harmonic series shows that this connection goes deeper than we think. Each musical tone is a complex mathematical configuration of vibrations. Looking at the data in Table 1.1, you can see that these extend over numerous octaves of the pitch register.

Table 1.1 Harmonic Series: The First Eight Harmonics of A

Harmonic	Note	Frequency	Ratio
First (Fundamental)	A1	110 Hz	1
Second	A2	220 Hz	2
Third	E3	330 Hz	3
Fourth	A3	440 Hz	4
Fifth	C#4	550 Hz	5
Sixth	E4	660 Hz	6
Seventh	Fx4	770 Hz	7
Eighth	A4	880 Hz	8

Many of the skills that you learn as a computer musician directly deal with this basic fact. Through the use of EQ, for example, you can attenuate the upper harmonics of a note, leading to a distinct brightening of its sound. In contrast, you can suppress the upper harmonics, leading to the opposite—a much duller and less obtrusive sound. The skill of successful equalization lies in getting the balance just right.

The harmonic series is also important in many other ways. When you go on to learn about musical harmony in subsequent chapters, you will discover that the harmonic series of each note determines what notes will actually harmonize with it. This is due to the harmonics that the notes share in common. The more harmonics the notes share, the better they get on together—a bit like common interests in human relationships. So, they are heard as a harmony rather than as a discord. You'll learn more about this in Chapter 8, "Chords."

So far we have only looked at musical tones produced by conventional instruments. What about musical tones produced by electronic instruments, such as synthesizers? Here it is important to realize that synthesizers only became viable in the first place through the application of the various sciences surrounding the understanding of musical tone. In simple terms, if you could devise an electronic instrument that could produce harmonic frequencies at various intensities, you could feasibly imitate the waveforms of those sounds produced by conventional instruments. This imitation is loosely called *synthesis*, and the instruments that employ it are called *synthesizers*.

Synthesis

The sound-producing component of a synthesizer is called the *oscillator*. The oscillator is capable of producing both frequency and harmonic content. This means that the oscillator can produce notes of a recognizable pitch and that the oscillator can impart to those notes a particular quality or timbre. This latter gives the synthesizer the capability to reproduce the characteristic complex waveforms associated with instruments such as pianos, violins, brass instruments, and so on.

The most basic waveform produced by oscillators is the sine wave, composed of only one specific frequency. Three other simple types of waveforms are the square, triangle, and sawtooth. Figure 1.12 shows all four of these.

The square wave is produced by emphasizing odd-numbered harmonics, and it produces notes of a quite hollow sound, which work a real treat in the basses of many different types of dance music. The triangular waveform emphasizes few specific odd-numbered partials and, as a result, produces a clear note that is good for imitating the sounds of flutes, for example. The most complex waveform here is the sawtooth, which is extremely rich in harmonics. These waveforms are used to imitate string and brass sounds, as well as those beautifully rich leads characteristic of trance music. The characteristic sounds of these waveforms can be heard in audio Track 4.

In the process of additive synthesis, the required waveform is obtained by adding harmonic waves to a given fundamental. The reverse process—subtractive synthesis—begins with a waveform that is rich in harmonic content and then selectively filters out certain frequencies.

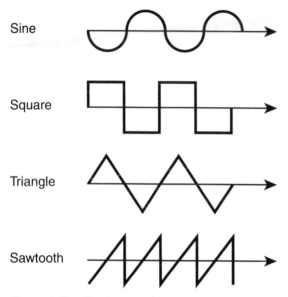

Sine

Square

Triangle

Sawtooth

Figure 1.12 Simple waveforms.

To accurately synthesize a sound, it is also necessary to take into account the sound envelope—the characteristic way in which a sound develops through time. There are four components to the sound envelope—attack, decay, sustain, and release. Attack represents the way in which the sound starts from an initial low and then reaches a peak value. Decay is the way a sound fades away. Consider the case of a piano: The attack is immediate, yet when the sound reaches a peak, it immediately starts to fade. Contrast this with the sound of an organ, which has no decay. Sustain is the period during which the peak value is maintained. Finally, there is the release, which is the time it takes for the sound to disappear once the note has been released.

By looking at the ingredients of the sound envelope, you can appreciate that it represents a pretty important part of the process of synthesis. By emulating the envelope of a sound as well as its harmonic content, you can create more or less realistic imitations of the sounds of conventional instruments. But of course that is not the entire picture. Because of the various parameters of electronically produced sounds—many of which are under your control—you can alter a sound in any way that you choose. You can also produce sounds that are totally unique. This is very much a matter for experimentation and represents one of the most fascinating features of electronically produced sounds. Through them, it is feasible to create entirely new kinds of music.

Yet whatever type of music you create using electronic instruments, it is still music. So any skills that you develop with regard to electronic music production need to be augmented and supplemented by an understanding and appreciation of music itself. It has been said that music is a language, and to be able to communicate effectively through that language, you must understand the language thoroughly. Here, one of the most important foundations for such an understanding is the recognition of the various terms and symbols surrounding the notes used in the language of music. These will be discussed and explained in the next chapter.

Exercises

You can download the answers to the chapter exercises from www.courseptr.com/downloads.

1. Fill in the missing words. Musical tone has three basic properties. These are
   _____, _____, and _____.

2. Fill in the missing words. The frequency of sound is measured in terms of
   _____. When abbreviated, this term appears as _____.

3. If the frequency of the first harmonic is given as 220 Hz, what are the frequencies of the following harmonics?
   - Second harmonic: _____
   - Fifth harmonic: _____

4. Fill in the missing words. Oscillators generate two main properties. These are
   _____ content and _____.

5. Name three examples of different timbres.
   A. _____
   B. _____
   C. _____

6. Fill in the missing words in this paragraph. The characteristic _____ of a sound is determined by its harmonic content. The harmonic content of a sound largely determines the _____. The simplest of all waveforms is the sine wave. There are three other important simple waveforms—the sawtooth, the _____, and the _____ waveforms.

7. Match these six to form three related pairs.

1	4
Wavelength	Tone Quality

2	5
Frequency	Volume

3	6
Waveform	Amplitude

8. Choose the correct answer. The master tune standard for Western electronic instruments is:

    A. 256 Hz

    B. 332 Hz

    C. 192 Hz

    D. 440 Hz

    E. 368 Hz

9. Fill in the missing word. How is the volume of sound measured? The volume of sound is measured in _____.

10. Fill in the missing words. The intensity of each note within a particular sequencer track or channel is also known as the _____. This is measured on a scale from _____ to _____.

11. If the frequency of the first mode of vibration shown below (A) is given as 64 Hz, what would be the frequencies produced by:

    B. _____

    C. _____

    D. _____

12. Fill in the missing words.: The first partial is also known as the _____ frequency. If subsequent partials are related by whole numbers to the _____ frequency, the series is called _____.

13. Fill in the missing words. A sound vibration of increasing amplitude manifests to the _____ as an _____ of _____.

14. Fill in the missing words. The sound envelope is the characteristic way in which a sound develops through time. It has four components, which are the _____, _____, _____, and _____.

2 The Notes

This chapter will extend your knowledge of pitch and will look at how the different notes used in music are universally represented in all music software programs. Learning how notes are represented and named is an important prelude to understanding and making effective use of many of the basic materials of music, including chords, scales, keys, modes, and so on.

Learning the Notes

A good way to learn the names of the notes is by using a MIDI keyboard (see Figure 2.1). Observe that the black and white keys together make up a particular pattern. The black keys tend to be grouped in twos and threes, and while there is a black key between some of the white keys, between others there is not. Getting a grasp on this pattern is the first step toward being able to identify the notes of the scale.

Figure 2.1 Learn the names of notes by using a MIDI keyboard.

Locating Note C

The most important note to learn first is C. This is the white key that is always to the left of any group of two black keys. Once you've located this key, notice that there is more than one of these keys. Depending upon the range of the keyboard, there are any number of note Cs—up to about seven. These represent note C as it occurs in different octaves. Look at the synthesizer keyboard in Figure 2.2—all of the note Cs as they occur in different octaves have been labeled. On the right-hand side, you can see the piano roll with which you may trigger, via MIDI, the equivalent note on the synthesizer.

The word *octave* relates to the number eight. From note C, count the white keys up until you reach note C again. This happens after eight keys. The distance between note Cs—eight notes either up or down—is thus called an octave (see Figure 2.3).

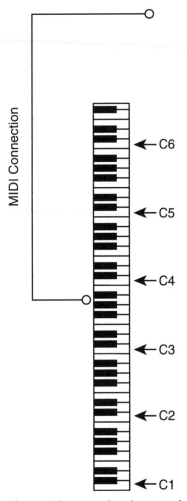

Figure 2.2 Note C as it occurs in different octaves (piano roll format).

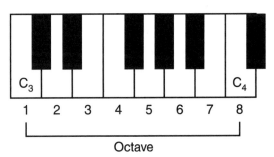

Figure 2.3 Octave relationship between notes of the same name.

Why are notes an octave apart called by the same note letter? The answer to this question comes down to the unique properties of the interval of the octave.

Each note generates harmonics. As discussed in Chapter 1, after the fundamental frequency—the first harmonic—there is the second harmonic, with a frequency double that of the first. Therefore, if the frequency of the fundamental is given as 220 HZ (the note A below Middle C), the frequency of the second harmonic will be 440 HZ (the note A above Middle C)—a frequency which would be heard as being an octave higher.

This relationship between the two frequencies is represented by the diagram in Figure 2.4. Observe how two waves of the second harmonic fit neatly into a single wave of the first harmonic. Because the second harmonic has a frequency double that of the first harmonic, their relationship can be represented in the form of a ratio—in this case, 2:1.

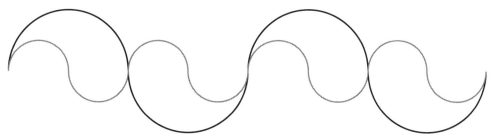

Figure 2.4   Sound waves of 2:1 frequency ratio.

If another note is played with a frequency double that of the lowermost note (a frequency ratio of 2:1), the ear thus recognizes a special relationship between them. This is because the upper note is simply reinforcing the second harmonic of the lower note. This connection that the ear recognizes between the two notes is the strongest one known in musical harmony. In fact, it is so strong that the two notes are heard as being virtually identical. This is why two notes an octave apart are *named by the same note letter*. They are related according to the frequency ratio of 2:1. Figure 2.5 depicts this relationship. The note C4, lying an octave above the note C3, has a frequency double that of C3. This is why they are both called note C. Note that it is a convention to depict the upper number of a frequency ratio first.

To distinguish between notes of the same name in different octaves, a number is used to indicate the octave in which the note occurs. Refer back to Figure 2.1. There you can see the number of each respective note C. Your main point of reference is usually C3, which corresponds to Middle C (see Figure 2.6). All of the notes above that carry the same note number until you reach C4, and so it continues.

Octave numbers make learning the note names much easier because you only need to learn the names of the notes in one octave. All other octaves have the same note names but with different

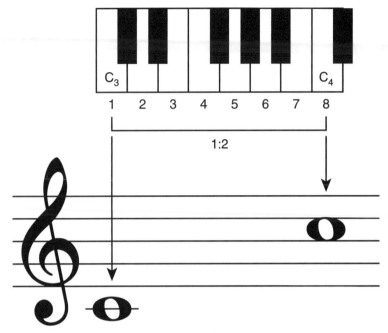

Figure 2.5   Octave relationship as 2:1 frequency ratio.

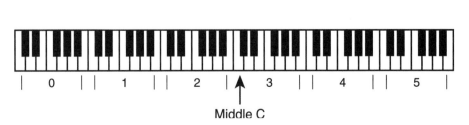

Middle C

Figure 2.6   Notes and their octave numbers.

numbers to distinguish the octave in which they occur. Music software programs include these numbers in the piano roll view so you can easily work it out for yourself.

The Musical Alphabet

Once you know the position of note C on the keyboard, the rest of the keys are easy to name because they follow the pattern of the musical alphabet, moving upward from C (see Figure 2.7). The musical alphabet only has seven letters: A, B, C, D, E, F, G. Once you reach G, you return to A.

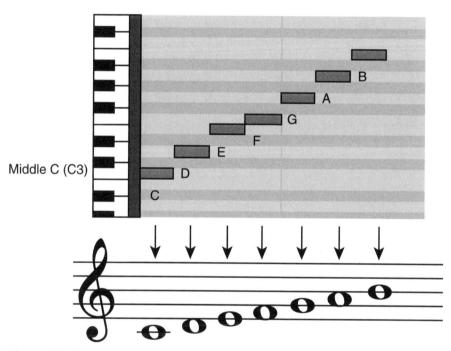

Figure 2.7 Names of the seven white keys.

When you are trying to memorize these names, remember to follow this procedure:

1. Locate C as the white key to the left of the two black keys.

2. Count forward in the musical alphabet for each white key.

When you've accomplished this, try a more difficult exercise:

1. Locate C as the white key to the left of the two black keys.

2. Count backward in the musical alphabet, going down from C for each white key.

The Names of the Black Keys

When you have the names of the white keys firmly planted in your memory, it is relatively easy to remember the names of the black keys. The black keys are all sharps and flats of the white keys.

Locate note D on the MIDI keyboard. Then go up to the nearest black key. Play this note to hear that it is slightly higher (sharper) in pitch than note D. This note is called *D sharp*. When written, it is expressed as the note letter followed by a sharp sign: D#.

Return to note D. Now go down to the nearest black key. You will hear that this note is slightly flatter in pitch than note D. This note is called *D flat*. When written, it is expressed as the note letter followed by a flat sign: Db. When represented on the staff, the sharp or flat sign precedes the note it affects, as shown in Figure 2.8.

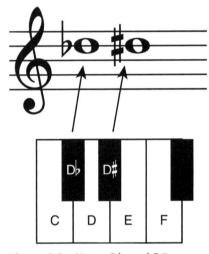

Figure 2.8   Notes Db and D#.

All of the notes of the original white-key scale can be treated in this way (sharpened or flattened). And this is how the black keys acquire their names—as the sharps or flats (alterations) of the white keys.

Notice that the same black key can have more than one name. The nearest black key up from note C is note C sharp. Yet this black key has already been named as D flat. Each black key can therefore have two names, depending upon whether it is used as a sharp of the white key below or as a flat of the black key above (see Figure 2.9).

Notes related in this way are called *enharmonic equivalents*. This is because really they are the same note. C sharp is the same note as D flat. The difference lies in the context in which the note

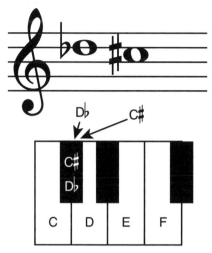

Figure 2.9   Enharmonic equivalence of D flat and C sharp.

is used. When we go on to look at different keys later in this book, you will understand this more clearly.

So the names of the black keys can now be given as shown in Figure 2.10.

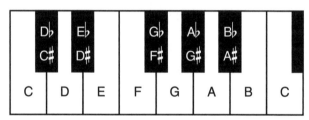

Figure 2.10   Names of the black keys.

Importance of Note Names

Knowledge of these note names is important for numerous reasons. First, it provides a foundation for the successful understanding and use of musical scales, keys, modes, chords, and so on, and the various musical values that arise from the use of these within musical compositions. Our study of these values will begin in earnest in Chapter 3, "The Major Scale."

Second, such knowledge enables you to know which note you are playing on your synthesizer or sampler. Here you can be pretty sure that note D#4 on one synth will correspond to note D#4 on another. In the case of samplers, you need to know the note names so that you know which key a sample is assigned to. On a sampled drum kit, if the open hi-hats are assigned to note A#2, you need to know where A#2 is.

This is useful knowledge when you are editing your compositions. Many musical software programs offer Event editors. The example in Figure 2.11 is from the Event editor in Cakewalk's SONAR.

Trk	HMSF	MBT	Ch	Kind	Data		
1	00:00:00:00	1:01:000	1 Note	F 7		80	240
1	00:00:00:00	1:01:000	1 Note	D 7		80	240
1	00:00:00:00	1:01:000	1 Note	G 6		76	240
1	00:00:00:00	1:01:000	1 Note	Bb6		66	240
1	00:00:00:15	1:01:777	1 Note	Eb6		82	224
1	00:00:00:15	1:01:780	1 Note	C 6		84	192
1	00:00:00:15	1:01:793	1 Note	Bb6		90	183
1	00:00:00:15	1:01:793	1 Note	G 6		84	219
1	00:00:00:27	1:02:480	1 Note	G 6		90	480
1	00:00:00:27	1:02:480	1 Note	Eb6		84	480
1	00:00:00:27	1:02:480	1 Note	C 6		96	480
1	00:00:00:27	1:02:480	1 Note	Bb6		90	480
1	00:00:01:14	1:03:432	1 Note	Bb6		96	112
1	00:00:01:14	1:03:432	1 Note	C 6		102	96
1	00:00:01:14	1:03:432	1 Note	Eb6		99	112
1	00:00:01:14	1:03:432	1 Note	G 6		99	96
1	00:00:01:24	1:04:000	1 Note	Bb6		96	480

Figure 2.11 Event editor in SONAR.

This editor offers much useful information about each event within a composition. Crucially, such events are represented by the note names you have just learned. Therefore, knowledge of these names gives you an immediate ability to recognize and edit each event within your composition.

In the case of samplers, knowledge of the note names is equally essential. In multi-sampled instruments, such as pianos, organs, and so on, it is generally accepted that note D#4 will produce a pitch corresponding to that note. In more generalized cases of sampling, such as the sampling of vocal phrases, natural sounds, and drum hits, the sample will be entered at its own natural pitch, regardless of the note to which it has been assigned. When a sample is assigned to a particular note of the keyboard in this way, this note is called the *root note* of the sample. To know and recognize these root notes, you must learn the names of the notes.

Through your study of this chapter, you have learned the names of the notes used in music. As a result, you have taken an important first step toward improving your grasp of the fundamentals of the language of music. And as a result of that first step, you can now begin to approach the raw materials from which music is made up. Consider, for example, the notes whose names you have just learned. Composers do not use these notes at random. In nearly all cases, the composer uses a selection of the available range of notes that suits his purpose. Such a selection necessarily includes some notes and excludes others. You have probably heard such a selection being referred to as a *musical scale*. To start you off with the study of these musical scales, the next chapter will look at the most basic scale used in our music—the scale of C major.

Exercises

You can download the answers to the chapter exercises from www.courseptr.com/downloads.

1. Draw in where the black keys should be on this keyboard. The position of note C has been given for you.

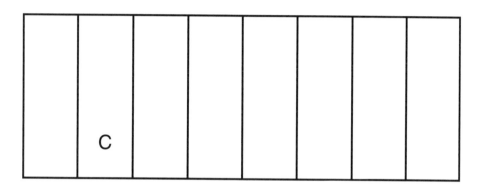

2. Choose the correct answer for the following statement. Note C is always:

   A. The white key to the left of the three black keys.

   B. The white key to the right of the three black keys.

   C. The white key to the left of the two black keys.

   D. The white key to the right of the two black keys.

3. Fill in the missing words. From note C, it is necessary to count up or down _____ notes to reach note C again. The distance between any two adjacent C's on the keyboard is called a(n) _____.

4. Fill in the missing words. The ratio between two notes an octave apart is _____:_____. If the frequency of the first note is given as 336 Hz, the frequency of the note an octave above will be _____.

5. Place the seven letters of the musical alphabet in the boxes provided, in order from the lowest to the highest.

6.   Fill in the names of all of the white keys on this keyboard.

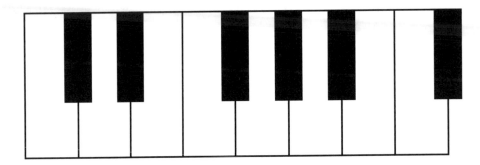

7.   Fill in the missing words. The first black key to the right of note D is called
_____, while the first black key to the left of note E is called
_____. Because these are the same key but spelled differently, they are
classed as being _____ equivalents.

8.   Answer the following questions.

A. What does the symbol # mean?

B. What does the symbol b mean?

C. Name five black keys that use the symbol #.

D. Name five black keys that use the symbol b.

9.   Label all of the notes correctly in the circles provided on this keyboard. Remember to
give each black key two names.

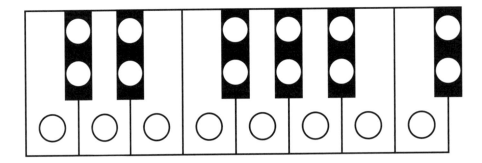

10.   Identify the key on the keyboard to which the following samples have been assigned.
The first key has already been labeled for you:

■ 1: Note F#3, closed hi-hat

■ 2: Note D#3, clap

- 3: Note A#3, open hi-hat
- 4: Note D3, snare
- 5: Note D#4, ride cymbal
- 6: Note F#4, tambourine
- 7: Note C#4, crash cymbal
- 8: Note G#4, vocal hit
- 9: Note C3, kick drum

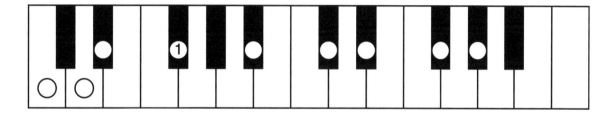

3   The Major Scale

You can put your knowledge of the names of the notes on the MIDI keyboard to good use when approaching musical scales. A *scale* is a rising or falling series of notes, usually within the range of an octave—and repeated in all other octaves. Music of every possible kind uses scales. Notes are selected from a scale for the purposes of melody and harmony. In a melody, the notes of the scale are used successively—that is, as a linear progression of notes, as shown on the left side of Figure 3.1—whereas in a chord, different notes of a scale are played at the same time, as shown on the right side of Figure 3.1. Both draw their notes from a particular scale.

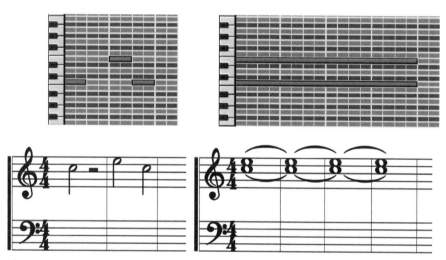

Figure 3.1   Notes C and E used melodically and harmonically.

Types of Scales

There are many kinds of scales used in the music of the world: the chromatic, major, and minor scales common to Western classical and popular music (as discussed in Chapters 3, 9, 11, and 15); the pentatonic scale popular in both folk and dance music (as discussed in Chapter 16); the microtonal scales found in the music of the Near and Far East (see Chapter 25); the modal scales also used in folk music and popular, experimental rock, and dance music (see Chapter 20); the octatonic and hexatonic scales often used as variants of the major and minor scales by modern classical and film composers (see Chapter 22); and the exotic scales commonly used by composers and music producers to create unusual atmospheres (see Chapter 22). Knowing these scales puts the music writer in a very good position because there is a scale for every musical purpose and situation. That knowledge also enables the writer to create music that has a clear sense of harmony and coherence. This book will look at all of these scales, together with their uses in the process of writing electronic music. The purpose of this chapter is to introduce you to one of the most popular scales used in music throughout the world—the major scale.

Introducing the Major Scale

The major scale is so named because, as you will learn later (in Chapter 9, "The Natural Minor Scale," and Chapter 10, "Melody and Motives"), the primary chords it offers are bright major chords as opposed to the darker-sounding minor chords of the minor scale. As a scale system in its own right, the major scale has been used by musicians for thousands of years, and it is difficult to estimate how many thousands of pieces of music have been written using it. Certainly today it accounts for a massive number of songs, and its popularity with songwriters shows no sign of waning. There is something universal about the major scale that appeals to everybody. Although it is a generally bright-sounding scale—unlike the more moody and introspective minor scale—it is also capable of expressing strong emotions. John Lennon's timeless song "Imagine" is a classic example of a song written in C major. Another example is the famous "Somewhere Over the Rainbow."

Key

To approach an understanding of the major scale, you must consider another important element of music—key. Scale and key are closely related. *Key* concerns the note upon which a scale is built. The MIDI keyboard—modeled upon the piano and organ of traditional music—has five black and seven white keys in any octave, thus giving a total of twelve notes. Any of these keys—white or black—can be the starting point upon which a scale is built. The keyboard thus enables use of any one of twelve separate keynotes—the individual names of which you learned in Chapter 2. A scale that has note C as the starting point is said to be in the key of C.

Scale

The easiest scale to learn is the major scale in the key of C. This is because its seven notes correspond to the seven white keys on the MIDI keyboard. So as long as you can locate note C, the C major scale is easy to recall. And the names of the notes in this scale are simply the seven letters of the musical alphabet starting at C: C, D, E, F, G, A, B. Each of the seven notes of the C major scale is given a number that shows its order in the scale, with the first degree—note C—being given the number 1 (see Figure 3.2).

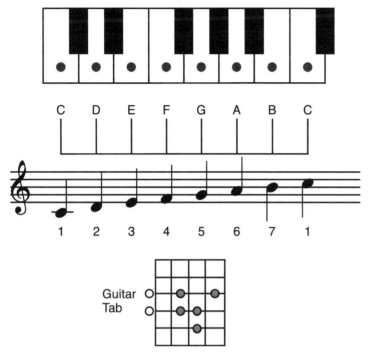

Figure 3.2 The C major scale.

The best way to come to grips with a scale is to learn to play it up and down on a keyboard, guitar, bass, or your favored instrument (see Figure 3.3). The process of learning the scale is a musical conditioning that puts that pattern of notes firmly in your memory. Once you've achieved the physical process of learning the scale, it becomes much easier to play, improvise, and write music comfortably using that particular scale. When learning how to play it, do not be tempted to go too fast. Play nice and slowly and try to get an even tone on each note. Track 6 on the CD indicates the speed for which you should be aiming.

Here, though, the edge will always be with the trained musician. There is nothing like playing songs in a particular key to give a person a feeling for that key. If decks or a MIDI keyboard are the only instrument used, then the situation is different. As a music technology tutor, I meet computer musicians all the time, many of whom do not play any conventional musical instruments. All of these musicians, without exception, express a desire to improve their keyboard skills. Because the MIDI keyboard represents the point of entry into the computer for vital musical information, it makes perfect sense that such students want to improve their keyboard skills. Some kind of ability in playing the keyboard makes it much easier to compose and record basses, drum patterns, leads, and harmonies. Generally, therefore, two choices present themselves to computer musicians. They can take up a conventional keyboard instrument, such as the piano, which will provide the musical experience needed. Alternatively, they can endeavor to patiently assimilate knowledge through use of the MIDI keyboard by playing and sequencing exercises, examples of which have been provided for you in this book.

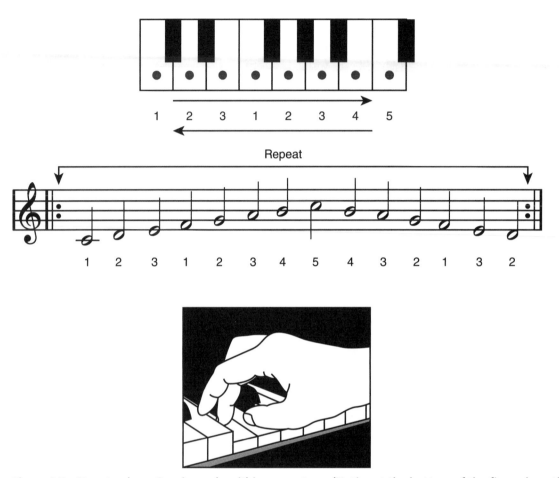

Figure 3.3 How to play a C major scale within one octave. (Notice at the bottom of the figure how the player crosses his thumb under to play the F note.)

Playing the C Major Scale

To play the C major scale on the MIDI keyboard, start with the thumb—which in keyboard terms is called *finger 1*—and then play D with the second finger and E with the third finger. For F, the thumb is passed under the hand, and the rest of the notes upward are then played using the next available finger (refer to Figure 3.3). When top C is reached, the descent begins where the fingering pattern is then reversed.

It is difficult to overstate the value of this simple exercise. All instrumentalists have to go through this training. The importance of the exercise lies in the fact that it combines theory and practice. It is one thing to know the names of the notes, but it is another to hear them clearly in your mind. Through such exercises, your inner ear and aural memory are developed. Until you can clearly "hear" the scale simply by imagining it, you must continue to practice. If you do not have

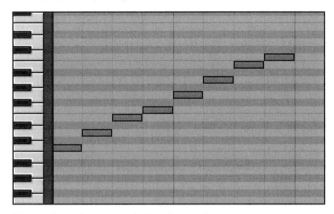

Figure 3.4 Sequenced C major scale.

access to a MIDI keyboard, an alternative is to sequence the scale up and down and listen very carefully to the result (see Figure 3.4).

Understanding Intervals

The C major scale is called a major scale because it follows a particular pattern of intervals. What is an interval? It is the gap between two notes. The octave considered earlier is an example of an interval. Another example is the major third between notes C and E, shown in Figure 3.1. You'll notice that the intervals between adjacent notes of the C major scale are not all the same size. This is important to know, so I will now explain it further.

The interval or gap between any two adjacent notes on the keyboard (or frets on the guitar) is called a *semitone* (see Figure 3.5).

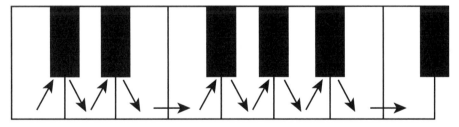

Figure 3.5 Semitone gaps on a keyboard.

If you count the number of arrows in Figure 3.5, you'll realize that there are 12 such gaps in a single octave. Each of these has an equal size of 1/12 of an octave. There are thus 12 semitones in the octave. This series of semitones embraces a scale of pitches, which is called the *chromatic scale*. Although the chromatic scale is not generally used as a musical scale in its own right, it offers those notes in the octave from which the notes for a given scale may be selected. The C major scale uses seven of those notes—the seven white keys. In this context, the five black keys are not needed.

Because there is a black key between the notes C and D, this means the gap between them is two semitones. A gap of this sort is also called a *tone*. Similar gaps are found between notes D and E, F and G, and A and B. However, between notes E and F (as well as B and C), there are no black keys. This means that the gap here is a semitone (see Figure 3.6).

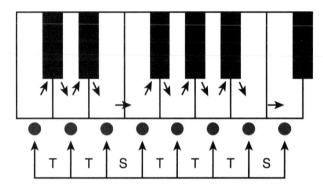

T = Tone   S = Semitone

Figure 3.6   Tone and semitone.

From this discussion, you can see that the major scale is defined by a characteristic pattern of tones and semitones that make it up. It is important to realize that this difference between tones and semitones in the major scale cannot be seen or recognized when the notes are placed on the staff. These differences only become apparent when the notes of the major scale are plotted on the keyboard (see Figure 3.7).

On a guitar, this pattern would translate as 2212221 of successive frets (see Figure 3.8).

The importance of this is that once the pattern of tones and semitones is known, it becomes possible to build a major scale on any note simply by counting up from that note: tone, tone, semitone, tone, tone, tone, semitone. You can work out major scales for other keys following this basic pattern.

For present purposes, you will find it useful to memorize this pattern. Two useful formats to memorize are numerical and letter. The numerical format goes 2212221 and describes the number of semitones between each of the steps of the major scale. The letter format uses the abbreviations of T for tone and S for semitone. It thus goes TTSTTTS. In Figure 3.9, you can see how this applies when we try to sequence a major scale on the note F# within a piano roll view of a MIDI track.

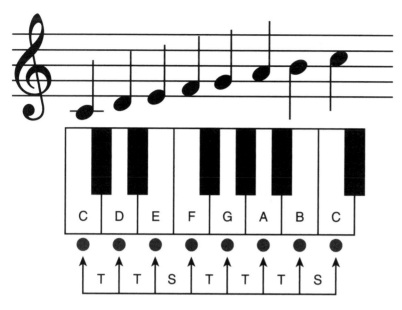

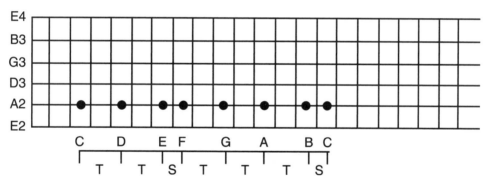

T = Tone   S = Semitone

Figure 3.7 Tones and semitones within the major scale.

Figure 3.8 Tones and semitones on the frets of a guitar.

TTSTTTS is a useful formula because it enables you to build the same scale system on other keynotes, thus giving you access to an entire range of keys. Chapter 15, "Expanding Your Knowledge of Keys," will discuss the further ramifications of this.

As a complete musical scale system in its own right, the scale of C major offers all the notes needed for an entire composition. You can use these notes to create lead melodies, basses, and beautiful harmonies. The art of doing so lies in using leads, basses, and harmonies that all go together. Recognizing and using a key and scale system is one of the first steps toward creating beautiful music because it means that all of your musical layers are in a particular scale and key and thus work together musically.

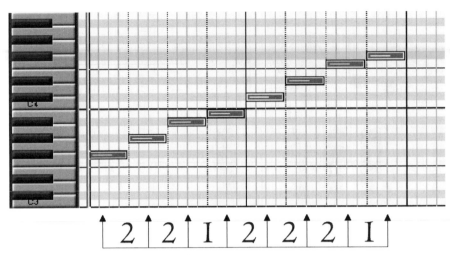

Figure 3.9 Building a major scale on F#.

Having looked at a musical scale, you now have a better understanding of the world of pitch—that is, the notes used in a composition with which you can make melodies and harmonies. Coupled with this, you also need to undertake an in-depth study of the world of musical time. How long each note lasts in the composition and the rhythms created by the combination of these note lengths is the topic for the next chapter.

Exercises

You can download the answers to the chapter exercises from www.courseptr.com/downloads.

1. Fill in the missing words: The C _____ scale has _____ notes per octave. Their names are _____.

2. List three kinds of scales used in music:

    A. _____

    B. _____

    C. _____

3. Fill in the missing words. A scale that takes note _____ as the tonic note is said to be in the _____ of C.

4. Which degree of the scale are these notes in C major?

    ■ D: _____

    ■ B: _____

- G: _____

- F: _____

5. The interval between any two adjacent notes on the keyboard or _____ on the guitar is called a _____. The octave is composed of _____ such semitones. These are called the 12-tone _____ scale.

6. The pattern of tones and semitones that makes up the major scale is:

    _____ _____ _____ _____ _____ _____ _____

7. Define the gaps between the following pairs of notes in terms of the number of semitones:

    A. C–D: _____

    B. B–C: _____

    C. A–B: _____

    D. E–F: _____

8. Fill in the missing words. The most important note in the C major scale is the _____ scale degree, which is also called the _____. This note serves as the _____ center of music written in that key.

9. Play the C major scale. Practice this exercise on the MIDI keyboard until it is fluent.

4 Rhythm, Tempo, and Note Lengths

It is time now to take a break from pitch values and to look at a parameter of musical sound we haven't explored so far—duration. Every sound used in a musical composition has a particular duration or length. This duration represents its value in the dimension of musical time. The succession of such values or events occurring in and through musical time is called the *rhythm*. In this sense, the parameter of duration is of great importance because it provides the building blocks upon which rhythm is based. Rhythm, of course, is and always has been an absolutely essential ingredient of music of all kinds. In fact, without rhythm there probably could not *be* any music.

A deep understanding of rhythm is essential to today's modern computer music producer, especially when it comes to the process of drum programming. Virtually every recognizable style of modern electronic music relies heavily on the presence of a good drum or percussion track. And when it comes to the various styles of dance music, the drum track is probably the most important feature. After all, it is the beat that we dance to.

These days it is not enough to rely on other people's loops when it comes to putting a percussion track into music. Any producer worth his salt will produce his own drum and percussion tracks. To do this successfully, it is invaluable to listen carefully to percussion tracks, to study and observe live drummers and percussionists, and to study the types of drums and percussion instruments used. For example, just what is a guiro? How do percussionists play it? What is the range of techniques used to play it, and what types of sounds are liable to be obtained from it? Suffice it to say, a careful study like this can bring your library of drum samples to life. In your imagination you can hear the guiro player and see how he is playing the instrument. (A guiro, by the way, is simply a washboard, and a stick is used to scrape it.) Figure 4.1 shows a variety of such percussion instruments.

A good grounding in rhythm will also put you in good stead when it comes to melodic and harmonic composition. One of the most important features of a successful and effective bass line is often its distinctive rhythm. Styles of music (such as house, hard dance, techno, and drum and bass) are often distinguished by the driving rhythms of their bass lines. Good melodic leads and riffs also tend to have a very recognizable sense of rhythm about them. Chapter 10, "Melody and Motives," goes more deeply into this.

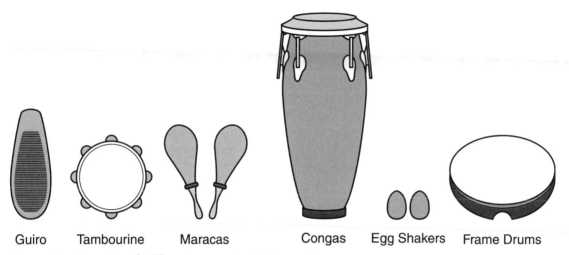

Guiro   Tambourine   Maracas   Congas   Egg Shakers   Frame Drums

Figure 4.1 A variety of different percussion instruments.

Harmonies and chords also have their own distinctive rhythm—called *harmonic rhythm*—which is the rhythm engendered by the chord changes in a song. And chords are often heard and presented in a strong and identifiable rhythmic context.

Pulse and Beat

An understanding of the nature of rhythm begins with observation of the world and ourselves as a part of it. It is immediately obvious that rhythm plays a vital part in the world—in fact, our lives are totally governed by it. There is the rhythm of the seasons, the tides, and the phases of the moon, as well as that important diurnal rhythm by which our lives are regulated and controlled—the alternation of night and day.

Looking at ourselves, we can also see rhythm in abundance—in the beating of our hearts, the inhalation and exhalation of breath, the rhythmic action of peristalsis, the process of walking. Rhythm, in fact, is everywhere, both within and without.

So it is perhaps no coincidence to discover that the rhythms of music tend to take their cue from such natural rhythms. Musical time tends to be divided up into regular beats—pulses of a consistent duration that emulate those regular rhythms of nature. Regardless of whether the music has a percussion track, an ability to listen to and understand the music heard often depends upon an ability to pick up and follow this beat.

Tempo

Once you accept the idea of a pulse or beat, it becomes apparent that the beat can be relatively fast or slow. This speed is called the *tempo*. Our psychological sense of tempo is strongly related to the heartbeat. It has been scientifically proven that beats faster than the average speed of the human heart (about 80 beats per minute) tend to stimulate and excite, whereas those slower than the heartbeat have a calming effect.

The tempo of music is determined by the duration of the beat—how long it lasts. This determines the number of beats that occur per minute. This value is used to precisely define the tempo of the music.

Table 4.1 lists some average beat lengths associated with different types of music.

Table 4.1 Various Tempos in Beats per Minute (BPM)

Tempo	Beats per Minute
Ambient	50–100 BPM
Hip-hop	70–95 BPM
Deep house	110–130 BPM
Trance	130–145 BPM
Hard dance/hardcore	145–170 BPM
Drum and bass	160–180 BPM

Note Lengths

The beat length determines how fast or slow the music is felt to be going. The relative beat length is something different—it describes the length of a given beat relative to others within a composition. Take a look at the example in Table 4.2, in which two notes of the hi-hat occur for every note of the kick drum.

Table 4.2 Kick Drum Quarters and Hi-Hat Eighths

	1	2	3	4	5	6	7	8
Kick drum	<	<	<	<				
Hi-hat	<	<	<	<	<	<	<	<

To hear what this table is trying to get across, listen to Track 7 on the CD. For your information, Tracks 8, 9, and 10, together with the text provided in Appendix B, offer further information and examples of rhythmic patterns in the process of drumming. In Table 4.2, we have all of the ingredients of an identifiable rhythm. The kick drum marks out the pulse by which the tempo is gauged, while the hi-hat marks out a two-to-one rhythm—two beats of the hi-hat for every beat of the kick drum. The hi-hat beats are consequently half the length of the kick drum beats, which represents a fractional expression of their length.

Although Table 4.2 crudely conveys the information in a graphic format, for musical purposes there is a much better system, in which the fractional note lengths by which rhythms are expressed and notated are given particular names and symbols. If you learn these, you can express and notate with total accuracy even the most complex and intricate of rhythms.

In this system, I am referring to crotchets, quavers, minims, and so on. This particular method of naming beats and their fractions, however, is known as the English way. The much simpler way universally adopted within musical software programs is called the American way. Within this system, each note is given a value that refers to its length as a proportion of a whole note. This method uses the terminology whole note, half note, quarter note, and so on.

Music software programs generally use this system in two ways. It is advisable to learn both. There are note fractions and the musical symbols used to represent those fractions. Excerpts from two well-known music software programs show use of both (see Figure 4.2).

Figure 4.2 Two ways of signifying note lengths.

On the left side of Figure 4.2, you can see note lengths referred to as fractions. On the right side of Figure 4.2, those same fractions are represented by symbols. Both refer to the same note-value scale. The symbol on the far left (of the right side of the figure) is called a *whole note*. It is easy to remember because it is an empty circle. The next symbol to the right is an empty circle with a tail. This is a half note, and there are two of these for every whole note. So if the whole note lasts for a second, each half note would last for half a second.

If you tapped a table with your right hand every second, you could write this down as a series of whole notes. If you tapped the table with your left hand twice as quickly, that would be two beats of the left to one beat of the right, and you could write that down either way, as shown in Figure 4.3.

Figure 4.3 Whole notes and half notes.

After that comes the quarter-note symbol, which is easy to remember because it is like the half-note symbol, except that the circle has a black fill. There are two quarter notes in each half note, and therefore there are four quarter notes in a whole note (see Figure 4.4).

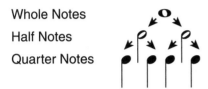

Whole Notes

Half Notes

Quarter Notes

Figure 4.4 Whole note, half notes, and quarter notes.

Most electronic music tracks use four quarter notes as a standard division of musical time. Each series of four quarters is called a *bar*. In the piano roll view with which most computer musicians are familiar, within each bar the quarters are represented as vertical lines. In Figure 4.5—showing the piano roll view in SONAR—the quarters are marked out by the red vertical lines. Each bar numbered in Figure 4.5 thus has four quarter notes. This is helpful when you are trying to memorize the note values. Each quarter note is also a quarter of a whole bar. A half note is also a half bar, and a whole note is a whole bar.

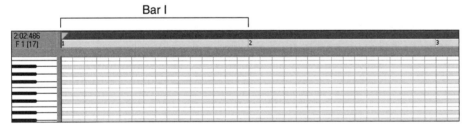

Figure 4.5 Vertical grid representing note values.

An eighth note is half the length of a quarter note. Its symbol is like a quarter note, except that it has a flag. When you are writing a series of eighth notes, this flag is used to beam the notes together (see Figure 4.6).

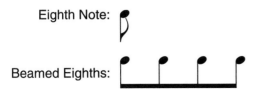

Eighth Note:

Beamed Eighths:

Figure 4.6 Eighth notes.

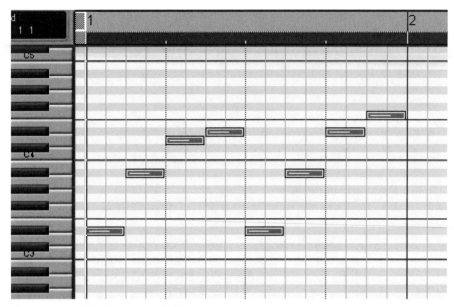

Figure 4.7 Eighth-note melodic sequence.

In Figure 4.7, the melody uses a series of eighth notes over the bar.

The 16th note is memorable because it has two flags, while the 32nd note has three flags. All note lengths after this follow the same pattern—64ths have four flags, 128ths have five flags, and so on. For most tracks it is very rare to see any note shorter than a 32nd. In fact, 32nd notes are so quick that their use is generally confined to, say, programming in a snare drum roll.

You can also beam 16th and 32nd notes (see Figure 4.8).

Figure 4.8 16th and 32nd notes.

To summarize, in Figure 4.9, you can see a list of the note values just discussed, together with their relevant symbols.

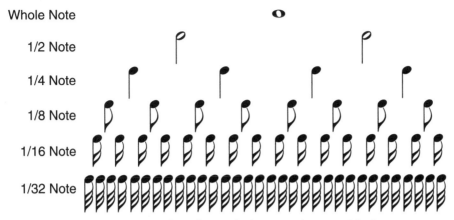

Figure 4.9   Range of note values from whole notes down to 32nd notes.

Dotted Notes

The note values just discussed are adequate for the purposes of expressing virtually any possible rhythm. On occasion, you'll find the use of various in-between beats. Examples include triplets, shuffle rhythms, and cross-rhythms. Another common type of in-between beat is the dotted note, which extends the value of a note category by another half. Therefore, a dotted half note (see Figure 4.10) is equivalent to a three-quarter note.

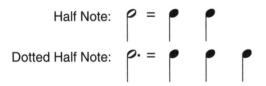

Figure 4.10   Dotted half note.

And a dotted quarter note (see Figure 4.11) is equivalent to a three-eighths note.

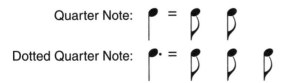

Figure 4.11   Dotted quarter note.

Rests

Rhythm can be defined as a pattern of sounds and silences. Silence is extremely important in music because it is the spaces between events that help to define them and give them shape. This is certainly true with rhythm—it is the gaps between the notes that give the rhythm its shape and identity. These gaps are called *rests*, and each of the note values discussed has a corresponding rest.

The use of rests in music software is generally confined to those programs that make use of score-writing facilities. Propellerhead's Reason, for example, does not make use of rests because it has no score-writing features. SONAR, Logic, and Cubase do have such abilities, and for programs such as Sibelius and Finale, the score-writing facility is the main point of the program.

If you are going to use score-writing facilities, you need to learn and memorize the corresponding rests for each of the note values. Figure 4.12 shows these rests.

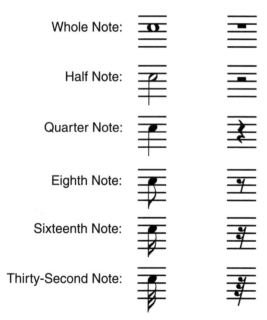

Whole Note:

Half Note:

Quarter Note:

Eighth Note:

Sixteenth Note:

Thirty-Second Note:

Figure 4.12   Notes rests.

Anything that comes in musical staff format will use these symbols, so it is worthwhile to learn them. In the piano roll view, rests are not represented because they appear simply as empty spaces. You can see this in the way the same arpeggio pattern is represented in Figure 4.13 in piano roll and score formats, respectively.

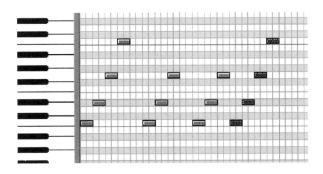

Figure 4.13 Piano roll and score representation of arpeggio pattern.

Resolution, Snap to Grid, and Quantization

Knowledge of note values is essential for the effective use of resolution, snap to grid, and quantization functions offered by music software programs. *Resolution* concerns the value of the notes set when using the Pencil tool to draw in notes. When the tool is set to an eighth, it will automatically pencil in an eighth note on the selected pitch (see Figure 4.14).

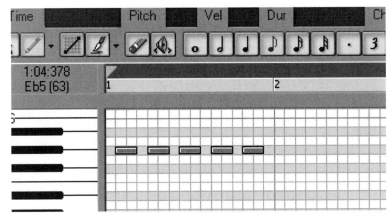

Figure 4.14 Eighth-note resolution of the Pencil tool.

The snap-to-grid function ensures that written notes are automatically set at the beginning of the beat—the beat being whatever resolution is set for it. If the beat is set to a half note, snap to grid will ensure that all of the notes occur at the start of each half note, and so on. In Figure 4.14, resolution is set to an eighth, and the snap-to-grid function has been turned on (see Figure 4.15).

Figure 4.15   Resolution and Snap to Grid selection buttons.

Quantization is a form of snap-to-grid function that occurs while recording. If quantization is set to an eighth, it will ensure that all of the notes recorded will be placed at the beginning of the nearest eighth note. In Figure 4.16, the example on the left is unquantized, while the example on the right has been quantized.

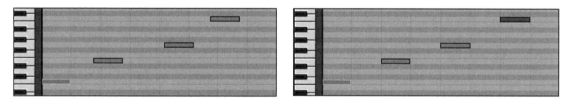

Figure 4.16   Unquantized and quantized to the nearest eighth.

In the unquantized version, some of the notes occur slightly before the beat, while others occur just after. Quantization—as seen on the right side of the figure—ensures that all of the notes occur on the beat. This is not always desirable though, because it can lead to a rigid, mechanical sound.

To effectively use snap-to-grid functions and quantization, it is clear that you need to learn the note values given in this chapter. By learning these note values, you will also gain a much clearer understanding of musical rhythms and the way in which rhythms are notated and expressed by composers. Allied with this is the important study of how composers choose to write their music. The facility called *score editing*, where notes are placed directly onto a musical stave, is not always a favorite option for computer musicians. I know of professional computer musicians whose musical productions rely solely on the use of the piano roll format. Yet there are others who also like the option of working within a score edit format. Personally, I like to use both. For those who are interested in score edit options, the next chapter offers an introduction to the basic concepts behind this process.

Exercises

You can download the answers to the chapter exercises from www.courseptr.com/downloads.

1. Fill in the missing word. Every sound used in a musical composition has a certain length or _____.

2. Complete the following sentence. The speed of music is called the _____, which is measured and described in terms of _____.

3. Name the following symbols (according to the American fractional method):

    ♩ =   ♪ =

    ♬ =   ♩ =

    𝅝 =   ♬ =

4. Name the note value that represents the sum of the following. One example has already been done for you.

    A) ♩ + ♩   = A Whole Note

    B) ♩ + ♩ + ♩ + ♩ = _____

    C) ♩ + ♪ + ♪ + ♩ = _____

    D) ♬ + ♪ + ♬   = _____

    E) ♬ + ♬ + ♬ + ♬ = _____

    F) ♩ + ♪ + ♪ + ♪ + ♪ = _____

    G) ♬ + ♬ + ♬ + ♬ = _____

5. Identify the durations in fractions of a whole note sequenced on this drum channel.

6. Choose the note symbol indicating the resolution required for quantization to the nearest:

    A. Sixteenth note:

    B. Half note:

    C. Eighth note:

    D. Quarter note:

7. Complete the following sentences:

    A. There are _____ sixteenth notes in a half note.

    B. Three quarter notes are equivalent to _____ eighth notes.

    C. There are _____ thirty-second notes in an eighth note.

8. Place next to the following rests the equivalent note length:

      =   =

      =   =

9. Complete the following statements:

    A. A dotted quarter note is equivalent to _____ eighth notes.

    B. A dotted whole note is equivalent to _____ quarter notes.

    C. A dotted sixteenth note is equivalent to _____ thirty-second notes.

10.   Place the note symbol required in the requisite space:

$\flat$ + $\flat$ + $\flat$ =

$\upharpoonleft$ + $\upharpoonleft$ + $\upharpoonleft$ =

$\eighthnote$ + $\eighthnote$ + $\eighthnote$ =

11.   Underneath the following notes and gaps, place the equivalent note value or rest required. The note resolution of the matrix grid is set to sixteenth notes.

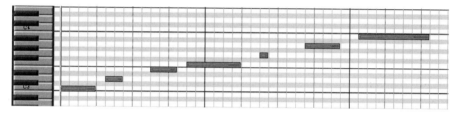

5 Score Editing

Generally, musical software programs offer two ways of drawing in notes—you can draw them in with the Pencil tool using either the piano roll or the score edit view. This choice also applies when you are editing note events that have been recorded directly via the MIDI keyboard. You can edit through the piano roll view or the score edit view, if available. Many computer musicians tend to prefer the piano roll method because that way they are not required to learn to read music within a staff format.

Both methods are equally useful, but without formal musical training, the task of score editing can seem daunting. This chapter will provide all of the information you need to initially use the score-editing facilities provided in software programs should you wish to do so. The information presented here is also useful if you want to make remixes from MIDI files—information for these is often conveyed in conventional musical notation.

In score editing, musical notes are simultaneously represented in two ways. Their duration is represented by the symbols shown in Chapter 4, while their pitch is represented by the position of the note on a staff.

Pitch Notation

The *staff* is a series of five lines upon which you can place musical notes. You can place notes both on and between the lines of the staff, as shown in Figure 5.1.

Figure 5.1 Whole notes on lines and spaces of the staff.

The Treble Clef

A staff is useless, however, without a clef. Score editors use two main clefs. First is the treble clef, which is placed at the beginning of the staff, as shown in Figure 5.2.

Figure 5.2   The treble clef.

This is generally used to represent all notes above Middle C. Middle C is placed at the bottom of the staff on a small line called a *ledger line*. This is used to supplement the staff. Rather than draw an entire line, a ledger line is used instead (see Figure 5.3).

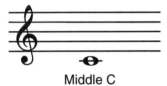

Middle C

Figure 5.3   Middle C on the treble staff.

When you know the position of Middle C, you can calculate the positions of all of the other notes on the treble staff. When you are initially learning, it is advisable to count up from Middle C. The count follows the musical alphabet from C upward. When you reach G, you return to A, and the series continues (see Figure 5.4).

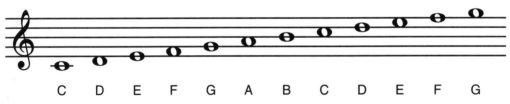

C   D   E   F   G   A   B   C   D   E   F   G

Figure 5.4   Notes above Middle C.

Counting upwards in this fashion is necessary until you can remember the positions of all of the notes. This takes time and practice. When you've acquired some experience, you can also learn various shortcuts. It is well worth remembering an alternative name for the treble clef, which is the *G clef*. It is called the G clef because the spiral of the treble clef is normally drawn around the line upon which note G above Middle C is drawn. As you can see in Figure 5.4, this is the second line up. If you remember this position, you can then also count up from G, which saves you time and effort.

Should notes higher than the limit of the staff be needed, they are placed on ledger lines as shown in Figure 5.5.

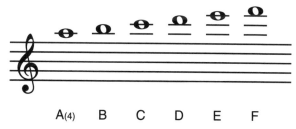

A(4)   B   C   D   E   F

Figure 5.5   Use of ledger lines on the treble staff.

The Bass Clef

Notes below Middle C are represented on a staff that has a bass clef. To learn the positions of the notes, you again use Middle C as a starting point. In this case, Middle C is represented as a note placed upon a ledger line immediately above the staff. The positions of all of the other notes are thus calculated by counting down from Middle C. Here it is important to remember to count backward in the musical alphabet, as shown in Figure 5.6.

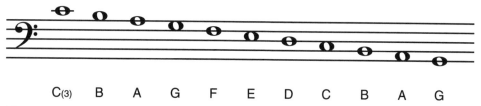

C(3)   B   A   G   F   E   D   C   B   A   G

Figure 5.6   Notes below Middle C on the bass staff.

Just as the treble clef bears an alternative name of G clef, so does the bass clef have an alternative name—it is called the *F clef*, so named because the symbol coils around the line upon which the F below Middle C goes. This is a useful place of orientation on the bass clef because it can save you time and effort counting down from Middle C. Of course, with sufficient practice, you will remember the positions of the notes automatically anyway.

When you reach the bottom of the staff, notes are again placed on ledger lines, as shown in Figure 5.7.

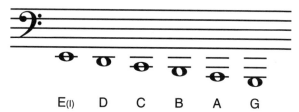

E(1)   D   C   B   A   G

Figure 5.7   Bass notes below the bass staff.

Alternative Clefs

When more notes would be on ledger lines than on actual lines of the staff, alternative forms of the treble and bass clefs are used. In terms of the treble clef, this form is called the *octave-treble clef,* and it is identical to the ordinary treble clef except for a small number 8 placed at the bottom of the symbol (see Figure 5.8). When used, it means that all of the written notes will sound an octave higher.

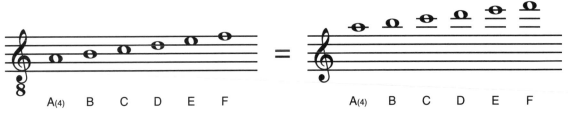

Figure 5.8 Octave-treble clef.

For the bass clef, there is an alternative called the *octave-bass clef* that is constructed along similar lines, with a number 8 added to the bass clef symbol (see Figure 5.9).

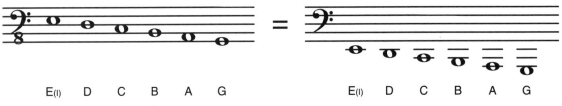

Figure 5.9 Octave-bass clef.

Owing to their characteristic registers, leads would ordinarily use the treble staff and basses would use the bass staff. Keyboard instruments, harps, and so on use a system of two staffs—one treble and one bass—bound together by a brace, as shown in Figure 5.10.

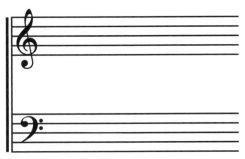

Figure 5.10 Staff system for keyboard instruments.

Sharps and Flats on the Clefs

There are only individual positions on the staff for the white keys of the keyboard. Positions for the black keys are not needed because these are provided for by sharp and flat signs. As originally discussed in Chapter 2, a sharp sign in front of a note signifies that it is to be played a semitone higher. For the note F#, therefore, you would write a note F and put a sharp sign in front of it. A flat sign in front of a note signifies that it is to be played a semitone lower. For the note Bb, therefore, you would write a note B and place a flat sign before it. See Figure 5.11 for examples of a sharp and a flat.

F Sharp   B Flat

Figure 5.11   Sharp and flat notation.

If the sharp or flat is no longer required, it is cancelled out through the use of a natural sign (see Figure 5.12). This indicates that the note is now to be played in its original, "natural," white-key version.

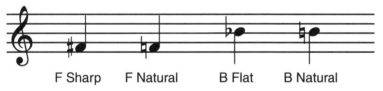

F Sharp   F Natural   B Flat   B Natural

Figure 5.12   Use of natural sign.

Rhythmic Notation

As well as signifying the pitch, note symbols also denote the duration of each note. These symbols are identical to those learned in Chapter 4. For note values with tails, there are particular conventions regarding the direction of the tails. Notes above the middle line of the staff have the tails pointing downward, while notes below the middle line of the staff have their tails pointed upward. Notes on the middle line can be pointing up or down. See Figure 5.13.

Figure 5.13   Directions of note symbols.

Beaming Notes

Beaming is where notes of a common value are connected together within the bar (see Figure 5.14). This occurs for all notes smaller than a quarter note—eighths onward. Don't worry about how to beam the notes unless you intend to produce scores of your own music. The software does it automatically for you.

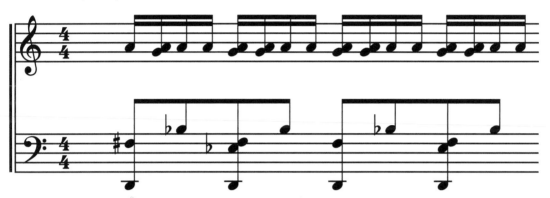

Figure 5.14   Beamed sixteenths and eighths.

Percussion Staffs

Percussion tracks use their own type of clef and staff. The staff for a single percussion part—such as a snare drum part, for example—is a single line upon which the note values are written as shown in Figure 5.15.

Figure 5.15   Single-line percussion staff.

The numbers 4/4 signify the time signature—that there are four beats in a bar. The short vertical line in the middle of the staff is a bar line placed to show each complete cycle of four beats. Chapter 7, "Meter," will provide more information on both of these topics.

For more complex percussion parts—such as a complete drum pattern, for example—a percussion clef is used, and it is customary to assign particular drums of the kit to particular lines. Figure 5.16 shows a typical assignment.

| Hi-Hat |
| High Tom |
| Snare |
| Lo Tom |
| Bass Drum |
| Hi-Hat Pedal |

Figure 5.16   Percussion staff.

For each drum, the assignment provides the type of note head with which the part is customarily written. Using different note heads—such as x-shaped note heads for the hi-hats—makes it much easier to read drum parts. This way, you can notate complete drum tracks, as shown in Figure 5.17.

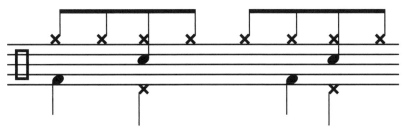

Figure 5.17   Drum pattern notated on percussion staff.

Score-Editing Symbols

If your software has score-editing facilities, it is liable to offer a menu of score-editing symbols. Logic has a good score-editing facility and offers, among others, the menu of symbols shown in Figure 5.18.

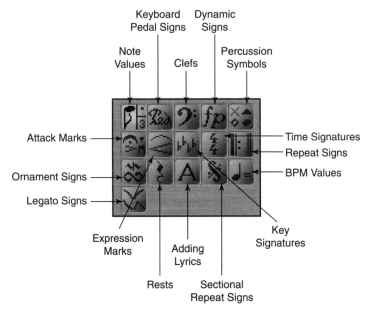

Figure 5.18   Logic score-editing symbols.

These symbols look extremely complex and daunting. However, you will not generally use many of these because they mostly apply to the process of producing a printed score of your work—a task that goes beyond the scope of this book. Where the use of such symbols is necessary, as in the case of key signatures and time signatures, I will give you all of the relevant information concerning their appropriate meaning and use.

Exercises

You can download the answers to the chapter exercises from www.courseptr.com/downloads.

1. Fill in the missing words. The _____ is a series of five lines upon which musical notes may be placed. Notes may be placed both _____ and _____ the lines of the staff.

2. Write down both of the names by which the following clefs are known:

    _____ or _____

    _____ or _____

3. Place note Middle C as a whole note in its correct position on the following staffs:

4. What are the following symbols called?

    A. # is called a _____.

    B. b is called a _____.

    C. A # before a note indicates that _____.

    D. A b before a note indicates that _____.

5. Write on each staff the pitch indicated using quarter notes:

    C3   G#3   B3   E♭4   A#4   D♭3   A3   C#4   D4

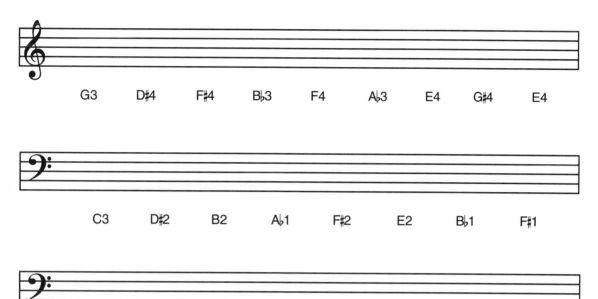

G3   D#4   F#4   B♭3   F4   A♭3   E4   G#4   E4

C3   D#2   B2   A♭1   F#2   E2   B♭1   F#1

G2   A#1   E♭2   D♭1   B1   D2   F2   F#2

6.   Name each of the following notes and their respective time values:

6 | Intervals

After you have learned the C major scale, you can make great progress in understanding and using other important elements of the musical language. This is because the C major scale represents a complete self-contained pitch system in its own right. It is possible for a composer to write all of his tunes using this scale. The music might end up being limited, but it is possible.

Understanding Intervals

The C major scale offers seven notes that can be used in any order or combination. When one note is heard after another, or even when two notes are played at the same time, the ear and mind analyze their relationship. This analysis takes place on numerous levels. When it occurs in relation to the pitch of the notes, the ear and mind are focusing on the pitch relationships. This relationship between notes in terms of their pitch—that is, how high or low they are—is called an *interval* (see Figure 6.1).

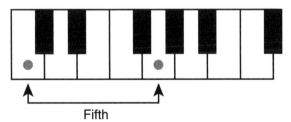

Fifth

Figure 6.1 Interval of fifth on a keyboard. (Be patient—you'll get an explanation of why this particular interval is called a fifth a bit later in this chapter.)

Intervals are vitally important components of music. In a lead melody, intervals occur between successive notes of the tune. These are called *melodic intervals;* see the upper-left portion of Figure 6.2. In a chord in which the notes are all struck at the same time, the intervals occur in a different way—they are harmonic (simultaneous), as demonstrated in the upper-right portion of Figure 6.2, as opposed to being melodic (successive) intervals.

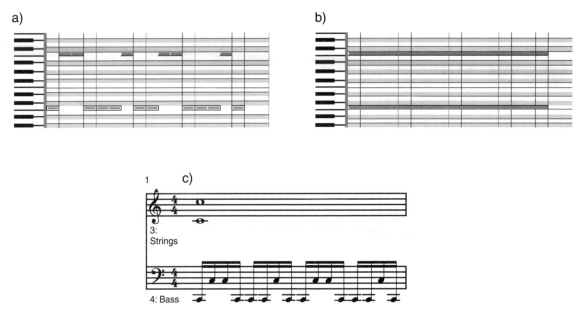

Figure 6.2 Melodic and harmonic uses of octave interval.

The important point is that the same intervals are used, but in two different ways—melodically, along a horizontal dimension, and harmonically, along a vertical dimension. So whichever way you look at it, intervals themselves are of tremendous importance because they represent the building blocks upon which the musical language is based. A comprehensive knowledge of intervals is therefore paramount to attain professional levels of musical composition. In this chapter, you will learn of the basic principles of recognizing and identifying these intervals.

In Figure 6.2, the interval of an octave occurs both melodically—sequenced as an eight-step bass pattern (a)—and then harmonically—as a sustained string chord (b). In the bottom portion of Figure 6.2, you can see how both tracks work together in score edit format.

Both harmonic and melodic intervals are described in the same way. There are simple intervals that lie within the range of an octave (see Figure 6.3).

Working Out Intervals

When you are trying to work out intervals, remember to include the starting note. From C to G, there are five notes including the starting note and the ending note: C D E F G. Therefore, the interval between C and G is a fifth.

The "first" is counted as an interval because it represents a situation in which two notes of the same pitch are sounding at the same time. Because two sound sources are producing the

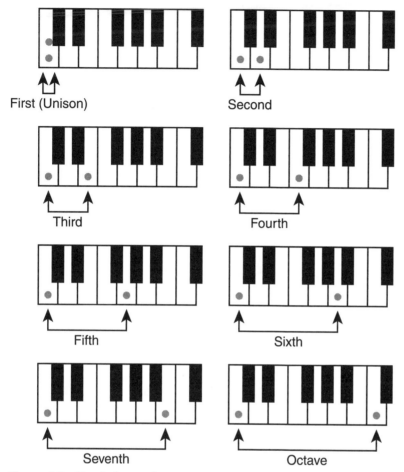

Figure 6.3 Simple intervals.

same note, there is a relationship between their pitches—in other words, they are the same. This interval is therefore called a *first*—or, alternatively, a *unison* or a *prime*. On polyphonic instruments (that is, instruments capable of producing more than one note at the same time), this interval would not usually occur because there is not much point in duplicating the same note. On monophonic instruments capable of producing only one note at a time (such as the human voice), the first *does* occur when, for example, two singers sing the same note.

Seconds, thirds, fourths, fifths, sixths, and sevenths occur when there is a difference between the pitches of two notes, and those differences occur within the range of an octave. Consequently, they are all classed as being simple intervals. You can hear each of these in succession on Track 11 on the CD. These occur when, for example, two singers or instrumentalists are playing notes of different pitches. They can also occur when a polyphonic instrument, such as

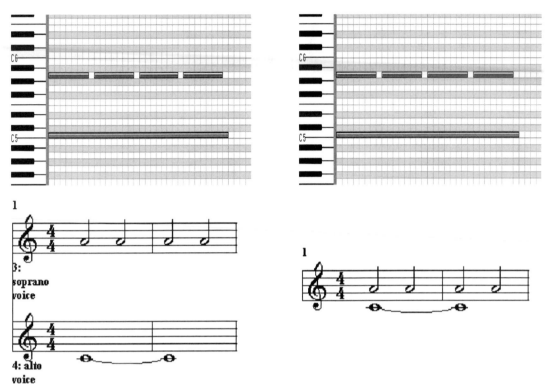

Figure 6.4 Interval of sixth used as a vocal harmony (left) and a warm pad harmony (right).

a piano, or a polyphonic synthesizer is used. In Figure 6.4, the interval of a sixth is employed, first as an interval between two separate monophonic voice parts, and second as a harmony on a polyphonic synthesizer pad patch.

Because in both cases two notes are heard together, the ear perceives a relationship between them. This relationship is loosely called a *harmony* or a *sonority,* and it is upon these relationships that the whole science of musical harmony is based. This has to do with the fact that some notes blend well with others—these are called *concords*—whereas others tend to disagree—these are called *discords.* Chapter 8, "Chords," will further discuss this fact, along with the reasons behind it and other related topics.

Intervals also occur between the successive notes of a melodic line. In Figure 6.5, some of the intervals occurring between the notes of a lead melody have been bracketed.

Compound Intervals

Intervals bigger than an octave are called *compound intervals.* This is because they represent a simple interval plus one or more octaves. Thus, an eleventh is also called a *compound fourth.*

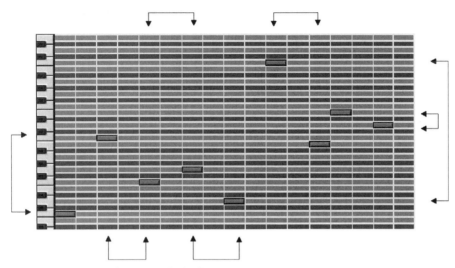

Figure 6.5 Intervals in a melodic line.

The logic of this is that the same relationship—for example, C to F—is being duplicated on a higher octave (see Figure 6.6).

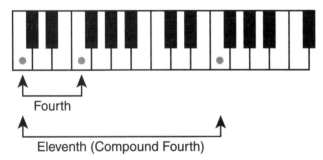

Fourth

Eleventh (Compound Fourth)

Figure 6.6 Eleventh as a compound fourth.

To work this out mentally, it is a matter of subtracting seven from the total number, which represents the compound interval. Therefore, a twelfth is a compound fifth because $12-7=5$. For larger compound intervals, keep subtracting sevens until you get down to a number below seven. Consider the case of a twenty-fourth—that is, the interval between notes C3 and E6. This is clearly a compound third because $24-7=17$, $17-7=10$, and $10-7=3$.

Compound intervals have very particular qualities that have been used to great effect in various kinds of electronic music. In the dance music of the late '90s, tenths (or compound

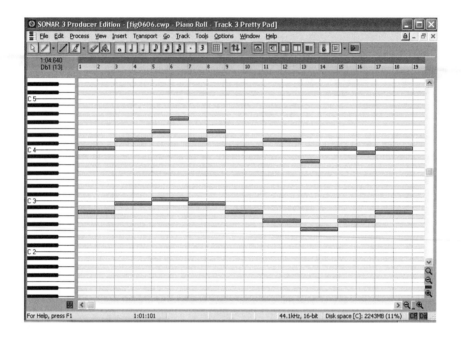

Figure 6.7 Trance breakdown. (Korg Triton "Pretty Pad Patch.") Sequenced in Cakewalk SONAR (piano roll and score edit formats).

thirds) were used to great effect in the breakdowns of trance tracks. Check out the audio CD included with this book, for an audio example of this. In Figure 6.7, you can see the compound intervals used.

You can hear Figure 6.7 directly by listening to Track 12 on the audio CD.

I cannot stress enough the importance of intervals. Everything written musically in terms of leads, basses, pads, harmonies, arpeggios, and so on uses intervals as the basic building blocks. Everything consequently depends upon intervals. For this reason, it is important to study them closely and find out as much as possible about them. The greater your knowledge of intervals, the greater your ability will be to use them effectively in the process of composition. Naturally, this knowledge includes being able to hear and recognize intervals by their characteristic aural qualities. Exercises for this can be found in the next section.

Exercises

You can download the answers to the chapter exercises from www.courseptr.com/downloads.

1. Complete the following statement. There are two types of intervals: _____ intervals, which are those that lie within the range of an octave, and _____ intervals, which are larger than an octave.

2.   Identify the following intervals:

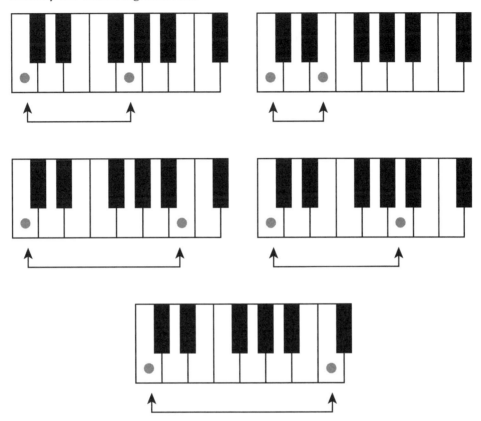

3.   Name the following melodic intervals:

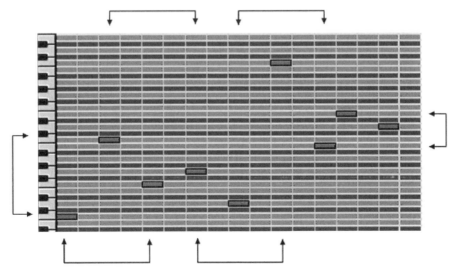

4.   Fill in the missing notes:

Note C. Go a seventh up: Note B. Go a fifth down: Note E. Go a fourth up: Note
_____. Go a third down: Note _____. Go a ninth up:
Note _____. Go a sixth down: Note _____.

5.   Complete the following list of fifths in the C major scale:

A. C — G

B. D — _____

C. E — _____

D. F — _____

E. G — _____

F. A — _____

G. B — _____

6.   Complete the following sentences:

A. A fifth above note D is note _____.

B. A ninth above note F is note _____.

C. A compound third above note G is note _____.

D. A seventh below note A is note _____.

E. A fourth below note B is note _____.

F. A sixth above note E is note _____.

G. An octave above note D is note _____.

H. An eleventh above note C is note _____.

7.   Sequence a random series of a dozen varied simple intervals using only the white notes
of the keyboard. Make each interval last a single bar. Use an acoustic piano patch.
Leave a gap of two bars between them. After you have done this, turn around with a
sheet of paper and try to identify each of the intervals. Do this as often as necessary until
you can recognize the intervals by their qualities.

7 Meter

Note lengths, as you studied in Chapter 4, show and describe how musical time is divided up into regular chunks called *beats*. Having considered note lengths in Chapter 4, it is now time to consider the various rhythmic frameworks in which these note lengths tend to be used. These are called *meters*.

Meter concerns the way beats are combined into larger units or groups that make sense to the ear. Each such unit is called a *metric cycle,* or a *measure.* They are also referred to as *bars*—a term which arose from the practice of drawing a vertical line on the score after the completion of each metric cycle (see Figure 7.1).

Figure 7.1 Use of bar lines in score-edit format.

Metric Cycles

Music of all kinds, styles, and genres uses such metric cycles. They are as important to the sense of rhythm in your music as a musical scale is to your melodies and harmonies. Consequently, the study of meter is vital if your music is going to make any rhythmic sense to your listener. So what is a metric cycle (or measure)? The simplest way to understand this is to consider the action of playing a hand drum, such as a conga. Some of the beats will be louder, and some will be softer. A metric cycle is a pattern of these stresses that makes sense to and satisfies the ear. As the word "cycle" implies, this tends to be repeated over and over again, establishing for the listener a clear framework for understanding and feeling the beats and rhythms.

The simplest metric pattern of all is a grouping of beats into twos, with the first beat being strong (*s*) and the second beat being weak (*w*); see Figure 7.2.

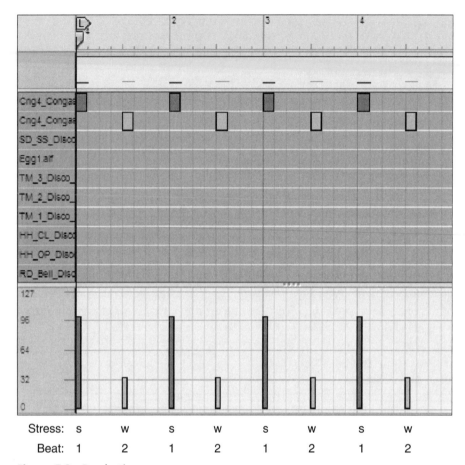

Figure 7.2 Duple time.

Another common grouping is into threes, with the strong beat occurring on the first of every three beats (see Figure 7.3). In this case, *m* signifies a medium stress between strong and weak.

The most popular grouping of all—the one used in most tracks today—is a grouping of beats into fours (see Figure 7.4).

There are therefore three basic meters or metric cycles, called *duple time*, *triple time*, and *quadruple time*, respectively.

Time Signatures

The metric cycle used in a composition is indicated by a time signature. Time signatures consist of a series of two numbers—the upper number (the numerator), which signifies the number of beats in the metric cycle, and the lower number (the denominator), which signifies the value of those beats in terms of halves, quarters, eighths, and so on (see Figure 7.5).

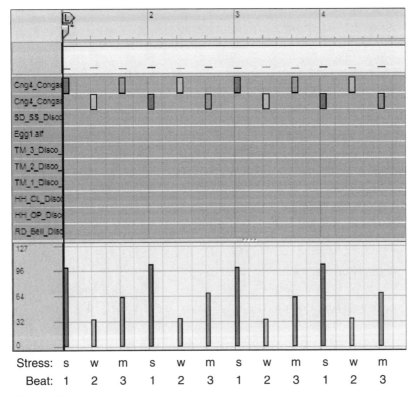

Figure 7.3 Triple time.

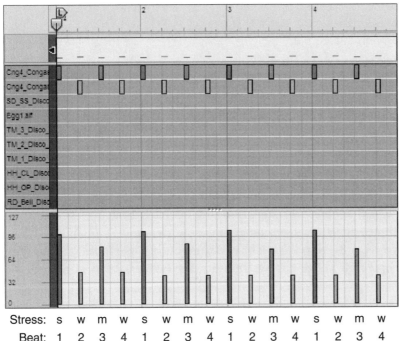

Figure 7.4 Quadruple time.

3 Numerator

4 Denominator

Figure 7.5 Time signature.

The time signature in Figure 7.5 signifies that each metric cycle has three beats and that the value of each beat is a quarter. On a staff, the time signature is placed at the very beginning, after the clef (see Figure 7.6). There is no need to place it in subsequent bars unless there is a change of time signature.

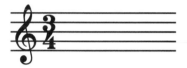

Figure 7.6 Time signature as it appears on the staff.

If you look at the bottom of an open Reason file, the time signature is clearly displayed (see Figure 7.7).

Time
Signature

Figure 7.7 Time signature display on Reason file.

In this case, the time signature retains the default setting of 4/4, which means that each metric cycle has four beats, and each beat is a quarter. This is a useful default because most music producers tend to prefer to work in 4/4. It is an easy, convenient pattern to work with, and it displays nice properties of balance and symmetry.

Compound Time Signatures

There is a further group of metric cycles recognized in conventional musical theory. Duple, triple, and quadruple time are called *simple time signatures*. When each beat of a simple time signature is subdivided into three, the equivalent compound time signature is obtained. Compound duple time—in other words, 6/8—thus has six beats. Compound triple time (9/8) has nine beats, while compound quadruple time (12/8) has twelve beats. See Figures 7.8 through 7.10 for examples of each.

You can hear the difference between these three kinds of metric cycles in Track 13 of the audio CD. Although compound time respects the same essential values as duple, triple, and quadruple

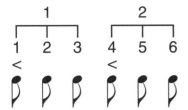

Figure 7.8   Compound duple time has six beats.

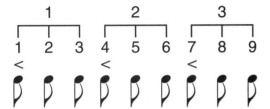

Figure 7.9   Compound triple time has nine beats.

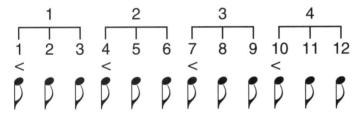

Figure 7.10   Compound quadruple time has 12 beats.

time, the division of each beat into three gives the rhythm a swinging, moving quality. A famous example of the use of compound time is J. S. Bach's "Sheep May Safely Graze," which is in 9/8.

Developing and Composing Rhythms

Note values show how musical time is divided up into beats and the various symbols and proportions that express those divisions. Your knowledge of these enables you to work out and express any rhythmic idea. In practice, as you have seen, most musical rhythms tend to occur within the framework of a metric cycle. Exceptions to this *do* occur, although they are not common: Christian plainchant is a rare example, its rhythms being more or less in free time with no sense of meter. Its gentle melodies simply meander from one note to another with no sense of beat, stress, or fixed pulse.

Most music is metric, and for a good reason. Many important rhythmic techniques depend upon the presence of such a cycle. A brilliant example of this is syncopation. Through use of meter, a pattern of stresses is set up in the music. And through repetition, your listener gets used to, for example, **1** 2 **3** 4 (with the numbers in bold indicating the strong beats of the bar). In syncopated rhythm, this expectation is played on to good effect, with stress being placed on a normally weak (rather than a strong point) of the bar. In other words, instead of **1** 2 **3** 4, it would be **1** 2 3 **4**.

Figures 7.11 and 7.12 present two examples. In the second bar of Figure 7.11, the strong beat comes on the second beat of the bar as opposed to the first and third beats of a more regular rhythm.

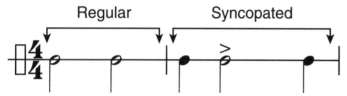

Figure 7.11 The strong beat comes on the second beat of the bar.

In the second bar of Figure 7.12, the strong beat occurs on the fourth quaver of the group instead of the fifth.

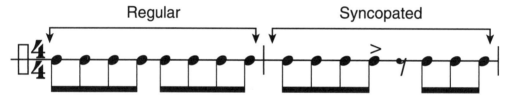

Figure 7.12 The strong beat occurs on the fourth quaver of the group.

You can listen to the effects of syncopation on Track 14 of the CD. From it, you will realize that you can use syncopation to generate energy and excitement in the rhythm. Its use is prevalent in all styles of electronic music—especially the faster, more upbeat styles, such as dance, breakbeat, drum and bass, and so on. Figure 7.13, for example, shows a commonly used alternative to the

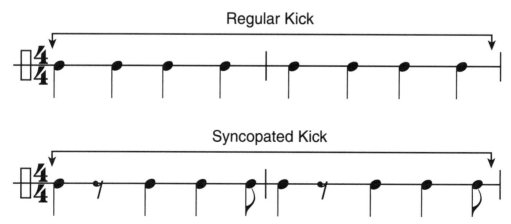

Figure 7.13 Syncopated kick drum pattern.

regular four-square beat of the kick drum found in dance music. It is syncopated because the second, third, and fourth beats arrive a quaver later than expected.

To use syncopation effectively, you need to learn the various metric cycles used in music. Having learned these, you then arrive at a position where you can start to experiment with placing stresses on unusual or unexpected points in that cycle.

Rhythmic Motives

Another rhythmic technique that depends upon the presence of a clear metric cycle is the use of rhythmic motives. A *rhythmic motive* is a short, identifiable unit of rhythm. Figure 7.14 shows a simple example that occurs in the context of quadruple time. This particular motive is extremely popular with dance-music writers.

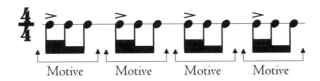

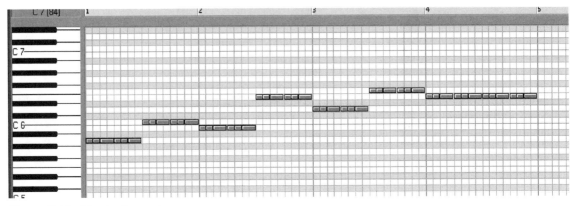

Figure 7.14 Rhythmic motive.

The same motive—consisting of two sixteenths followed by an eighth—is simply repeated throughout the bar. This creates a strong, driving rhythmic energy.

Often a rhythmic motive will be transformed into other related motives to create rhythmic variety. In compound quadruple time, a common motive (Motive A) and its main variant (Motive B) are as shown in Figure 7.15.

All modern and popular music uses rhythmic motives in one way or another. Such motives often feature syncopation, such as the example shown in Figure 7.16, which is a Cuban jazz motive.

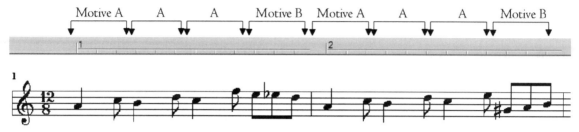

Figure 7.15 Compound quadruple motives.

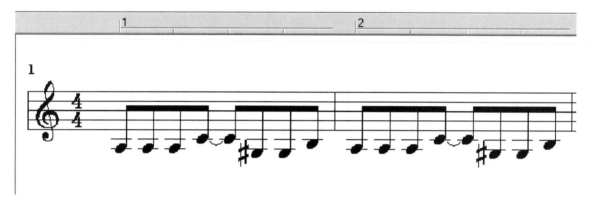

Figure 7.16 Syncopated motive.

Note: The symbol between the fourth and fifth of these eighth notes is a tie. This means that the value of the two notes is added together—in other words, the second note of the pair does not sound.

To develop an ability to use and write motives, you must spend some time listening carefully to music with an ear for the motives used. Once you have identified a motive, you can then work it out in terms of the note values used. This enables you to use that motive in your own compositions. Often particular genres will use characteristic motives, and the ability to use these can help you when writing music in these particular styles.

Triplets

Sometimes motives involve three notes being played in the time of two. These are called *triplets* and they are written as shown in Figure 7.17:

In this case, the three triplet quavers would be equivalent to the value of one quarter note. As a technique, triplets are very useful—they can bring an element of variety to rhythms. Used in

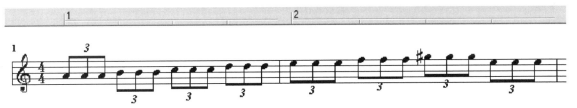

Figure 7.17 Notated triplets.

percussion on the hi-hat sixteenths, they can generate a sense of more pace as three sixteenths are being heard in the space of two (see Figure 7.18). This technique is often used in drum and bass and can be heard on Track 15 of the CD.

Figure 7.18 Hi-hat sixteenths in triplets.

Shuffle Rhythm

When the central note of each triplet is missed, the result is a shuffle rhythm. Originally starting with jazz and swing styles, the shuffle has come to pervade all types of modern music, from dance to popular (see Figure 7.19). To get an idea of shuffle rhythms listen to Track 16.

Figure 7.19 Shuffle rhythm.

To obtain a decent shuffle on a drum machine, you must select the correct resolution—in other words, triplets. Triplets are indicated in software programs in different ways. In Logic, eighth-note triplets are called *twelfths*, whereas sixteenth-note triplets are called *twenty-fourths*. Cakewalk's SONAR refers to them directly as *triplets*. See Figure 7.20.

In Reason, triplets are indicated by the note value that they affect, followed by a T for triplet. On the Redrum drum machine, options for both 1/8 and 1/16 triplets are offered, as shown in Figure 7.21.

Looking at the right side of the drum machine, you can see a Shuffle button. When you press this, shuffle will be applied automatically to all pairs of sixteenth notes. In this case there is no need to change the resolution; it can be set to a straight sixteenth. You can also alter the degree of shuffle. The more shuffle you apply, the greater the value of the first note of the pair and the lesser the value of the second note, and so on.

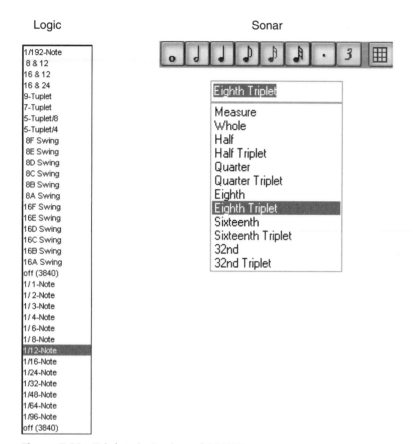

Figure 7.20 Triplets in Logic and SONAR.

Figure 7.21 Resolution dial on Reason's Redrum.

Cross Rhythm

You can gain an interesting effect when you play triplets against pairs. Track 17 on the CD gives an example of this. This is three notes in one part being heard in the same time as two notes of another part. This is known as a *cross-rhythm*, and in classical times this particular cross-rhythm was known as *hemiola* (see Figure 7.22).

Figure 7.22 Hemiola rhythm.

You get this effect in drum and bass music when the tambourine produces sixteenth triplets and the closed hi-hats produce straight sixteenths. The result is a nice, exciting, dense rhythm that gives the drum track more edge. In East African drumming, cross-rhythm has been developed to a fine art, and it is no rare thing to hear some really dense rhythms in which two is played against three which is played against five. This is a technique that seems to be neglected in modern electronic music, although one that would be well worth experimenting with.

Through your study of this chapter, you have learned about the various metric cycles used and recognized in the theory of modern music. This represents a very good introduction to this particular area. Yet modern electronic musicians can and do use far more intricate metric cycles in their music, often employing odd-numbered beats to the bar, such as 7/8 or 11/4. Called *asymmetric meters*, these have not been mentioned in this chapter because they represent a more advanced concept of rhythmic theory. It is enough as a first stage to learn the basic theory before you consider more advanced features. Resulting from the influence on electronic music of the music of Eastern and Middle Eastern cultures, these asymmetric metric cycles provide an interesting alternative to the basic metric cycles presented in this chapter. You'll study these in Chapter 14, "Additive Rhythms," together with information on how they are put together and used.

For now, it is time to look again at the values of pitch, in particular those combinations of musical notes that we call *chords*. You'll study these in the next chapter.

Exercises

You can download the answers to the chapter exercises from www.courseptr.com/downloads.

1. Complete the following sentence. Each complete metric cycle is called a
   _____. There are three basic types of metric cycle recognized in
   traditional musical theory. These are _____ time,
   _____ time, and _____ time.

2. Set up a metronome beat or click track on your sequencer and set the tempo to
   60bpm. Each click represents a complete bar or metric cycle. Then count out loud the
   following:

   A. Duple time: Two beats to each beat of the click track.

Click:		<		<		<		<	
Count:	1	2	1	2	1	2	1	2	etc.

B. Triple time: Three beats to each beat of the click track.

Click: <   <

Count: 1   2   3   1   2   3   etc.

C. Quadruple time: Four beats to each beat of the click track.

Click: <   <

Count: 1   2   3   4   1   2   3   4   etc.

3. Complete the following. A time signature consists of _____
    numbers—an upper number that is the _____ and a lower number
    that is the _____. The upper number tells you _____
    beats there are in a bar, while the lower number tells you their _____.

4. What is the meaning of the following time signatures?

    $\frac{2}{4}$ signifies _____

    $\frac{3}{8}$ signifies _____

    $\frac{9}{16}$ signifies _____

    $\frac{2}{4}$ signifies _____

5. What is the correct time signature for the following drum lanes? The grid resolution
    is set to 1/16.

    a) ——

    b) ——

    c) ——

6. Fill in the missing note values to complete the bars. Question marks have been placed where the notes are required.

7. Place the correct time signature at the front of each of these patterns.

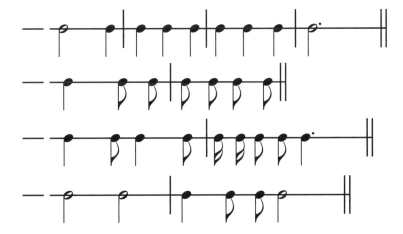

8a.   List the rhythmic motives that can be devised from two sixteenth notes and one
      eighth note, with each value appearing only once.

      1. _____

      2. _____

      3. _____

8b.   Compose a four-bar rhythm in quadruple metre that uses at least two of these motives.

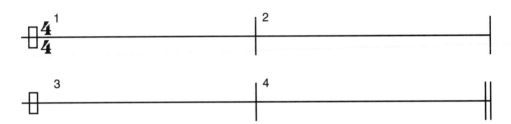

9.   What note values are the following triplets equivalent to?

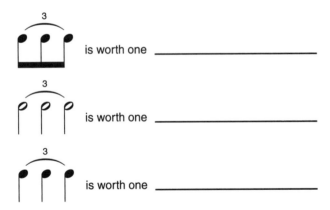

is worth one _____

is worth one _____

is worth one _____

10.   Below you will see the 16 buttons of a drum machine, such as Redrum. The resolution is set to a 1/16. Place a tick in those boxes required to give the following rhythms for these separate drum parts.

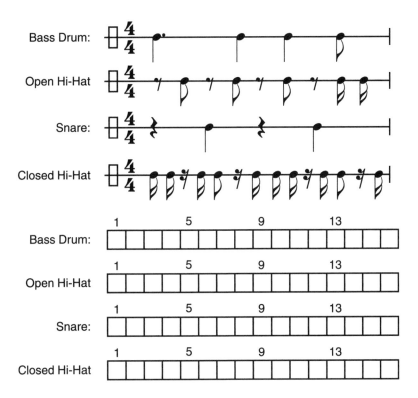

8 Chords

In Chapter 6, I introduced the concept of intervals and how important they are for all types of music. Any kind of music you write will use intervals. By now, you should know how they are measured and described in terms of the number of diatonic scale steps they span. Recall that simple intervals are those that lie within the range of an octave, whereas compound intervals are those that exceed it.

Another important feature of the interval is that it represents the simplest possible unit of harmony—in other words, a chord. Any kind of music you write will use chords. These chords are made up of intervals. Consequently, to come to grips with musical harmony and, as a result, to be able to create effective chord progressions, you need to study intervals very carefully. And don't just learn what they are; play and listen to them. Get to know them and their characteristic sound. Intervals are for the musician what the colors of the palette are for the visual artist.

An interval occurs when you play two notes together. It is a universal fact that when two notes are played together, the ear detects a relationship between them, and we hear this in terms of agreement or disagreement. Some combinations of notes sound really good and pleasing to the ear. Others can sound quite harsh and unpleasant, as if the two notes are in conflict with one another. So what is happening here?

Mathematics has a lot to do with it. Between the frequencies of any two notes, there is a relationship that can be expressed in the form of a ratio. Long ago, it was discovered that the simpler the ratio of the two frequencies, the more pleasing the sound is to the ear. The reasons for this are rather complex and are bound up with the workings of the internal mechanism of the ear and the fact that both notes in an interval generate their own spectrum of harmonics. The ear very cleverly compares these notes: The more the harmonics they share in common, the better the two notes seem to blend.

Because of this, there are some intervals that sound harmonious to the ear—called *concords*—and some that express a certain tension or unease—called *discords*. This is entirely due to the relative simplicity/complexity of their ratios.

It is upon this experience, which we all more or less share, that the whole art and science of musical harmony is based. Some combinations of notes are musically more preferable than others. This applies to combinations of two, three, four, or even more separate notes. Such combinations we call *chords*. So learning about harmony is really learning about those note combinations that musicians through the ages have discovered to be really effective.

Perfect Concords

The most concordant interval of all is the octave—discussed in Chapter 2—where the ratio of the two frequencies is virtually the simplest possible: 2:1. Here the two notes are so concordant that they register to us as being virtually the same. Harmony by octaves occurs naturally when, say, men and women sing the same song. Women sing in a higher register, while men sing in a lower register. Both sing the same notes, but separated by one or more octaves.

After the octave, there are two very important intervals that also have simple ratios. These are the perfect fifth, which has a ratio of 3:2, and the perfect fourth, which has a ratio of 4:3 (see Figure 8.1). Both intervals produce a very natural, distinctive, and strong harmony. So effective are these harmonies that they are used in all kinds of music the world over, and they have been used in this way since the very early beginnings of music itself. Along with the octave, they count as true universals of the musical language of humanity.

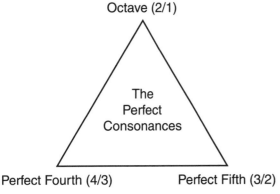

Octave (2/1)

The
Perfect
Consonances

Perfect Fourth (4/3)   Perfect Fifth (3/2)

Figure 8.1 The three perfect consonances.

In Western musical theory, these three intervals were given a high place of recognition, being classified as the three *perfect* consonances. Early forms of musical harmony in the West were based exclusively upon these intervals. Perhaps you have heard reconstructions of the chanting of monks during Medieval Christianity. The monks would sing the same tune, but separated by fourths, fifths, and octaves. The result was a harmony that by today's standards sounds very "old world."

As a general type of musical harmony, the technique used by these monks is called *parallelism* because the same tune is simply being shadowed at a higher and/or lower pitch. Traditional Chinese music used this type of harmony, and its use has become a cliché among writers of film music who want to create an Oriental atmosphere (see Figure 8.2). You can hear a representative example of this type of harmony in Track 18 of the audio CD.

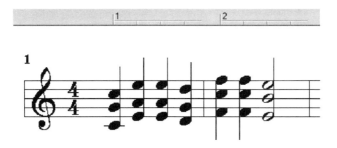

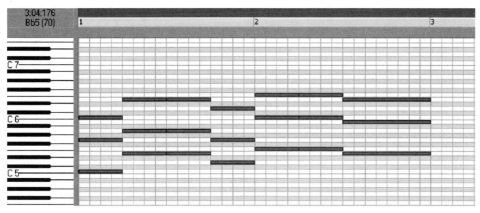

Figure 8.2   "Chinese"-sounding harmony by fifths, fourths, and octaves. (Score edit and piano roll views.)

To create an effect reminiscent of parallel harmony on some synthesizer patches, you can tune the second oscillator a perfect fifth (seven semitones) higher than the first. This gives the effect of harmony by fifths. Sometimes, though, the second oscillator is tuned up a fourth, giving the effect of harmony by fourths. The result in both cases is a strong but empty plaintive kind of sound. In Track 19 of the audio CD, the second oscillator has been tuned up by a perfect fifth so you can hear this kind of effect.

This type of harmony is also a strong feature of modern rock, where it provides the basis for so-called *power chords*. Popularized by bands such as Black Sabbath (*Paranoid*) and Deep Purple (*Black Knight*), their use has since become an extremely common feature of rock music (see Figure 8.3).

Looking at the C major scale, you will see that it is possible to build a fourth or fifth upon all of the notes of the scale (see Figure 8.4).

Try this out: Sequence what you see in Figure 8.4 and listen. There is nothing like hearing the real thing. Notice that at one point in the scale, the interval sounds different. This is the fifth between notes B and F. This is a different kind of fifth than the others—it is called a *diminished* fifth. It is very distinctive because of its strange and even eerie sound. For the monks of old who sang in fourths and fifths, it was officially banned from use; because of what was seen to be its

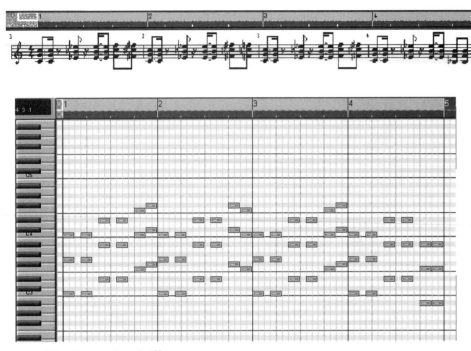

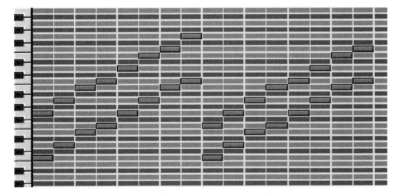

Figure 8.3 Power chord riff.

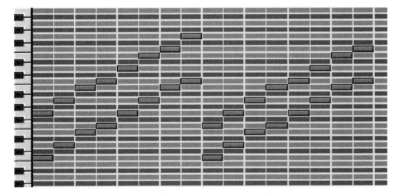

Figure 8.4 Harmony by fifths/fourths in C major scale.

sinister sound, it came to be called *diabolus musica*—the devil in music. Its counterpart—the fourth from F to B—was also called the *devil's fourth* for the same reason!

Imperfect Concords

After octaves, fifths, and fourths—the perfect consonances—there are other kinds of intervals that are vitally important for musical harmony. These are the thirds and the sixths. In the major scale, it is possible to build a third or a sixth upon any of those seven scale degrees (see Figure 8.5).

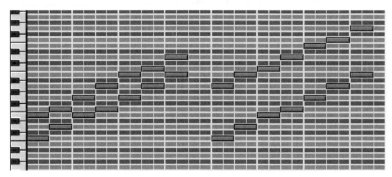

Figure 8.5 Thirds and sixths in the major scale.

Thirds and Sixths

Musical traditions describe these intervals as being concords, due to their comparatively simple ratios. You will find it useful to play these intervals on your MIDI keyboard to learn to recognize their characteristic qualities. Bear in mind that some thirds are major, whereas others are minor. What is the difference? Looking at the third between notes C and E, you can discern a gap of four semitones between the two notes. This kind of third is called a *major third* (see Figure 8.6).

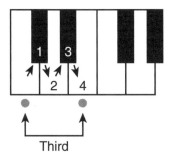

Figure 8.6 Major third between notes C and E.

Looking at the next third up between notes D and F, there are only three semitones between them. This is called a *minor third* (see Figure 8.7).

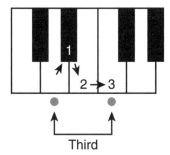

Figure 8.7 Minor third interval between notes D and F.

The same is true of sixths. Some of the sixths in the scale are major—those that have a gap of nine semitones—while some are minor—those with a gap of eight semitones (see Figure 8.8).

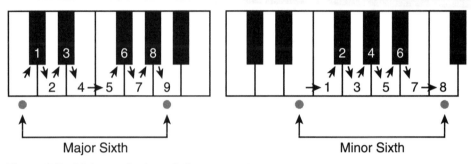

Figure 8.8 Major and minor sixths.

Because thirds and sixths are of two kinds (major and minor), they are classified as being *imperfect intervals*—imperfect because they occur in two forms. Because their ratios are all comparatively simple, thirds and sixths have a very agreeable sound to the ear. Table 8.1 gives the simple ratios of these intervals.

Table 8.1 Ratios of Major and Minor Thirds and Sixths

Interval	Ratio
Major third	5:4
Minor third	6:5
Major sixth	5:3
Minor sixth	8:5

Because of their harmonious quality, thirds and sixths are very important in musical harmony, and they are often used instinctively by backing singers to provide a descant or harmony over a particular tune. They have a particularly rich, full sound that blends very well with the main melody.

Seconds and Sevenths

The two types of intervals remaining are seconds and sevenths. These have a much rougher sound than thirds and sixths, owing to the complexity of their ratios. Intervals with complex ratios tend to sound discordant due to the presence of beats. The explanation for this belongs with the more advanced study of acoustics. But basically, it is due to a clash of wavelengths that don't marry well because they are not mathematically regular.

Formerly classed as being discords, seconds and sevenths have a recognizable element of tension about them. In terms of seconds, there are two types—major seconds and minor seconds (see Figure 8.9). Major seconds have a gap of two semitones, as between notes C and D, D and E, F and G, and A and B. Minor seconds have a gap of only one semitone, as between notes E and F, and B and C. The former are generally thought to be quite mild discords, while the latter have a much sharper discordant quality.

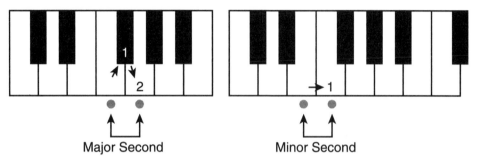

Figure 8.9 Major and minor seconds.

The tense, sharp quality of minor seconds is often used to good effect in film music. String stabs of minor seconds were used in the film *Psycho* during the murder in the shower scene. Since then, their use has become a horror-movie standard.

Play these intervals on the keyboard. It is important that you directly hear and experience intervals, rather than just reading about them. Intervals are the building blocks of melody and harmony. The different qualities of the intervals you use determine much about the emotional impact of the music. Is the music calm and peaceful? Is it tense or fraught? Check out Track 20 on the audio CD, which builds up a texture based on purely discordant intervals. You will know immediately what I mean.

Sevenths can also be major or minor (see Figure 8.10). There are the minor sevenths (gaps of 10 semitones) between D and C, E and D, G and F, A and G, and B and D, which are mild discords. The major sevenths (gaps of 11 semitones) between F and E, and C and B are more intensely discordant.

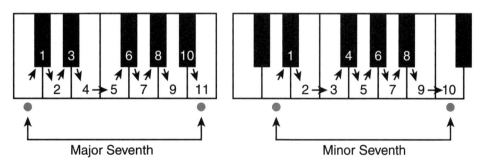

Figure 8.10 Major and minor sevenths.

Types of Intervals

In this chapter, I have described intervals both in terms of their aural quality and in terms of their mode. Aural quality tends to be generalized in terms of whether an interval sounds concordant or discordant. To a large degree, these qualities are relative to the type of music being considered. Jazz harmony is full of sevenths and ninths, which traditionally are regarded as being discordant. However, when discord becomes the norm, as in jazz, the ear comes to accept such discords as being relatively stable harmonies. Consequently, the classification of whether an interval is concordant or discordant is not absolute.

In terms of the *mode* of interval, this concerns whether it is perfect or imperfect. Perfect intervals —the fourth, fifth, and octave—are fixed in the sense that they have only one mode. Imperfect intervals—the second, third, sixth, and seventh—are variable in the sense that they can be major or minor. The difference between them is also reflected in their usage. Perfect intervals tend to provide the stable background structure for chords, while imperfect intervals determine whether the chord is major or minor.

Table 8.2 summarizes these intervals, and Figure 8.11 shows them on a staff.

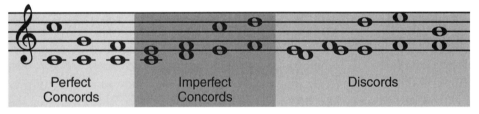

Figure 8.11 The three types of intervals.

Triadic Harmony

Through the study of intervals, you have no doubt learned more about the C major scale as well. This, however, represents only a small beginning. You can acquire knowledge of a particular scale system in this way, but you also need to build upon it and extend it. One of the most important areas to learn about a particular scale is the possibilities it offers for building chords, especially those involving more than two notes. I use the word "building" in this context because in a chord you are piling up a stack of musical notes to be heard at the same time. Hopefully, you will put together that stack using tangible principles—hence the notion of building chords.

Chord Progressions

Every scale offers a characteristic series of chords. These, when used and placed in a logical sequence for the ear, give rise to chord progressions. Chord progressions underpin virtually every song that has ever been written. When learning a new song, the most essential feature for the musician to grasp is the underlying chord progression. Once the musician has worked

Table 8.2 Major, Minor, and Perfect Intervals

Interval	Type	Mode	Quality	Number of Semitones (Gap)
First	Perfect	Perfect	Perfect concord	0
Second	Imperfect	Minor	Discord (sharp)	1
Second	Imperfect	Major	Discord (mild)	2
Third	Imperfect	Minor	Concord	3
Third	Imperfect	Major	Concord	4
Fourth	Perfect	Perfect	Perfect concord	5
Fourth	Chromatic	Augmented	Discord (sharp)	6
Fifth	Perfect	Perfect	Perfect concord	7
Sixth	Imperfect	Minor	Concord	8
Sixth	Imperfect	Major	Concord	9
Seventh	Imperfect	Minor	Discord (mild)	10
Seventh	Imperfect	Major	Discord (sharp)	11
Octave	Perfect	Perfect	Perfect concord	12

out the chord changes and their timing, the rest is often a matter of improvising around that framework.

We are all unknowing experts on the subject of chord progressions. We have all heard so many songs and pieces of music that our ears have become educated to a very high degree. In fact, our ears have become so educated that we can often spot a single wrong note among what may be thousands of other notes in a piece of music. This is because the wrong note doesn't go with the particular chord being used at the time.

As a computer musician, you are required to call upon all of that education. The knowledge of all of the pieces of music that you have ever heard is faithfully stored in your subconscious, guiding your choices of what and how to write. Often a feeling of frustration can arise where you can mentally hear the sound that you want, but you find it difficult to achieve in practice. This frustration is usually due to a lack of clear knowledge of underlying principles. Consequently, you can overcome it by learning what these principles are.

This especially applies to musical harmony. For the ear, harmony is what holds your different tracks together. In other words, it is the connection for the listener between, say, your bass line, your lead, and any fills. All three need to work together to create a strong and logical sense of harmony. The ability to create decent chord progressions is thus vitally important for your song-writing. Through the chord progression, your song acquires impetus, logic, and a sense of forward movement and flow. Naturally, to be able to create logical chord progressions, you must learn the chords available to you, along with how to use them. To start you off, we'll discuss the various chords you can use in the scale of C major.

You have already seen that when two notes are played simultaneously, the ear senses the harmony (or lack thereof) between them. In musical terms, this harmony is called a *sonority*. Therefore, a sonority occurs when more than one note is sounded at the same time, with the simplest sonority being the interval. In this chapter, you have already studied the various qualities possessed by these intervals.

Triads

After the interval come triads, in terms of the graduated progression of sonorities from the simplest to the most complex. Triads occur when three different notes are sounded simultaneously. In modern music there is only one rule when it comes to the use of sonorities: Any note may be combined with any other note. When this rule is applied to chords of three notes, a great number of potential sonorities is possible. Among these are particular sonorities that, through their widespread use over the history of music, have acquired a more or less universal status.

One such sonority is the major triad. Early forms of harmony tended to focus on the properties of fifths and fourths. However, in the 14th century, an English monk named Walter Odington discovered that by combining thirds and fifths, it was possible to create chords of three notes, all of which were in a concordant relationship to one another.

When a fifth is combined with a major third, the result is a *major triad* (see Figure 8.12). All three intervals involved are concords, with the perfect fifth being a perfect concord and the major and minor third being imperfect concords.

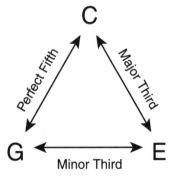

Figure 8.12 The major triad.

The result is a beautiful chord that has provided the mainstay of musical harmony for hundreds of years now. When the fifth is combined not with a major, but with a minor third, the result is another chord of three notes—all of the intervals of which, again, are concordant. This is called the *minor triad* (see Figure 8.13).

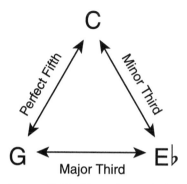

Figure 8.13 The minor triad.

You can hear the difference between the major and the minor triad in Track 21 of the audio CD. Between them, the major and the minor triads account for most of the chords used in chord progressions. They have been used in this way since at least the 15th century and probably will continue to be. Every generation of musicians rediscovers them and puts them to good use within whatever styles of music are predominant at the time. Today is no exception.

Triads in the C Major Scale

Each note of a triad has a name. The most important note is called the *root*. This, like the foundation of a house, is the vital note upon which the triad is built. It is also logically the note by which the triad is identified and named. To build a triad, above the root you place another note from the scale a third higher, and then a final note a fifth higher than the root.

So, for the triad of C major, you have:

Root (C) + Third (E) + Fifth (G)

A triad whose root note is C is thus called a triad of C.

Each note of the C major scale can be taken to be the root of a particular triad. Because there are seven notes in the scale, this means there are seven triads. So how do we distinguish between one triad and another? There are two ways in which you can do this. First, each triad can be represented by a number that tells you the degree of the scale that is its root. The numbers used traditionally are Roman numerals. Because some triads in the scale (see Table 8.3) are major and some minor, it is useful to identify them in different ways. Major triads in the scale are given an uppercase Roman numeral, whereas minor chords in the scale are given a lowercase Roman numeral. The usefulness of Roman numerals will become apparent in the "Chordal Functions" section, soon to follow in this chapter.

Along with Roman numerals, popular music song formats also recognize a series of symbols used to describe chords and used by guitar players. These often occur along with specific guitar tablature (see Table 8.3).

Table 8.3 Triads in the Key of C Major

Chord	Root	Third	Fifth	Name	Guitar Symbols
Chord I	C	E	G	C major	C
Chord ii	D	F	A	D minor	Dm
Chord iii	E	G	B	E minor	Em
Chord IV	F	A	C	F major	F
Chord V	G	B	D	G major	G
Chord vi	A	C	E	A minor	Am
Chord vii	B	D	F	B diminished	Bo

For the computer musician, you might find it helpful to see the seven chords sequenced in matrix view. From this perspective, the seven triads of C major would appear as shown in Figure 8.14.

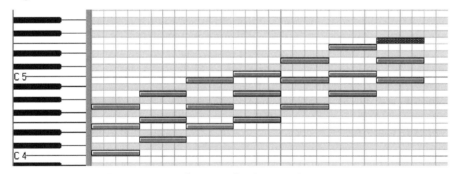

Figure 8.14 Triads in C Major. (Piano roll edit view.)

Alternatively, you can view them through the score edit facility, in which case the group of chords would appear as shown in Figure 8.15.

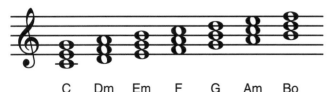

C   Dm   Em   F   G   Am   Bo

Figure 8.15 Triads in C Major. (Score edit view.)

It is very important to learn to play these on a MIDI keyboard. This group of chords figures in a huge amount of music. Certainly today, they figure in some 90 percent of all popular music tracks.

Some are major chords and some are minor chords. What is the difference? You can understand the difference by looking at a triad as a stack of two thirds superimposed upon one another (see Figure 8.16). A major triad consists of a major plus a minor third. In the minor chord, this reverses.

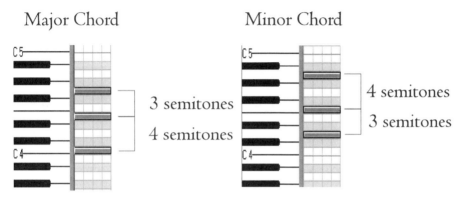

Figure 8.16   Major and minor chords.

Note that a major third spans a gap of four semitones, and a minor third spans a gap of three semitones. This is a very useful formula for working out major and/or minor chords from any given root note. For the major chord, you count up four semitones to get the third, and then three semitones to get the fifth. For the minor chord, you count up three semitones to get the third, and a further four semitones to get the fifth. Look more closely at Figure 8.16, and you will get the idea.

Another way of recognizing each chord is by its characteristic sound. The major chord is emotionally bright in comparison to the darker, moodier minor chord.

Chordal Functions

When chords are placed into a sequence, the result is a chord progression. A good chord progression is never haphazard—it is guided by principles of musical intelligence and good sense. Over time, many of these principles have been studied and formulated into a good working theory, which helps to explain the logic behind chord progressions. That there *is* a logic, there can be no doubt.

The main principle underlying the logic of chord progressions is tonality. Tonality raises one chord as being more important than all of the others. This chord is called the *tonic chord,* and it is built on the first degree of the scale. In the case of C major, the tonic chord is therefore the triad of C major. As the tonic, it is the main chord of the composition in the sense that chord progressions tend to arise from it and return to it at the end. It is the home chord, as it were.

The tonic is backed up by the dominant chord. The dominant chord always occurs on degree five of the scale. Therefore, in the scale of C major, the dominant chord is a G major triad. Table 8.4 shows the tonic and dominant chords of the key of C major.

Table 8.4 Tonic and Dominant Chords of the Key of C Major		
Degree	Notes	Name
Chord I	C E G	Tonic chord
Chord V	G B D	Dominant chord

Tonic and dominant chords represent the passive and active poles of tonality, respectively. Proceeding from the tonic pole, the chord progression tends to head toward the dominant pole. Once it reaches the dominant pole, the progression can then return satisfactorily to the tonic. This return is called a *cadence*—the way in which a chord progression is satisfactorily brought to a close. The progression from dominant chord to tonic chord is called a *perfect cadence* because it alone creates a complete sense of closure for the progression. You can hear this type of cadence in Track 22 of the audio CD.

Tonal chord progressions are analogous to, say, going out from home in the morning, doing your activities, and coming home again. Without the process of coming home, you would feel incomplete. In this way, tonality—rooted in the sense of a tonic chord—offers the equivalent in chord progressions to that satisfying psychological feeling of returning home. The return home, in the case of the chord progressions used in songs, is the cadence to the tonic chord.

One of the most important chords often touched upon along the way is the chord built on degree four of the scale. Called the *subdominant triad*, in the key of C major this is the triad built on F and having the notes F, A, and C. You can hear this chord used in Track 23. The name of the subdominant reveals its function: It serves as a counterbalance to the dominant. Its fifth, note C, tends to reinforce and back up the tonic. This serves to stabilize chord progressions and give them a sense of balance (see Figure 8.17).

For this reason, this group of chords forms a related group—they are called the three primary triads. Their job is to lay the foundations for the tonality of any particular key.

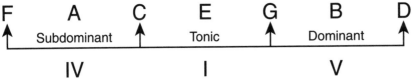

Figure 8.17 Tonic, dominant, and subdominant chords in the key of C major.

Notice that between them, the primary chords define all seven notes of the scale. In effect, this means that it is possible to give all tunes within that scale a harmony based on these chords alone. Songs that do this are extremely common. Some rock bands have used these same three chords in virtually all of their songs for periods of years. This type of music has come to be known as *three-chord rock*. Classic examples are The Troggs' "Wild Thing," the Clash's "Should I Stay or Should I Go," and Led Zeppelin's "Rock and Roll."

Chords I, IV, and V also provide the basis for the 12-bar blues progression used in rock, pop, and folk songs (see Figure 8.18). Called *three-chord songs*, they provide a chord sequence that is very familiar and easy to remember.

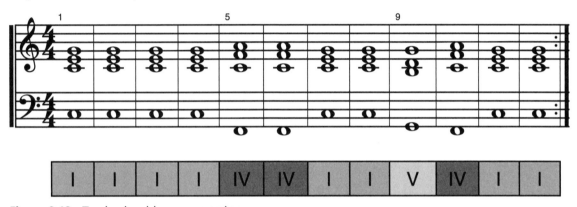

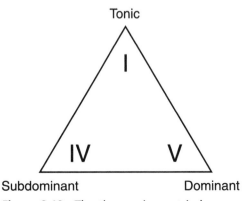

Figure 8.18   Twelve-bar blues progression.

The most important chords to locate, understand, and learn in any key are therefore chord I (the tonic), chord V (the dominant), and chord IV (the subdominant); see Figure 8.19. This means being able to play them comfortably at the MIDI keyboard. Being armed with chords I, IV, and V will equip you to start creating sound logical chord progressions for use in songs. The progressions they produce might sound very familiar. But you need to learn them initially as a foundation for more colorful and interesting chord progressions.

Figure 8.19   The three primary triads.

When you are familiar with chords I, IV, and V, it is time to start developing chord progressions with more than three chords. You can achieve this by incorporating secondary triads. These are all the minor chords in the key—Dm, Em, and Am. The last chord of a progression would usually be I, and the second-to-last chord would be IV or V. This final pair of chords is called a *cadence*, of which there are two basic types—the *perfect* cadence, which is V to I, and the *plagal* or "Amen" cadence, which is IV to I. It is called the Amen cadence because of the many hymns that tend to end in this way. Some popular songs use this type of cadence because it has a nice mellow feel to it, a feeling of settling upon the tonic triad. A famous song that uses

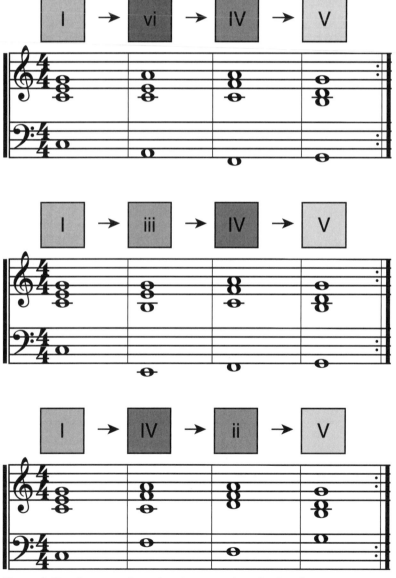

Figure 8.20 Common four-chord progressions in C major.

this type of cadence is Bob Marley's "No Woman No Cry." Most songs, though, tend to use the more familiar V to I progression. It creates a really strong and unambiguous sense of the music coming to an end. For example, listen to Bob Dylan's "Blowing in the Wind." This song in its entirety only uses the three primary chords—tonic, subdominant, and dominant.

A good place to start with developing chord progressions that go beyond use of the three primary chords is to try composing some four-chord progressions. Figures 8.20 and 8.21 provide some examples to start you off. You can hear these progressions, too, in Track 24 of the audio CD.

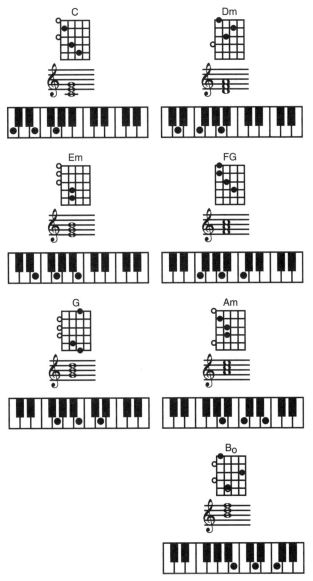

Figure 8.21 Table of the triads in the key of C major.

While learning the chords, you might find Figure 8.21 useful. It shows all of the seven triads in C major in score edit format, how to find those triads on the MIDI keyboard, and their names in popular sheet music format, together with their appropriate guitar tablature.

Once you have learned these, you will then be in a position to extend your knowledge beyond the limits of the C major scale. As you probably already know, as well as there being major scales, there are also minor scales. Having learned about a major scale, the intervals within it, and the various chords it offers for use in chord progressions, it is thus appropriate to learn about a minor scale in the next chapter.

Exercises

You can download the answers to the chapter exercises from www.courseptr.com/downloads.

1.   Complete the following statement. All musical intervals have a characteristic aural quality. In terms of aural quality, there are two main types of intervals: _____, which includes all of those intervals that have a generally agreeable sound to the ear; and _____, which have an element of tension about them.

2.   Complete the following statement. There are three perfect concords—the octave (ratio 2:1), the perfect _____ (ratio _____), and the perfect _____ (ratio _____).

3.   There are four imperfect concords—the _____ (ratio 5:4), the minor third (ratio _____), the _____ (ratio 5:3), and the minor sixth (ratio _____).

4.   Pencil in the notes required to harmonize this melody in C major in fifths.

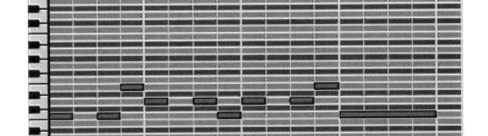

5.   Pencil in a note a fourth above each of these notes of the scale of C major. When you have done so, circle the so-called *devil's fourth*.

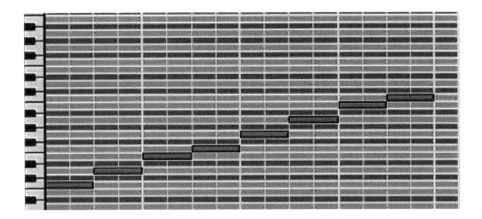

6.   Complete the following statement. There are two kinds of third in the major scale: There is the major third, which has a width of _____ semitones, and the minor third, which has a width of _____ semitones.

7.   Pencil in the notes required for a third above each of the following notes of the scale of C major. When you have done this, underline the third as being major or minor.

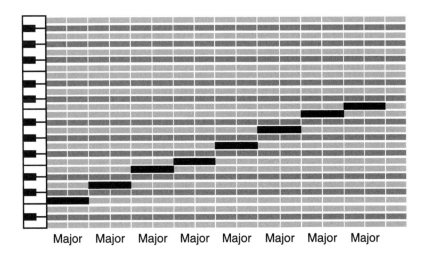

Major   Major   Major   Major   Major   Major   Major   Major

Minor   Minor   Minor   Minor   Minor   Minor   Minor   Minor

8. Complete the following statement. There are two kinds of sixth in the major scale: There is the major sixth, which has a width of _____ semitones, and the minor sixth, which has a width of _____ semitones.

9. Pencil in the notes required for a sixth above each of the following notes of the scale of C major. When you have done this, underline the third as being major or minor.

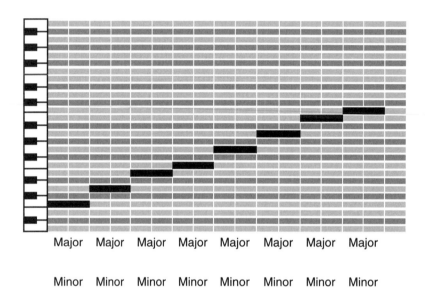

    Major   Major   Major   Major   Major   Major   Major   Major

    Minor   Minor   Minor   Minor   Minor   Minor   Minor   Minor

10. Identify the following intervals, both in terms of their size and whether they are major, minor, or perfect. The second note is always above the first.

Notes	Interval	Notes	Interval
C–D	Major second	F–C	_____
G–B	_____	C–B	_____
D–F	_____	G–F	_____
E–F	_____	D–B	_____
A–G	_____	A–F	_____
B–C	_____	E–A	_____

11.   List the intervals that belong in these categories:

Perfect Concord	Imperfect Concord	Discord
a) _____	a) _____	a) _____
b) _____	b) _____	b) _____
c) _____	c) _____	c) _____
	d) _____	e) _____
	e) _____	e) _____

12.   Fill in the missing words. The simplest sonority of all is the _____, which results from the simultaneous combination of two notes. Combinations of three notes are called _____, two examples of which are the _____ triad and the _____ triad.

13.   Fill in the missing words. The major triad has three notes, which are called the _____, the _____, and the _____. In the case of the major triad, the third is _____, while in the case of the minor triad, the third is _____.

14.   Fill in the missing notes to complete the series of triads in C major. Then identify those triads. The first chord has already been named for you:

Chord I	C	E	G	C major
Chord II	D	_____	_____	_____
Chord III	_____	_____	_____	_____
Chord IV	_____	_____	_____	_____
Chord V	_____	_____	_____	_____
Chord VI	_____	_____	_____	_____
Chord VII	_____	_____	_____	_____

15.   Fill in the missing whole notes required to complete the following triads.

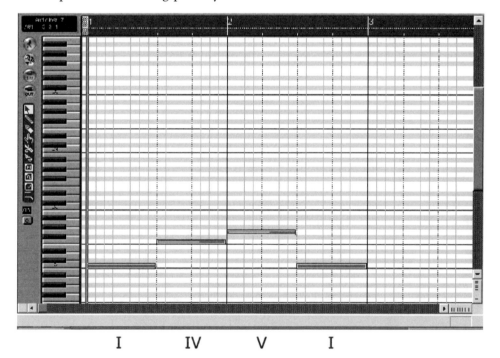

I   II   III   IV   V   VI   VII

16.   Fill in the missing words. The progression from _____ triad to
tonic triad is called a _____ cadence. The _____ triad
is built on the first degree of the scale, while the _____ triad is built
on the _____. In the key of C major, the three notes belonging to
the tonic triad are therefore _____, _____, and
_____, while the three notes belonging to the _____
triad are _____, _____, and _____.

17.   Program the notes given below into your sequencer. Then pencil in the notes required
to complete the following primary triads.

I   IV   V   I

18.   In the boxes provided, note all the possible three-chord progressions involving chords I, IV, and V, with each chord appearing only once. Having done so, you will find it very beneficial to play each of these through on your MIDI keyboard or to sequence them and listen to them.

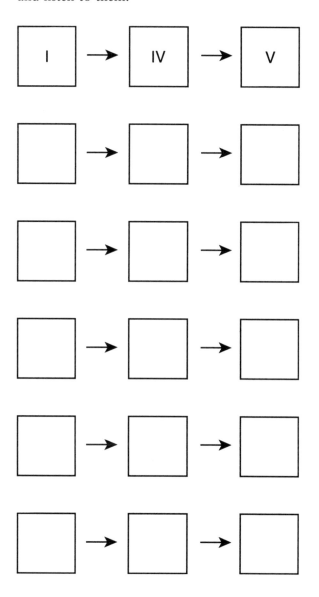

19.   Compose your own chord progressions in the key of C major involving at least one secondary chord, using the boxes provided to indicate the chord. When you have done so, spend some time either playing through or sequencing each chord progression. Listen carefully for the qualities of each progression and the particular merits of each. The number of chords required is indicated by the number of boxes.

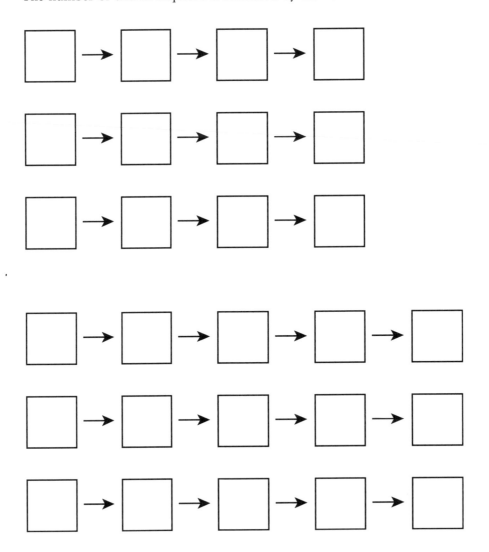

9 The Natural Minor Scale

For the computer musician, the key of C major provides a very good place to start the study of the various musical scales, chords, and chord progressions that underlie both popular and electronic music. Because C major uses only the white keys of your MIDI keyboard, it is quite easy to remember. It is also easier to play and record music in this key. Yet it would be a mistake to allow your knowledge to stop with the scale of C major. There are many other interesting keys and scales used by musicians. Initially, it is important to look closely at one key because the same principles apply equally to another. The difference is the starting pitch—tonic—upon which the key is built. Knowledge you acquire about one key, therefore, effectively equates to knowledge of all keys.

Having looked at a major key, it is now time to look to the other side of the coin. As well as major keys, you are no doubt aware that there can be minor keys. The existence of these two types of keys—major and minor—is one of the main features that underpins the tonal system of Western music. To write music effectively within that system—which still prevails today in popular music—you need a complete knowledge of both major and minor keys.

Understanding Minor Keys

Learning about keys is best accomplished in a certain order. Otherwise, the task can seem too daunting. After learning about the key of C major, you should then learn about the relative minor key—A minor. This uses the same white-key scale as C major, the difference being that note A is the starting point (see Figure 9.1). Note A is consequently the tonic of that key.

The key of A minor is called the *relative minor* of the key of C because it uses the same notes. The corollary to this is the key of C major, which is called the *relative major* of A minor. From this a useful rule of thumb, you can work out that to find the relative minor key from a major key, you simply count three notes down. Sequenced, the scale of A minor would appear as you see in Figure 9.2.

Like the key of C major, the key of A minor is easy to learn because it uses only the white keys. The difference is that A in the musical alphabet is the start of the scale: A B C D E F G (see Figure 9.3).

As with the C major scale, you should learn to play the A minor scale up and down on the MIDI keyboard. This kick-starts the process of becoming familiar with the scale—an essential step

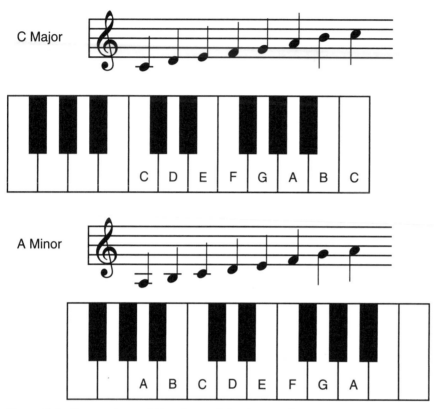

Figure 9.1   Comparison of C major and A minor scales.

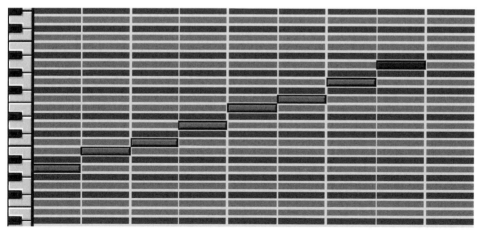

Figure 9.2   The scale of A minor sequenced in half notes.

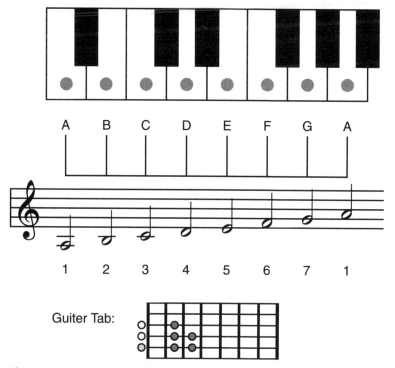

Figure 9.3 The A natural minor scale. The numbers below the notes indicate the degrees of the scale.

toward writing music in the minor key with ease and confidence. You play the minor scale up and down in the same way that you play the major scale. Start with the thumb on note A and play upward, remembering to move your thumb under for the fourth note. Reverse the fingering pattern when you are coming down, as shown in Chapter 3.

Earlier on, I showed you that the major scale produces a characteristic pattern of tones and semitones that remains true for all major scales: T T S T T T S. The same is true for the minor scales, except that because these begin on a different note, the pattern is slightly different (see Figure 9.4).

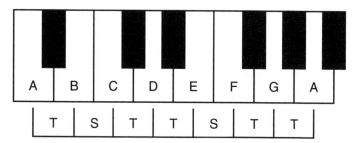

Figure 9.4 Pattern of tones and semitones in the minor scale.

Knowing this pattern of tones and semitones makes it easy to build a minor scale on any key of the keyboard or from any fret of the guitar. Each construction will represent a different key of the minor scale. Here a distinction between key and mode needs to be made. *Key* concerns the note upon which a scale is built. *Mode* concerns the type of scale—major or minor. The difference in the respective patterns of tones and semitones in the major and minor scales is thus a difference of mode.

Both major and minor are types of seven-note scales. Within that category, each is classified as being a different mode of seven-note scale. Hence the terms *major mode* and *minor mode* are sometimes used in reference to them.

- Major Mode: T T S T T T S
- Minor Mode: T S T T S T T

Chords in the Minor Scale

Once you know a particular scale, it is not enough just to learn it and be able to play it through. You also need to make an effort to become familiar with the various chords within the scale. Each song in the minor key will use these chords in a particular chord progression. The chord progression itself will involve at least two chords. To use such progressions effectively, you must find out what is available in terms of that scale.

A little thought will show that because the A minor scale uses the same notes as the C major scale, both keys share the same chords. And so they do. The difference between them is how they are used (see Table 9.1).

Table 9.1 Triads in the Key of A Natural Minor

Chord	Root	Third	Fifth	Name
Chord i	A	C	E	A minor
Chord ii	B	D	F	B diminished
Chord III	C	E	G	C major
Chord iv	D	F	A	D minor
Chord v	E	G	B	E minor
Chord VI	F	A	C	F major
Chord VII	G	B	D	G major

In the key of C major, the triad of C—C E G—was considered to be the tonic. Although the key of A minor uses the same scale, there is a different value there—the triad of Am is the tonic chord. The key of A minor has similarly different values for the chords built on the fourth and fifth degrees of the scale—that is, the subdominant and dominant triads. These two, along with the tonic, represent the primary chords of that key. The subdominant triad of the key of A minor is Dm, whereas the dominant triad is Em.

This observation raises some interesting issues with respect to the nature of the major and minor tonalities. In the major tonality, the three primary triads (I, IV, and V) are all major, while in the minor tonality (i, iv, and v) they are all minor. And because the primary triads are the most important chords in each key, this explains why the minor tonality leans toward more mellow moods. Its three primary triads are all minor (see Table 9.2 and Figure 9.5). You can hear the mellowness of this type of harmony on Track 25 of the audio CD.

Table 9.2 Primary Triads of C Major and A Minor

	Key of C Major	Key of A Minor
Tonic Chord	C: C E G	Am: A C E
Subdominant Chord:	F: F A C	Dm: D F A
Dominant Chord:	G: G B D	Em: E G B

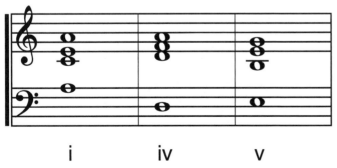

i	iv	v

Figure 9.5 The three primary triads of A minor in score edit view.

Here are a few important facts to remember:

- The tonic chord of any key is always built upon the first degree of either major or minor mode.

- The subdominant is always built upon the fourth degree of either major or minor mode.

- The dominant is always built upon the fifth degree of either major or minor mode.

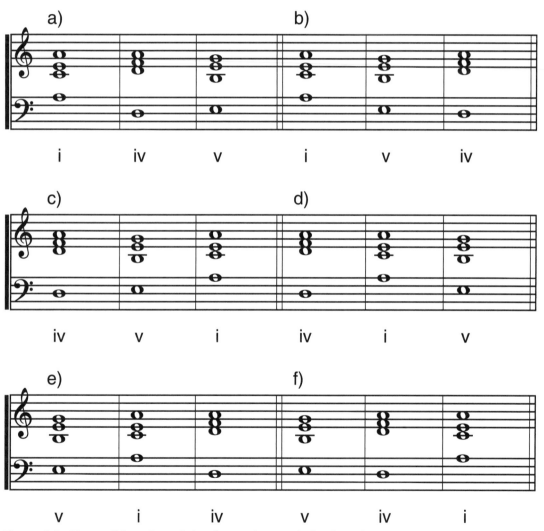

Figure 9.6 Six possible orders of the three primary triads of A minor.

Table 9.3 Six Possible Orders of the Three Primary Triads of A Minor

Roman numerals	Chords
i iv v	Am Dm Em
i v iv	Am Em Dm
iv v i	Dm Em Am
iv i v	Dm Am Em
v iv i	Em Dm Am
v i iv	Em Am Dm

When developing chord progressions within the minor key, start with the three primary chords and get to know the characteristic ways in which they lead one into the other. A good starting point would be their six possible orders in a three-chord progression (see Figure 9.6 and Table 9.3).

This practice gives you familiarity with the chords of Am, Dm, and Em, and it is also a good introduction to the composition of chord progressions in the minor mode. When you are famil-iar with these, then start to develop four-, five-, or six-chord progressions, which also involve the secondary triads: C, F, and G. Figure 9.7 shows some common four-chord progressions used in the minor mode.

Major and minor chords—collectively called *common chords*—represent the staples of most popular music. So far in this book, you have learned about six of these: three major chords—the chords of C, F, and G—and three minor chords—the chords of Am, Dm, and Em. Armed with these, you are now capable of producing chord progressions in either the major or the minor key. This gives you a great freedom of expression in your music writing. You can create bright, upbeat songs in the major mode or moodier songs in the minor mode.

Using the same set of six chords, you can even change key if you want—such as from C major to A minor and vice versa. This is a useful facility that enables you to create structurally contrasting sections in your songs. If you write your verses in the minor key, for example, you can switch up to the relative major for the choruses. Called modulation, this allows you to create refreshing contrasts of mood in your songs. We'll discuss this subject further in Chapter 11, "The Har-monic and Melodic Minor Scales."

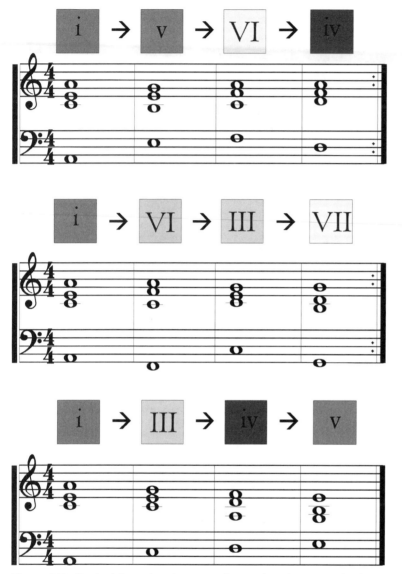

Figure 9.7 Typical four-chord progressions using the natural minor mode.

Exercises

You can download the answers to the chapter exercises from www.courseptr.com/downloads.

1.   Fill in the missing words. The relative minor key of C major is _____.
     To find the relative minor key from a major key, you must count _____
     notes down.

2. Fill in the six missing notes required to complete a rising A natural minor scale.

3. Fill in the missing words. _____ concerns the note upon which a scale is built. _____ concerns the type of scale—major or minor.

4. In the space provided, indicate the pattern of tones and semitones that belongs with each scale.

   Major Mode:　　　_____　_____　_____　_____　_____　_____　_____

   Natural Minor Mode:　_____　_____　_____　_____　_____　_____　_____

5. Which degree of the scale are these notes in A natural minor?

   - D: _____
   - B: _____
   - G: _____
   - F: _____

6. Fill in the notes required to give the three primary triads of the key of A natural minor.

   - Chord i: _____ _____ _____
   - Chord iv: _____ _____ _____
   - Chord v: _____ _____ _____

7. Play the A natural scale. Practice this exercise on your MIDI keyboard until you are fluent.

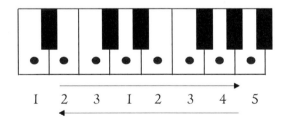

I　2　3　I　2　3　4　5

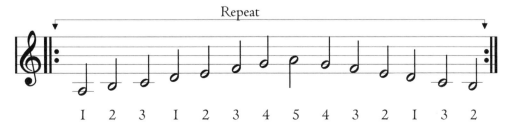

Repeat

I　2　3　I　2　3　4　5　4　3　2　I　3　2

8. Compose your own chord progressions in the key of A natural minor, involving at least one secondary chord, using the boxes provided to indicate the chord. When you have done so, spend some time either playing through or sequencing each chord progression. Listen carefully for the qualities of each progression and the particular merits of each. The number of chords required is indicated by the number of boxes.

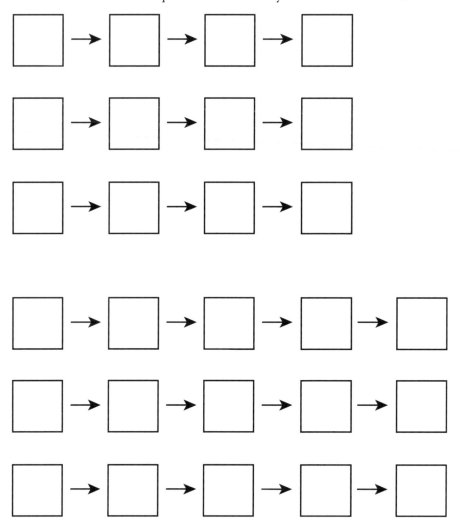

9.   Arpeggios of the chords of A natural minor. Play the following through on your MIDI keyboard. The fingers to use are given below each note.

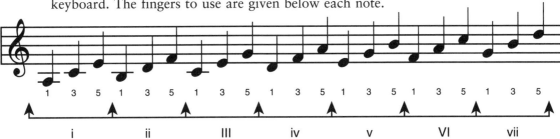

10 Melody and Motives

When you are writing music, you'll spend a lot of time thinking about leads and basses—in other words, melodic lines. Melodic lines involve a series of pitch changes. These changes define the melodic intervals that make up the line. Thus, you can think of a melodic line as having two distinct axes—an axis of pitch (the vertical axis) and an axis of time through which changes in pitch occur (the horizontal axis); see Figure 10.1.

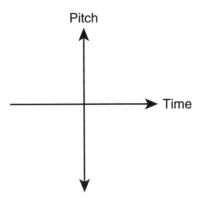

Figure 10.1 Axes of pitch and time in melody.

To accommodate both of these elements, sequencer windows are organized along the same lines (see Figure 10.2). On the left side is a keyboard representing the vertical dimension of pitch. The horizontal lines extending from it represent the theoretical extension of that pitch through time. Above the window are the bar numbers and all of the divisions of the bar necessary to use any given pitch with any note value.

Because they occur in two basic dimensions—pitch and time—you can think of melodic lines as simply being a series of changes of pitch occurring through time. Against this broad definition, you can construe any random succession of pitches to be a melodic line. But there is more to it than that. A good melodic line has some craft behind its construction. The rhythms and intervals it uses have all been selected by the writer for a particular expressive purpose. Expressing something definite in the writer's mind, it has a strong and clear identity that makes it memorable to us. But what gives it that identity?

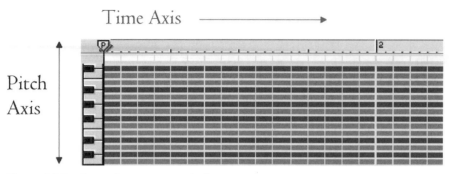

Figure 10.2 Axes of sequencer window.

Motives

More often than not, the strongest and most recognizable feature of the line is the motive/s from which it is built. All memorable tunes are made up of recognizable motives. A motive is simply a short snippet of melody that is readily recognizable to the ear because of its distinctive rhythm.

The best-known example of a motive is in Beethoven's Fifth Symphony: da - da - da - daaaa....! But this principle doesn't just apply to classical music. It is a universally recognized principle behind melodic composition. Whatever tunes you write, if they are to be memorable, they will be built up from motives.

Motives of one sort or another are used in all types of music. They generally employ two or three notes played with a strong, readily identifiable rhythm. The opening theme from *Mission Impossible* is a great example (see Figure 10.3). The underlying rhythm of the track is based on a 10/8 motive and is very distinctive.

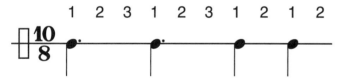

Figure 10.3 *Mission Impossible* theme: 10/8 motive used.

The opening—played on flutes, strings, and bass synth—uses three pitches in the first motive and another three as the motive repeats in the next bar. Together, the two statements of the motive balance each other in a question/answer type of relationship. In this way, the two motives combine to form a larger unit. This is called a *phrase* (see Figure 10.4).

The motive consequently represents the shortest piece of catchy music that it is possible to write. It is the strong rhythmic identity that makes it catchy. So memorable are some of these motives that they can often get stuck in our heads. Advertisers know this well—as a result, we are

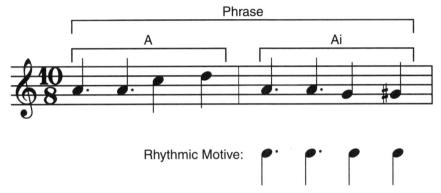

Figure 10.4 Phrase in *Mission Impossible* theme.

constantly bombarded by catchy motives in TV advertisements. Entering the subconscious, they also carry with them that engendered link to the intended product. Such is the power of motives.

Motives are usually the building blocks of a greater structure. In loop-based music, they are used to create a sense of forward motion, impetus, and drive, as shown in the chordal stab motive in Figure 10.5.

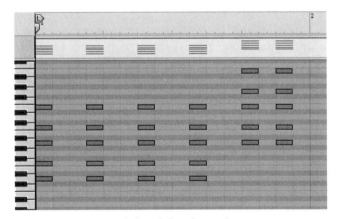

Figure 10.5 Looped chordal stab motive.

Writing a Strong Motive

To write a good motive, work on the rhythm first. Create a strong, distinctive rhythm that the ear will immediately recognize. For example, look at the two motives in Figure 10.6. Both have played a significant part in dance music of various styles. They are especially suited for bass lines. The driving rhythm gives both motives a sense of forward motion and impetus.

When it comes to melodic leads, you also need to think about the characteristic melodic intervals to use. Determining these is best accomplished by considering the emotional context. What does

Figure 10.6 Two dance music bass motives.

the motive represent? Is the energy rising or falling? Is it major or minor? Does the motive energy leap erratically, or is it smooth and stepwise? The example in Figure 10.7 is a Latin American motive, and the intervals it uses are large leaps, which give a sense of energy and excitement.

Figure 10.7 Latin American motive.

Film composers use motives all of the time, linking particular motives to certain characters. The way they treat the motive then informs you of the emotional context. John Williams's "Jaws" motive is a great example of this. He uses a rising semitone played low down on double basses to create a strong sense of threat. Then, to build tension during the shark attacks, he continually repeats the motive, getting louder and faster as the shark approaches.

This is where the power of melodic intervals starts to assert itself. There are major, minor, augmented, and diminished intervals—all of which have particular emotional affiliations. Many of these might be subjective, but that does not matter. If an interval causes you to feel something, it is liable to cause the same feeling in your listeners.

Experiment with the intervals we've looked at so far. What is the difference between a rising major third and a rising minor third? What is it about the rising minor sixth that evokes such a strong feeling of angst? And why does the rising major sixth sound so content? You will need to answer many of these questions for yourself as you build up your own catalog of intervals and their associated feelings. Once you do, you will gradually learn how to construct motives that serve your own particular expressive purpose.

You will also find it useful to listen to songs with an ear for the motives used. Because all songs—both traditional and popular—use motives, there is a great variety of material to study. You will find some suggestions in the following list, although you can also listen carefully to the kind of music that you enjoy. Keep an ear out for the motives used and ask yourself the following questions: Why has the writer used this motive? What do the intervals suggest?

Some useful songs—both traditional and modern—you can look at for their particular use of motives include:

- "Somewhere Over the Rainbow": Rising octave motive

- "Angels" (Robbie Williams): Rising major sixth motive

- "Right Here, Right Now" (Fatboy Slim): Scalar motives

- "Amazing Grace": Pentatonic motives

- "Insomnia" (Faithless): Loop-based motives

- "Shuffle Your Feet" (Black Rebel Motorcycle Club): Triadic motives

You can also hear some examples of the use and treatment of motives on Tracks 26–29 of the audio CD.

The motives you do use will draw their notes from a particular scale. Your ability to write motives thus also depends upon your knowledge of scales. To ensure that your knowledge is extensive, in the next chapter we will consider some further features relating to the minor scale.

Exercises

You can download the answers to the chapter exercises from www.courseptr.com/downloads.

1.   Fill in the missing words. A melodic line can be thought of as having two axes: There is the axis of _____ (the vertical axis) and the axis of _____ (the horizontal axis).

2.   Fill in the missing words. _____ generally employ two or three notes played with a strong, readily identifiable _____.

3.   Answer the following questions about the given two-bar melody.

A. What scale does this melodic extract use?

B. Using a pencil, identify and mark out the motives used, assigning to each identified motive a letter (A, B, and so on).

C. Mark out and indicate the phrase structure of the melody, giving each phrase a letter (A, B, and so on).

4. Build up a four-bar rhythm in compound quadruple time using the following motives.

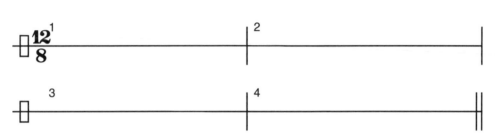

5. Using the rhythm you created in Exercise 4, compose a four-bar lead melody based around the motive of a rising fifth, in the key of C major.

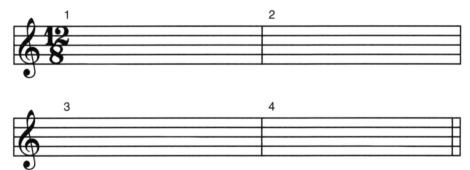

6. Build up a four-bar rhythm in quadruple time using the following motives.

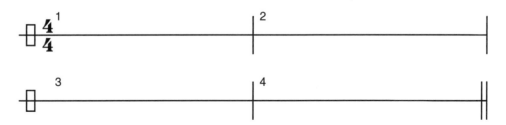

7. Using the rhythm you created in Exercise 6, compose a four-bar melody based around the motive of a falling third, in the key of A natural minor.

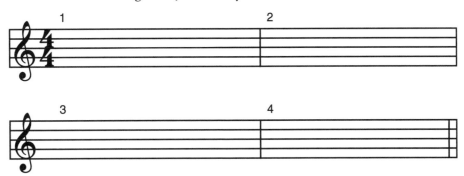

8. Compose and sequence a lead for a solo flute patch based around the following melodic intervals. The meter and time signature are optional.

11 The Harmonic and Melodic Minor Scales

Having by now studied both major and minor scales, you are in a good position to start using that knowledge to good effect in your music. Major/minor represents the total spectrum of scales recognized in conventional music theory. There are other scales that we'll consider later in this book, but for now we'll concentrate on these two.

The minor key is much more complex than the major. This is because the minor scale occurs in a number of different forms. The form we have considered so far is the natural minor scale. Popular music without the natural minor scale would not be as rich or varied. It is and does remain, along with the major scale, one of the staple resources for songwriters, composers, and musicians everywhere.

In addition to the natural minor scale, there are a further two forms of minor scale to consider—the harmonic minor scale and the melodic minor scale. Both represent variations of the natural minor scale. Although the natural minor scale represents the basic default for the minor key, both harmonic and melodic minor variations of that scale are worthy of study. In this chapter, we'll study first the harmonic minor scale, and then the nelodic minor scale.

Ancient Greek musical scales developed from the tetrachord: a series of four notes spanning a fourth (for example, C D E F). The scales used today use two such tetrachords—a lower tetrachord and an upper tetrachord. Between them they make up the eight notes of the octave. In the case of the natural minor scale, this is easy to see in Figure 11.1.

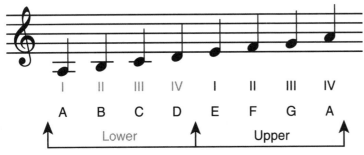

Figure 11.1 Lower and upper tetrachords in the natural minor scale.

The tetrachord system is very good for understanding and portraying differences of mode, as found, for example, in the difference between the natural minor and harmonic minor modes.

The Harmonic Minor Scale

In the harmonic minor mode, the lower tetrachord is the same as the lower tetrachord in the natural minor mode. The upper tetrachord differs slightly because the seventh note of the scale—G—is sharpened to give note G#. Try playing the scale in Figure 11.2 through on the MIDI keyboard.

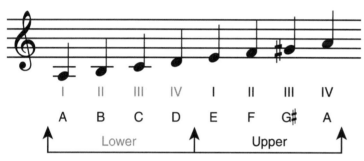

Figure 11.2 The harmonic minor scale.

Alternatively, sequence it and listen to the scale as it rises and falls, as shown in Figure 11.3.

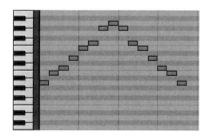

Figure 11.3 Sequenced harmonic minor scale.

The upper tetrachord has an exotic sense owing to the charm of its intervals. This is largely due to an interval we have not encountered so far—the augmented second between notes F and G#. So what is this about?

The main reason for the use of the note G# is that it gives a better harmony. Chord progressions tend to be guided between two basic poles—a passive pole represented by the tonic chord and an active pole represented by the dominant chord. In the natural minor mode of A, the tonic chord is Am and the dominant chord is Em. A long time ago, musicians discovered that when the chord of Em is changed to E—that is an E major chord—the cadential progression from dominant to tonic was that much more convincing. This was primarily because the G#—only a semitone below the tonic—rose nice and smoothly up to the tonic (see Figure 11.4).

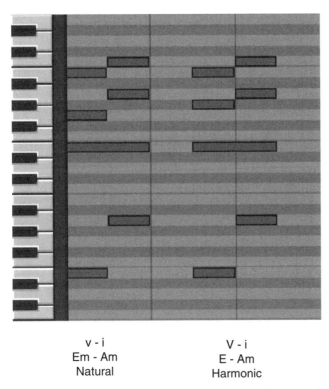

v - i
Em - Am
Natural

V - i
E - Am
Harmonic

Figure 11.4 Comparison of V–I in natural and harmonic minor scales.

To appreciate this, sequence it and listen carefully to the two progressions. The first (v–i in the natural minor scale) is quite mellow, and it has a more quiescent feel to it. The second (V–i in the harmonic minor scale) is much more incisive and powerful. You can hear the difference between these two progressions in Track 30 of the audio CD. Hence, the reason for the name given to this particular variety of minor mode: the harmonic minor scale, which is named after its characteristic harmony.

To use the harmonic minor scale effectively, you need to learn the chords within it. You can do so by following the same procedure as before.

1. Learn to play the scale up and down until you are familiar with it. See the list of scales in Appendix A, "Scales," for the correct fingering and best way to play it.

2. Start to learn the chords. These are the same as the chords in the natural minor scale except for one crucial difference—the note G is always sharp. A good way to learn the

chords in a scale is to play them as arpeggios. An arpeggio is where the notes of a chord are played as a sequence of notes. For further information on arpeggios, consult Chapter 24, "Arpeggiation." In this exercise, the root is played with the thumb, the third with finger three, and the fifth with finger five (the little finger), as shown in Figure 11.5.

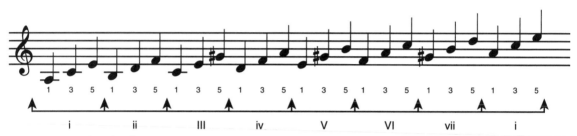

Figure 11.5 Chords of A harmonic minor sequenced as arpeggios.

3. Now that you have learned the chords, you can start to develop three chord progressions, beginning with chords i, iv, and V—the three primary chords.

4. When you have mastered the three primary chords, you can start to bring in some of the secondary chords. Also, try out the chord progressions developed using the natural minor mode and substitute chord V for chord v. Listen to the difference. Sometimes chord V is a much better option, especially at the cadence, because it gives a more final sense of closure on the tonic chord. To illustrate this, Figure 11.6 shows some typical four-chord progressions in the harmonic minor mode.

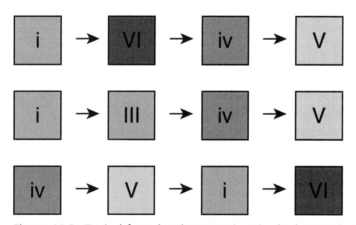

Figure 11.6 Typical four-chord progressions in the harmonic minor mode.

The chart in Figure 11.7 summarizes the information given about the chords in the harmonic minor mode, showing the seven chords, their representation in staff format, the guitar tablature for each chord, and a diagram that illustrates how each chord can be found on the keyboard.

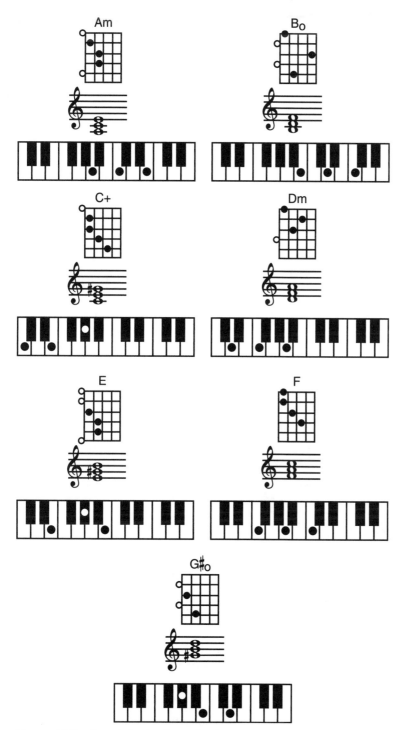

Figure 11.7   Chords in the key of A harmonic minor.

The Melodic Minor Scale

The melodic minor scale is the third member of the minor family group of scales. Bringing this scale into the picture makes the minor key seem even more complex. The major mode has only one form, whereas the minor mode has three—natural, harmonic, and melodic. So why is the minor key so complicated? Really, it is very much a holdover from classical music theory.

Classical composers were dissatisfied with the way in which the natural minor mode lent itself to their purposes. Although beautiful in themselves, the harmonies of the natural minor scale were not incisive enough for the dramatic kind of narrative favored by classical composers. To remedy this problem, the first step was sharpening the seventh, giving rise to the harmonic minor scale. This solved a lot of the problem. Sharpening the seventh yielded a powerful major dominant chord that suited their purposes.

However, in some melodic contexts that exotic-sounding upper tetrachord did not sound right. Composers arrived at a solution by sharpening the sixth as well. The result of this was a smooth stepwise motion up to the tonic—exactly like the upper tetrachord of the major mode. To counterbalance that major feeling, on descent the minor mode was re-established. This means that the melodic minor mode is different in its ascending and descending forms (see Figure 11.8).

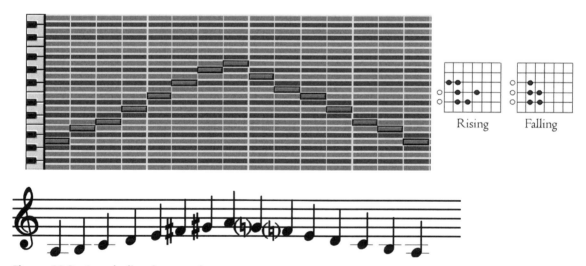

Figure 11.8 A melodic minor mode.

As a holdover from classical times, the melodic minor mode plays a larger role in theory than in practice. That said, the scale has some interesting facets, and your efforts to understand and use it will give you great rewards. Jazz musicians have made good use of the ascending form—so much that it is sometimes called the *jazz minor scale*. Some of the seventh chords it gives—which we will study in Chapter 21, "Chords of the Seventh"—are beautiful. Hawaiian traditional music uses the melodic minor mode to good effect, too.

Now that you have learned to play the scale up and down—remembering that the descent is identical to the natural minor mode—you can learn the chords by practicing them as arpeggios. When you get to the top, come back down again using only the white keys (see Figure 11.9).

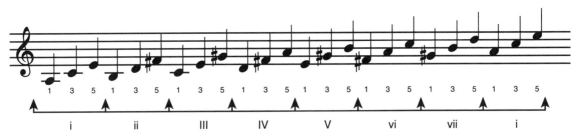

Figure 11.9 Chords of a melodic minor sequenced as arpeggios.

When you are familiar with these chords, start putting them together in chord progressions. To start you off, Figure 11.10 provides some examples. Track 31 of the audio CD also presents an interesting example, using the major subdominant triad of the melodic minor mode.

Figure 11.11 shows a table of chords in the A melodic minor mode.

In this chapter you have seen that the complexities of the minor scale are due to some of its inherent defects as far as harmony and melody are concerned. The natural minor doesn't offer a convincing dominant triad, so the seventh is sharpened. The sharp seventh in its turn creates an awkward-sounding augmented second (see the next chapter for a full explanation of this term) between the sixth and seventh degrees. So the sixth gets sharpened. The variations of the minor scale are thus due to musicians changing elements of it to suit their purposes. As such, you will find that as your knowledge increases and you gain more experience writing in the minor mode, the three forms will tend to merge into an overall minor scale complex that you will find fascinating and delightful to use.

In theory, the major mode looks pristine when compared to the minor mode, but you will often find that in practice musicians tend to change elements of the major mode, too. This is done by borrowing elements from the minor mode, as seen in the harmonic major mode and the major/minor mode. For more information on these interesting variations of our traditional scales, see Chapter 22, "Exotic Scales."

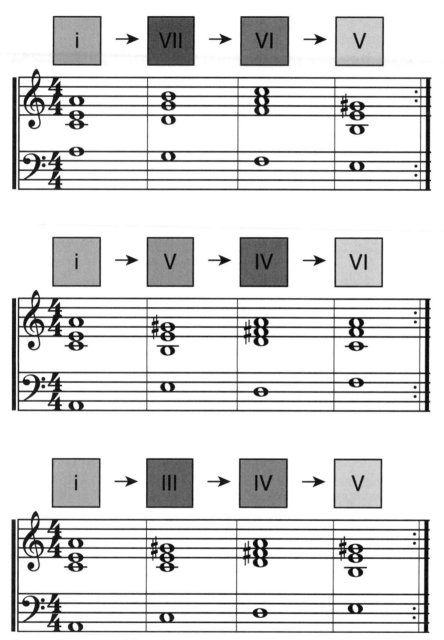

Figure 11.10   Typical four-chord progressions in the A melodic minor mode.

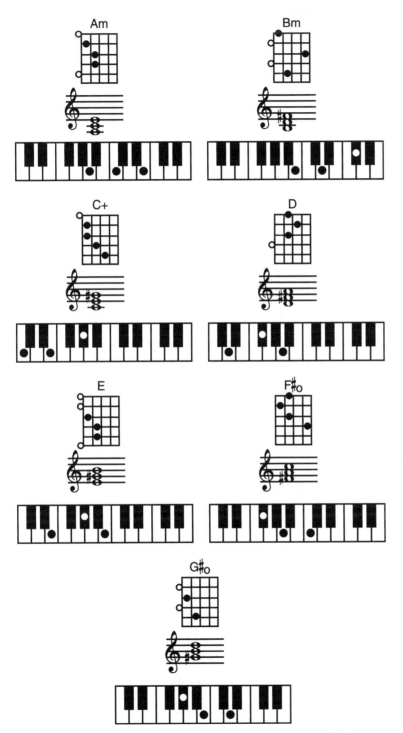

Figure 11.11 Chords in the melodic minor mode (ascending).

Exercises

You can download the answers to the chapter exercises from www.courseptr.com/downloads.

1. Fill in the missing words. Although there is only one kind of major mode, there are _____ types of minor mode: the natural minor, _____ minor, and melodic minor. The difference between the natural and harmonic minor is that the harmonic minor mode has a sharp _____ in order to give a leading note up to the _____ degree. The ascending form of the melodic minor mode also has a sharp _____, while on descent it is identical to the _____ minor mode.

2. Fill in the six missing notes required to complete a rising A harmonic minor scale.

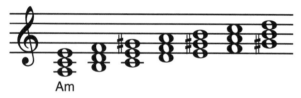

3. Identify the following triads from the A harmonic minor mode. The first triad has already been identified for you.

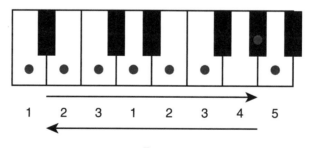

4. Play the A harmonic minor scale. Practice the following exercise on your MIDI keyboard until you are fluent.

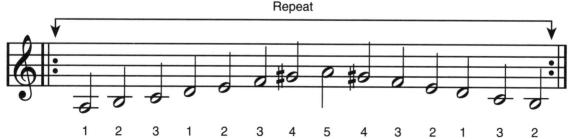

5. Sequence the following bass in A harmonic minor. Then, on another track, add a pad or string part over it using the chords indicated—the three primary chords of A harmonic minor.

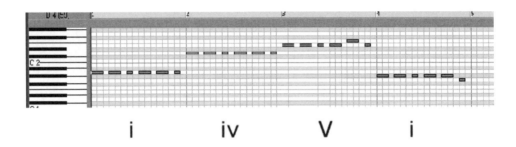

        i   iv   V   i

6. Play the arpeggios of the chords of A harmonic minor. Practice this exercise until you are fluent.

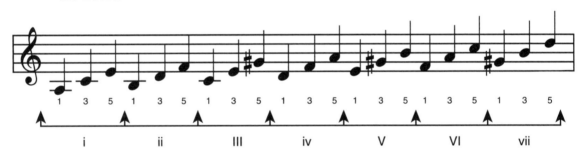

7. Compose your own chord progressions in the key of A harmonic minor, involving at least one secondary chord, using the boxes provided to indicate the chord. When you have done so, spend some time either playing through or sequencing each chord progression. Listen carefully for the qualities of each progression and the particular merits of each. The number of chords required is indicated by the number of boxes.

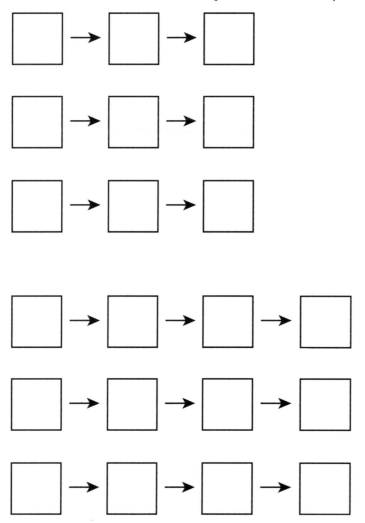

8. Play the A melodic minor scale. Practice the following exercise on your MIDI keyboard until you are fluent.

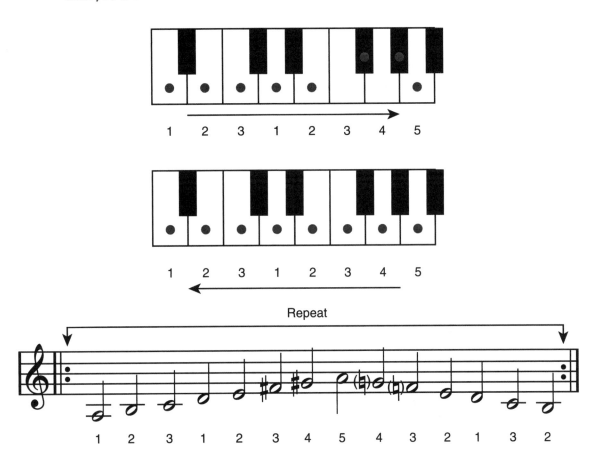

9.   Compose your own chord progressions in the key of A melodic minor, involving at least one secondary chord, using the boxes provided to indicate the chord. When you have done so, spend some time either playing through or sequencing each chord progression. Listen carefully for the qualities of each progression and the particular merits of each. The number of chords required is indicated by the number of boxes.

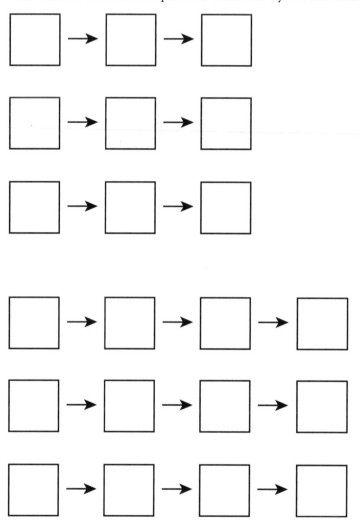

12 Augmented and Diminished Intervals and Interval Inversions

So far, we have studied two distinct families of intervals—the perfect intervals, which include the first, fourth, fifth, and octave, and the imperfect intervals, which include the second, third, sixth, and seventh. There is yet a third family of intervals that we have not yet considered—the family of augmented and diminished intervals. Knowledge of these represents an essential foundation for the understanding and use of the augmented and diminished triads you will study in Chapter 18, "Chord Progressions and Root Movement." It is also important knowledge for the understanding and use of artificial and exotic scales, which you'll study in Chapter 22, "Exotic Scales," and the use of complex harmony, which you'll study in Chapter 23, "Complex Harmony." So what is the family of augmented and diminished intervals?

Augmented and Diminished Intervals

The best way to understand the family of augmented and diminished intervals is to look at the interval of, say, a third, as found between the notes F and A. You already know that a third can occur in two forms—a major third of four semitones and a minor third of three semitones. When a major third is increased in size by a further semitone—say, for example, by sharpening the A—it becomes an augmented third. Similarly, when a minor third is decreased in size by a semitone—say, for example, by again flattening the Ab—it becomes a diminished third. You will see these intervals illustrated in Figure 12.1. Notice that to represent the diminished third, a double flat sign is needed in the score edit view. This means that the note concerned is flattened twice and therefore is lowered by two semitones.

In this way, the interval of a third can occur in four forms: diminished, minor, major, and augmented. This also applies to seconds, sixths, and sevenths. It does *not* apply to the perfect intervals because these do not occur in major or minor forms. This can be further understood as follows: When an interval is augmented, it is increased in size by a semitone. Therefore, the perfect fifth—C to G—can become an augmented fifth by sharpening the top note G, as shown in Figure 12.2.

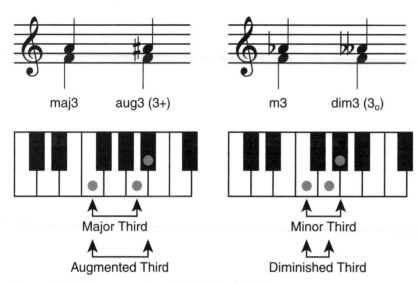

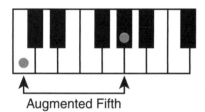

Figure 12.1   Augmented and diminished third.

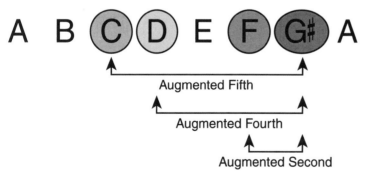

Figure 12.2   Augmented fifth interval.

This is the interval found between the third and seventh degrees of the harmonic minor scale. Figure 12.3 shows other augmented intervals in the same scale.

A   B   C   D   E   F   G#   A

Augmented Fifth

Augmented Fourth

Augmented Second

Figure 12.3   Augmented intervals in the harmonic minor scale.

You can augment any perfect or major interval in this way. This rule doesn't apply to minor intervals because augmenting a minor interval gives a major interval. Figure 12.4 shows all of the main augmented intervals.

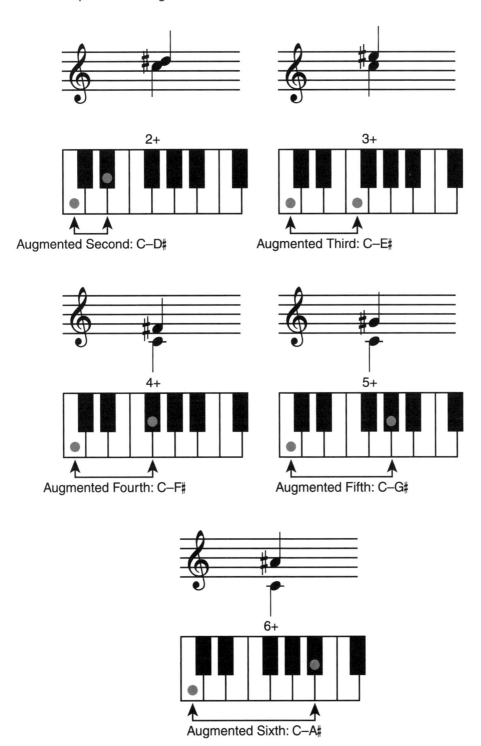

Figure 12.4   Augmented intervals.

The opposite of an augmented interval is a diminished interval. A diminished interval is a perfect or minor interval that has been shrunk by a semitone. A good example is the diminished fifth interval found in the C major scale between notes B and F. Recall that earlier, you were shown that all of the fifth intervals in the C major scale were perfect intervals bar one—the fifth between notes B and F, the so-called *diabolus en musica*. This is a diminished fifth because it is smaller than the perfect fifth by one semitone. You can easily verify this by doing a simple semitone count. Whereas the perfect fifth (as found, for example, between the notes C and G) has a measurement of seven semitones, the diminished fifth (as found between notes B and F) has a measurement of six (see Figure 12.5).

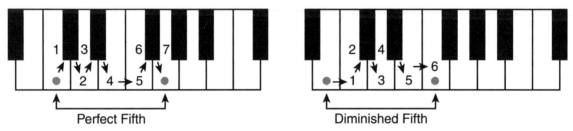

Figure 12.5 Comparison of perfect and diminished fifth intervals.

You will find more diminished intervals in the minor scale. Diminished intervals in the A harmonic minor scale are shown in Figure 12.6.

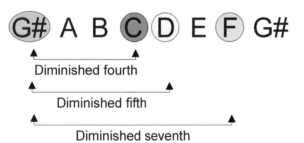

Figure 12.6 Diminished intervals in the A harmonic minor scale.

Only perfect and minor intervals can be diminished. They are shown in Figure 12.7.

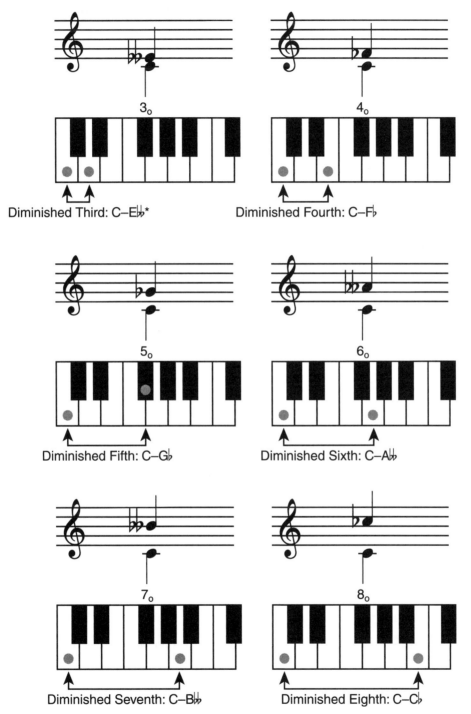

Figure 12.7   Diminished intervals.

In summary, therefore, seconds, thirds, sixths, and sevenths can occur in four forms: diminished, minor, major, and augmented. Perfect intervals—the prime, fourth, fifth, and octave—can occur in three forms: diminished, perfect, and augmented. In this way, you can see that our musical system recognizes a total of 28 intervals.

Interval Inversions

Viewed overall, there are three basic families of intervals: perfect, major/minor, and augmented/diminished. These are related in a special way. Each interval has what is called its *inversion*. The notes C to G give a perfect fifth. G to C, on the other hand, is a different interval—a perfect fourth—but it uses the same notes. It is thus like an "upside down" perfect fifth. Having this relationship to the perfect fifth, the perfect fourth is said to be the *inversion* of the perfect fifth (see Figure 12.8).

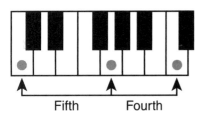

Figure 12.8   Perfect fourth as inversion of perfect fifth.

Each of the intervals considered earlier has an inversion. Notice that the inverted interval has opposite qualities—in other words, when inverted, a major interval gives a minor interval (and vice versa). Similarly, when inverted, an augmented interval gives a diminished interval (and vice versa). See Figure 12.9 for a table of inversions.

Through study of this chapter, you now have knowledge of all of the intervals used in our music, together with their pairing by inversion. Although this knowledge is quite technical, it is nonetheless essential for a full understanding, use, and treatment of scales, melodic motives, and harmonies. This is because all three of these use these intervals as their building blocks.

Knowledge of intervals and their inversions is of special importance when it comes to harmony. This is because any chord that you use can be scored in a variety of ways. The notes can be widely spaced over the pitch register, which is called *chordal spacing*. You can also double notes of a chord to create particular kinds of chordal emphasis, which is called *octave doubling*. The bass line of your tracks can use different notes of the chord as the foundation for your harmony. This is called *chordal inversion*, in which each chord can be used in numerous positions. You'll study all of these important features of scoring chords in the next chapter.

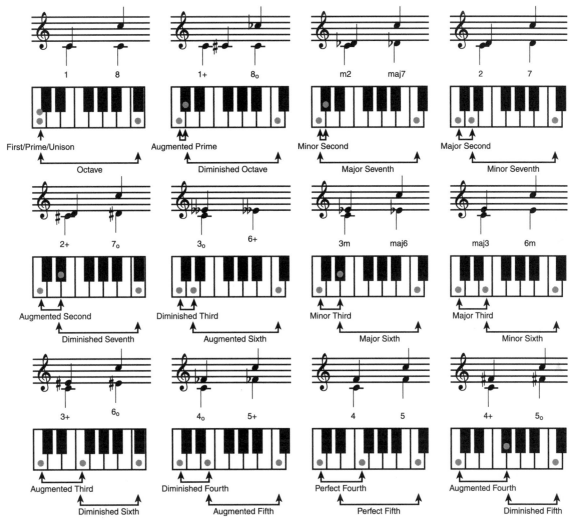

Figure 12.9 Table of inversions.

Exercises

You can download the answers to the chapter exercises from www.courseptr.com/downloads.

1. Fill in the missing words. When an interval is _____, it is increased in size by a semitone. Therefore, the perfect fifth—G to D—can become an augmented fifth by _____ the top note D or _____ the bottom note G.

2. Fill in the missing words. When an interval is diminished, it is _____ in size by a semitone. Therefore, the perfect fifth—G to D—can become a diminished fifth by _____ the top note D or _____ the bottom note G.

3.   Identify the following augmented intervals in the spaces provided.

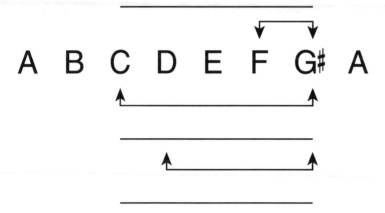

4.   In the spaces provided, identify the following augmented intervals.

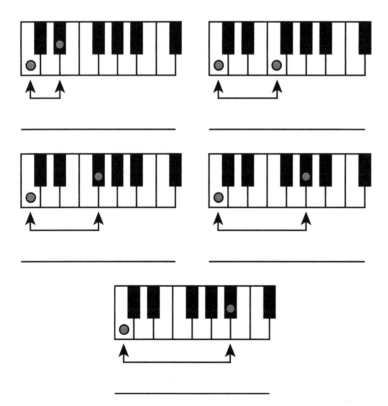

5. In the spaces provided, identify the following diminished intervals.

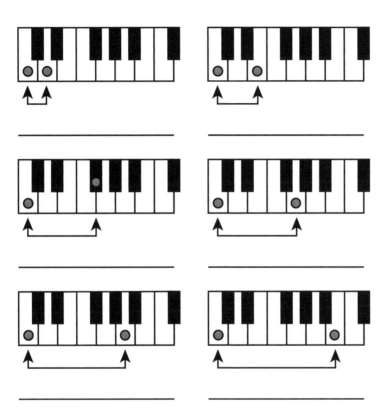

6. What are the three families of intervals?

A. _____

B. _____

C. _____

7. Fill in the missing words. When inverted, a major interval gives a
_____ interval (and vice versa), and an _____
interval, when inverted, gives a diminished interval (and vice versa).

8.   Identify the following intervals.

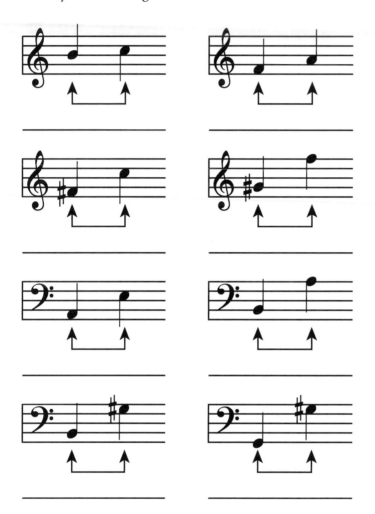

9.   Name the inversions of each of these intervals.

Interval	Inversion
First (unison, prime)	_____
Augmented prime	_____
Minor second	_____
Major second	_____
Augmented second	_____
Diminished third	_____
Minor third	_____

Interval	Inversion
Major third	_____
Augmented third	_____
Diminished fourth	_____
Perfect fourth	_____
Augmented fourth	_____

13 Chordal Inversions, Octave Doubling, and Spacing

A ny piece of music that you write will no doubt be based on a sequence of chords. From previous chapters, you have gathered that such a sequence is called a *chord progression*. The use of such chord progressions gives the succession of individual events within your composition a sense of coherence and logic. The ear recognizes the progression and makes sense of the music accordingly.

Chord progressions also serve to connect the different simultaneous layers of your tracks. Examples of these layers are the main lead, bass line, accompaniment (such as guitar strums or keyboard arpeggios), pads, strings, and so on. Each of these layers contributes its own particular part to the music. But the factor that allows them all to work together is the chord progression. This working together of different layers or tracks within the song is called the *harmony*. To write effective music, therefore, you must have knowledge of harmony.

In Figure 13.1, you can see two separate views of the same two-bar extract. The score edit view shows you the different tracks involved, which include piano, strings, synth, and bass. When all of the tracks are combined in piano roll view, you can see that they all fit together, being based on an E minor chordal harmony.

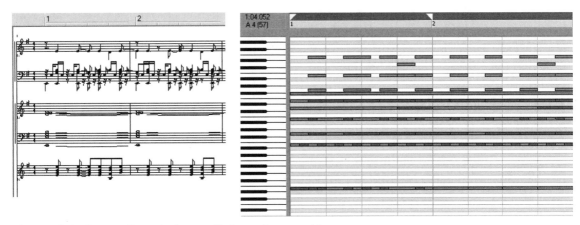

Figure 13.1 Score edit and piano roll view of composition.

Harmony

To acquire a knowledge of harmony, you need to know about the chords that are used in chord progressions. It is important to realize that triads of three notes form the basic units of any chord progression. Detailed knowledge of these is essential for those wishing to write their own music, especially since all other more complex chords used in chord progressions (such as sevenths, added sixth chords, ninths, and so on) build upon this foundation of triadic harmony.

Recall that a triad has three notes, each of which can be named as follows:

C	E	G
Root	Third	Fifth

The root is the most important note of a chord. Without a root, it would be impossible for the ear to tell which chord one is. So the root is the note from which the chord acquires its identity. This is fairly simple and straightforward. A chord whose root note is, say, F is called a chord of F, and so on. In the table you saw a moment ago, the root note is C, so it is called a chord of C.

The next most important note in a triad is the fifth, which gives the chord strength and back-bone. Try playing a fifth on its own—it is a very strong and stable interval. This strength and stability is imparted to the chord that uses it.

The third is also important because it gives the chord richness and fullness. In popular music harmony, the third is often called the *sweet* note. Consequently, when the third is absent, the chord has a bare, empty quality. When the third is played on its own, the chord also sounds incomplete—it has richness but no backbone. The third is also important in that it can be major or minor—a factor that will determine whether it is a major triad or a minor triad. All three notes of a triad are therefore important: Each note has a job to do within that sonority.

In harmony—especially with many styles of popular music—the most important contributors are the bass and the lead. The art of harmony at this level involves developing a bass and lead that harmonize with one another and follow an effective chord progression. The importance of this can vary depending upon the style of music. Some forms of modern music rely on fairly static harmonic fields—that is, they are based on a single chord.

Inverted Chords

As a triad has three notes, it follows that at any given time, any of the three notes of a triad might occur in the bass. When the root note is in the bass—in other words, it is heard as the lowermost note—the chord is said to be in *root position*. Chords in root position give a very strong and stable harmony compared to inverted chords. Consequently, most songs tend to end with a root position chord (see Figure 13.2).

Inverted chords occur when a note other than the root occurs in the bass. There are two kinds of inverted chords: In first inversion chords, the third is in the bass, and in second inversion chords, the fifth is in the bass. See Figure 13.3.

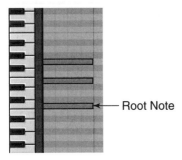

Figure 13.2   C major triad in root position.

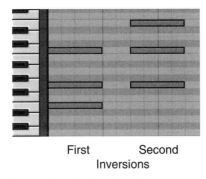

Figure 13.3   C major triad in first and second inversions.

Although they are not as stable as root position chords, both inversions find a frequent use in modern popular and electronic music. In popular music song sheets, inverted chords are often represented by the note letter indicating the root, followed by the note letter that represents the bass (see Figure 13.4).

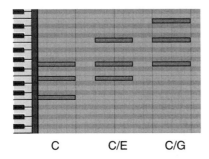

Figure 13.4   Chord symbols for C major triad in three positions.

For this reason, inverted chords are sometimes referred to as *slash* chords. Slash chords give more flexibility to the bass line. The bass can take any of the three notes of the chord. The freedom this offers enables smoother and more melodic bass movement.

When writing a chord progression, you must make a further choice: What is the best position for the chord? Should it be root or first or second inversion? To decide which position is best, you need to know the three positions as they apply to a given chord. You can only acquire this knowledge by studying the inversions of chords. Play them over and over until your ear learns to recognize their particular qualities.

Here's a useful tip: When you are trying to find the inversions of chords, follow this simple procedure.

1.   Locate the root position chord.

2.   To get first inversion, simply place the lowermost note up an octave.

3.   To get second inversion, place the lowermost note of the first inversion triad up an octave.

Figure 13.5 will help to explain these instructions.

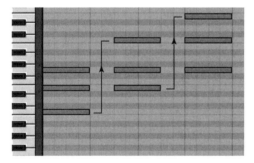

Figure 13.5   The three positions of C.

Octave Doubling

When you are choosing a chord for a progression, the issue of doubling will probably arise. Coming to grips with octave doubling is a precursor to writing professional-sounding harmonies. The best way to consider octave doubling is to think of the case of a whole orchestra playing a triad of A minor. Flutes and piccolos would play notes high up in the register, while strings would have a spread from the bass up to the middle register. The double bass, contra-bassoon, or tuba would play notes very low down.

Writing a minor chord effectively for these forces would necessitate the use of far more than three notes. To solve this problem, certain notes are doubled at the octave. The best notes to double tend to be the root and fifth because these give the chord its identity and backbone. Through octave doubling, a simple A minor triad could appear as in Figure 13.6, for example.

In Figure 13.6, the root has been doubled twice, the fifth once, and the third once. The result is a chord of seven notes that, because of octave doubling, still only uses root, third, and fifth of the

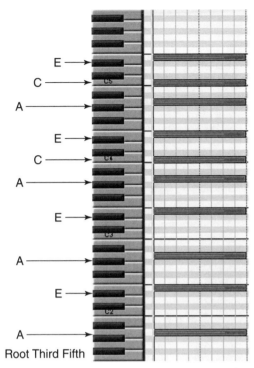

Figure 13.6 Sequenced A minor triad with octave doubling.

triad. Note that through octave doubling, the chord gains a nice, even spread of notes over the pitch register. You can hear the effect of this for yourself in Track 32 of the audio CD.

Spacing

Another important facet of chordal harmony is spacing. Spacing concerns the way the notes of the chord are spread within a balanced sonority. There are two kinds of spacing: closed and open. *Closed spacing* is when the notes of a chord are crowded together as closely as possible (see Figure 13.7).

Open spacing is where the chord is given a wider spread over the register. Each single chord can be spaced in a variety of ways, closed and open. Each type of spacing will contribute to the overall effect of that sonority. Figure 13.8 shows some examples of open spacing of an A minor triad.

To get a good grasp on inversions, doubling, and spacing, take a single chord and arrange it in many different possible ways. Then listen to the chords and ascertain their strengths and weaknesses. In this way, you will soon learn the best positions for your chords. In Track 33 of the audio CD, you will hear examples of the same chord being varied through the use of these principles.

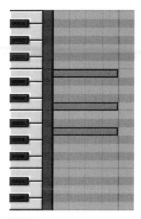

Figure 13.7 A minor triad in closed position.

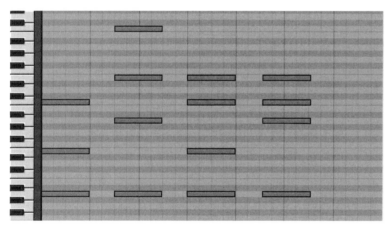

Figure 13.8 A minor triad in open spacing.

Knowledge of inversions, doubling, and spacing can give your chord progressions spread, coherence, and logic. It enables you to write music with a smoothness and flair that otherwise might be lacking. Look at the difference between the two versions of the same chord progressions in Figure 13.9.

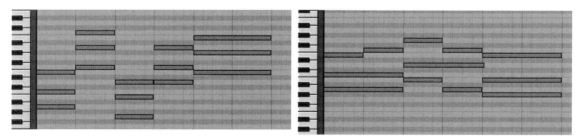

Figure 13.9 Awkward and smooth voice leading.

The first version ignores inversions, doubling, and spacing. It is awkward, blocky, and very unmusical. The second version takes these principles into account. It is smooth, musical, and coherent. Notice the sustained notes obtained by exploiting notes that the chords share in common. The use of this technique helps knit the chords together.

In classical harmony this smooth, flowing connection between the different voices is called *voice leading*. Imagine if Figure 13.9 was scored for three vocalists. The arrangement on the left would be very awkward to sing and would sound disjointed. The arrangement on the right would sound smoother because each individual melodic part falls much easier to the voice. Listen to Track 34, and you can compare the two versions for yourself.

In this chapter you have learned that a single chord can be used in a great variety of ways. The notes can be spaced differently to give different sonic slants on the same harmony. The chord can be thickened out by doubling certain notes. A chord can also be used in different positions determined by which note of the chord lies in the bass. You have also learned that these principles give smoothness and effective voice leading in the transition between one chord and another.

At this stage, it is time to take a short break from concerns of musical harmony. In the next chapter, you will look at rhythm a bit more closely—in particular, ways and means of finding refreshing alternatives to the four-square 4/4 rhythms that dominate much of our music.

Exercises

You can download the answers to the chapter exercises from www.courseptr.com/downloads.

1. Complete the following sentence. A triad has three notes, which are called the root, the _____, and the _____.

2. Name the positions (inversions) as determined by the bass notes of the following C major triads.

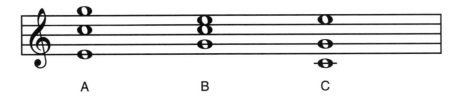

A is a C major chord in _____

B is a C major chord in _____

C is a C major chord in _____

3.   Identify the following chords, including their respective inversions.

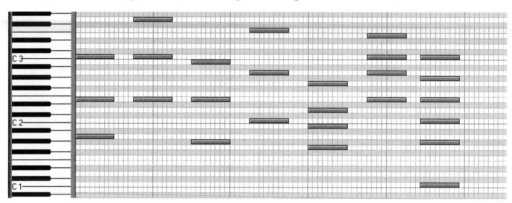

4.   In the spaces provided, write out the inversions of the following chords.

Example	A	C	E	First Inversion:	C	E	A
	C	E	G	Second Inversion:	_____	_____	_____
	F	A	C	First Inversion:	_____	_____	_____
	E	G#	B	Second Inversion:	_____	_____	_____
	C	E	G#	First Inversion:	_____	_____	_____
	G	C	E	Root Position:	_____	_____	_____
	A	D	F	First Inversion:	_____	_____	_____

5.   Fill in the missing words. There are two kinds of chord spacing: Closed and
_____ spacing is where the notes of a chord are crowded together
as closely as possible, while _____ spacing is where the chord is given
a wider spread over the register.

6.   Sequence the following chords in as many different types of spacing as you can think
of. An acoustic piano patch would be suitable for this, or even a string orchestra
patch. Feel free to double notes at the octave to give a full and rich-sounding sonority.
When you have done so, listen carefully to each sonority and assess the merits
and/or shortfalls of each.

A. A minor triad—root position

B. C major triad—first inversion

C. F major triad—second inversion

D. D minor triad—root position

7.   Fill in the missing harmony parts using the chords indicated.

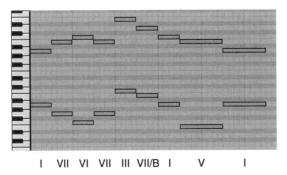

I   VII   VI   VII   III   VII/B   I   V   I

Tips:

A. Make sure each chord is a complete triad.

B. To ensure smooth voice leading, look out for shared notes that can be carried over through successive chords.

C. Score for at least four separate parts, meaning that with each chord, one or more of the notes needs doubling.

14 Additive Rhythms

Why 4/4 is used so often in Western music is something of a mystery. Perhaps it has more to do with habit than anything else. Other cultures of the world—such as in India or the Middle East, for example—think nothing of using more exotic groupings of beats, such as 7/8 or 11/4, and so on.

For those of a more adventurous mind, such groupings are well worth looking into. They have figured in some very beautiful and adventurous music. Mike Oldfield's classic, "Tubular Bells," is a good example. And of course there is that famous theme from *Mission Impossible*, mentioned in Chapter 10, which is in 10/8.

These more unusual asymmetric metric cycles result from a different way of thinking about rhythm. In the West, beats are viewed from an outmoded classical standpoint and subdivided into twos and threes. This results in those simple and compound time signatures considered earlier. Sometimes called *divisive rhythm*, time signatures such as 7/8 or 11/4 just do not figure in this system. In this sense, the theory lies behind the practice.

Understanding Additive Rhythms

However, there is another way of looking at rhythm—the modern musical approach, which is called *additive rhythm*. This is when a short beat—such as a sixteenth—is multiplied to produce various groupings of beats. Here the numbers two and three play a crucially important part.

String two beats together, and one type of rhythmic grouping results. String three beats together, and another results.

Beat	1	2	Beat	1	2	3
Stress	s	w	Stress	s	w	m

When these groups are combined in the additive fashion, interesting results ensue. If two such groups or rhythmic cells are combined, four possibilities are obtained (see Figure 14.1)—a grouping of two plus two (a), two plus three (b), three plus two (c), and three plus three (d).

When you think about rhythmic groupings in this way, really interesting time signatures result. Two plus two gives four beats to the bar, which we are already familiar with. But two plus three

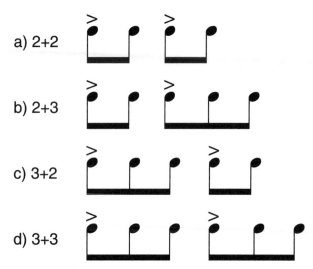

Figure 14.1 Four additive rhythms.

and three plus two give five beats to the bar—a time signature that has no place or origin within conventional simple and compound rhythms (see Figure 14.2).

Figure 14.2 Quintuple time.

The principle of additive rhythm is that a small note value—for example, a sixteenth—is grouped into twos or threes. This gives the two cells (duple and triple) from which additive rhythms are built up. In the aforementioned case, two cells were combined to give four possible additive rhythms. But it is also possible to combine these cells into threes, fours, fives, and so on.

If you combine three cells (figured one, two, three), as there are two kinds of each—duple and triple (figured A and B)—this means that, using three cells, there are eight possibilities, which you will see illustrated in Table 14.1.

With four cells, there are sixteen possibilities, and with five there are thirty-two possibilities, and so on.

The principle of additive rhythm, in other words, generates a virtual infinity of metric groupings.

Consider 13/8—easy! It is just 3+3+2+3+2, a combination of five rhythmic cells (see Figure 14.3).

Table 14.1 Additive Rhythms Using Three Cells

1 2 3

A A A	2+2+2	6 beats to the bar
A A B	2+2+3	7 beats to the bar
A B A	2+3+2	7 beats to the bar
B A A	3+2+2	7 beats to the bar
A B B	2+3+3	8 beats to the bar
B A B	3+2+3	8 beats to the bar
B B A	3+3+2	8 beats to the bar
B B B	3+3+3	9 beats to the bar

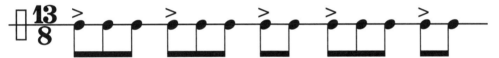

Figure 14.3   13/8 additive rhythm.

Practical Exercises

Figures 14.4 through 14.7 present some exercises so that you can start to acquaint yourself with the amazing world of additive rhythm. If you have a hand drum in the house, great. If not, use

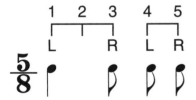

Figure 14.4   Exercise 1.

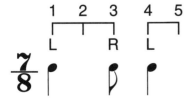

Figure 14.5   Exercise 2.

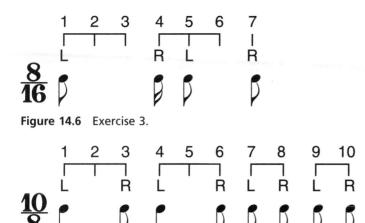

Figure 14.6 Exercise 3.

Figure 14.7 Exercise 4.

whatever is on hand—even a tabletop will do. "L" signifies a left-hand beat, while "R" signifies a right-hand beat. The tempo is flexible.

A bit of advice: When practicing these exercises, set up a count—either out loud or, if you are more experienced, in your head. Once you have a clear and regular count set up, you can think about the coordination of your hands.

This next rhythm is sometimes called the *house skip*.

Through the study and use of additive rhythms, you can learn to create rhythm tracks with great interest and variety. You no longer have to remain within the stricture of 4/4 all of the time. But even if you prefer writing in 4/4, additive rhythms can still add a lot to your music. Cuban and Latin American music uses additive rhythms all the time within a 4/4 framework. This is achieved by using combinations of two and three beats that fit into 4/4. A good example is three plus three plus two beats, totaling eight. Further interesting possibilities for the use of additive rhythms in a 4/4 framework are those combinations of twos and threes that total sixteen—for example, 3+3+3+3+2+2=16. These are used frequently in many styles of dance music.

Additive rhythms are also useful because they get you thinking about beats and looking at fresh ways of using beats in your music. How about combining different rhythms together? This is called *polyrhythm,* and you'll study some examples of this in Chapter 24 "Arpeggiation," where cycles of five and seven beats are heard against a cycle of four beats. These are called *five-step* and *seven-step* patterns.

But of course additive rhythms do not just have to be a feature of your rhythm tracks. They also offer fascinating ways to string together melodic motives. Track 35 of the audio CD is simple sine wave lead that puts together motives within a framework of 15 beats to the bar. Have a listen, and you will discover that 13, 15, 17, or any other type of unusual combination *does* actually sound effective.

Exercises

You can download the answers to the chapter exercises from www.courseptr.com/downloads.

1.   Fill in the correct time signatures for each of these rhythms.

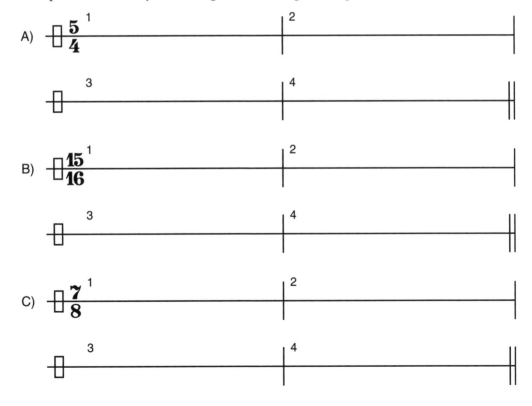

2.   Compose four-bar rhythms using the following time signatures.

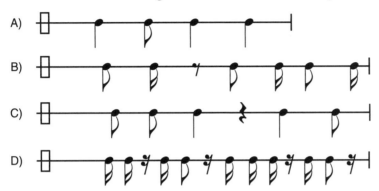

3.   Complete the following. 7/8 can consist of the following groupings of two and three:

A. 2 plus 3 plus 2

B. 2 plus 2 plus 3

C. 3 plus 2 plus 2

11/8 can consist of the following groupings of two and three. (Give four possible different types of groupings.)

A. _____

B. _____

C. _____

D. _____

8/8 can consist of the following groupings of two and three:

A. _____

B. _____

C. _____

4.   Compose and sequence a lead line using the following time signatures and keys.

A. 7/8 in the key of C major.

B. 5/8 in the key of A natural minor.

C. 13/8 in the key of A harmonic minor.

5.   Fill in the missing notes required to complete the following rhythms.

A)

B)

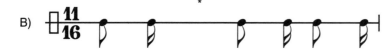

C)

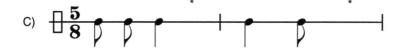

15 Expanding Your Knowledge of Keys

Music composers generally write their music in a key. An example of a key with which you are already familiar is C major. Other examples are A minor, F major, and so on. To write music with any proficiency, you need knowledge both of individual keys and of the system to which they belong. This applies to whatever type of music you are writing.

A glance at any popular songbook will show music written in a variety of keys. And when mixing, a DJ needs a certain degree of key awareness—an awareness that is honed to its maximum within the process known as *harmonic mixing*.

When writing tunes, knowledge of the key system is essential. You need to know what key the music is in and be comfortably familiar with the scale of that key and the range of chords that belong to it. Otherwise, it is like working in the dark.

Understanding Keys

You can acquire this knowledge and ability in stages. The first stage is to get to know the scale itself. Starting with the white keys of C major and A minor is easier in this respect because they use the white keys of the keyboard. So you avoid the complexities of sharps and flats, which use the black keys.

Knowing the keys of C major and A minor offers a firm foundation for the study of other keys. Thankfully, the key system is a fairly simple one. This is because the scale from which the notes of a key are selected only has 12 notes—the chromatic scale as defined by the black and white keys on the keyboard or the frets on a guitar. Because the chromatic scale only has 12 notes, this means that, practically speaking, there are only 12 possible keynotes. You can take any of these 12 notes to be the prospective keynote (or tonic) of a major or minor scale.

To construct a major scale upon any keynote, you must apply the formula Tone-Tone-Semitone-Tone-Tone-Tone-Semitone. In Figure 15.1, you can see this applied first to the key of C major and then to the key of G major. Here we are building the same scale, except that the starting note is different: In the first case, the starting note—or tonic—is C; in the second case, the tonic is G.

From this example, you can see that to build a major scale upon the keynote of G, you must use one of the black keys of the keyboard—an F#. This is because you need a whole tone between

C Major

G Major

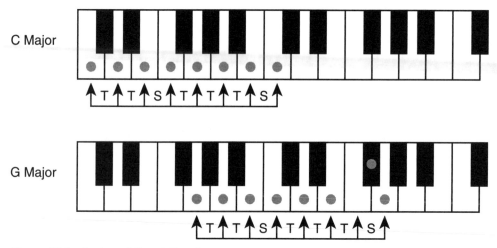

Figure 15.1 Scales of C and G major.

the sixth and seventh degrees of the scale. If you used the note F, there would only be a semitone between them. So for the scale of G major, the note F is raised to give note F#.

Similarly, a major scale constructed upon the keynote of D requires you to use two black keys. You need the note F# (instead of F) to give the whole tone required between the second and third degrees of the scale, and you need the note C# (instead of C) to give the whole tone required between the sixth and seventh degrees (see Figure 15.2).

D Major

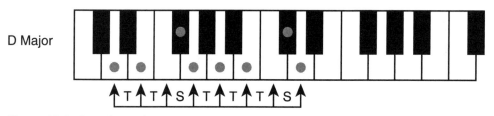

Figure 15.2 D major scale.

When sequenced, the three scales we have looked at so far would appear as shown in Figure 15.3.

Some scales use the black keys, but as flats. Two good examples are the keys of F and Bb major (see Figure 15.4).

Because music written in a particular key will use the sharps or flats that belong to it, you can identify each key by a key signature, which indicates the notes to be sharpened or flattened. This is placed on staff systems at the beginning of the piece of music (see Figure 15.5).

In the case of F major, this means that every time a note B occurs, it is to be played flat. Similarly, in the key of D, all F's and C's will be played sharp.

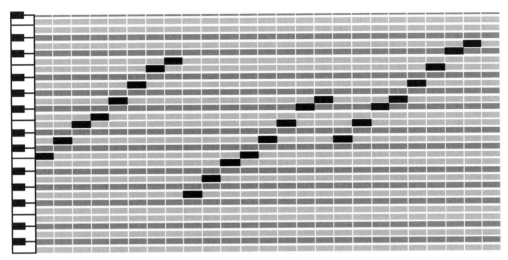

Figure 15.3 Sequenced scales of C, G, and D major.

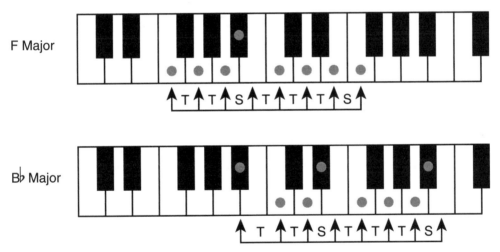

Figure 15.4 F and Bb major scales.

If your musical output is confined to software programs, such as Reason or Ableton Live, the use of key signatures is not necessary. You still need to learn them, though, in order to know which notes to select on the piano roll view or matrix pattern sequencer for the particular key used in your current song.

And the staff format used here will be very useful when you are downloading MIDI files, for example, in order to obtain musical material for a remix or a song arrangement. Staff notation is a universal format for the transmission of important information that you must be able to access in order to do an effective job with your remix or arrangement. Such information necessarily includes the key of the song.

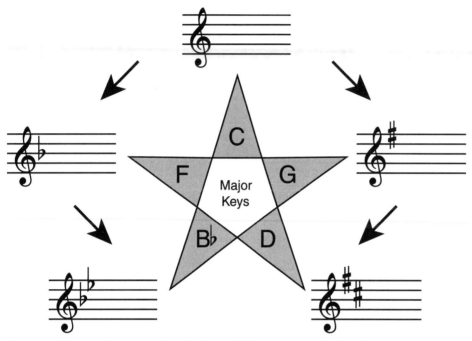

Figure 15.5   Key signatures for the keys of C, G, D, F, and Bb major.

Major and Relative Minor Keys

The relationship between major and relative minor keys—first studied with the keys of C major and A minor—is an extremely close one. Both scales use the same notes, the difference being the placement of the tonic. To work out a relative minor key, count down three notes (or up six notes) from the tonic of the equivalent major key. Figure 15.6 shows the relative minor keys of the five major keys we just considered.

Because the major and relative minor keys use the same set of notes, the key signatures for both scales are the same. This applies to all types of minor scale.

To learn these keys, follow the same procedures you used to learn the C major and A minor scales. First, learn to play the scales through. You'll find these in the appendix. Second, define the triads of the scale. The chord progressions produced earlier will also be useful. Keep them handy and play or sequence them in these new keys. Called *transposition*, this is the transference of music from one key to another.

Having studied this chapter, you have now acquired a deeper knowledge of musical keys, so you no longer need to be limited to C major and A minor. Having acquired such knowledge, you are well on the way to understanding the complete key system of Western music—a system that you'll study in more depth in Chapter 19, "The Cycle of Fifths."

Having this deeper knowledge of musical keys also helps to cement the basic principles that you have learned with regard to musical scales and scale formation. When those principles are clear

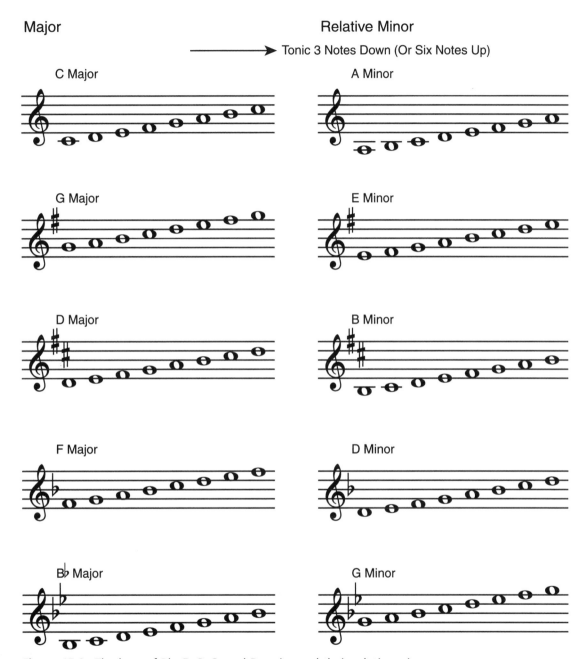

Figure 15.6 The keys of Bb, F, C, G, and D major and their relative minors.

in your mind, it then becomes possible to look at alternative scale systems—such as the pentatonic scale, the seven diatonic modes, and various exotic scales—without any confusion. In the next chapter, we will study the pentatonic scale, a scale of five notes that, although not really accorded much recognition in classical music theory, is nonetheless of great importance in all types of modern music.

Exercises

You can download the answers to the chapter exercises from www.courseptr.com/downloads.

1. Fill in the missing words. The scale from which the notes of a key are selected has 12 notes and is known as the _____. Any of these 12 notes can be taken to be the prospective _____ (or tonic) of a major or minor scale.

2. To construct a major scale upon any keynote, it is necessary to apply the formula: tone - _____ - _____ - _____ - _____ - _____ - _____.

3. Fill in the notes required to complete the following scales:
    - C major: C _____
    - D major: D _____
    - F major: F _____
    - Bb major: Bb _____
    - G major: G _____

4. Identify the following major key signatures:

5. Fill in the missing words. To work out a relative minor key, count down _____ notes (or up _____ notes) from the tonic of the equivalent major key. The relative minor of the key of G is therefore _____ minor.

6. Write down the relative minor keys of the following major keys.

Major Key	Relative Minor
C major	_____
F major	_____
G major	_____
D major	_____
Bb major	_____

7. Fill in the notes required to complete the following triads.
    - Key of Bb major, Chord ii, first inversion: _____ _____ _____

    - Key of D natural minor, Chord III, root position: _____ _____ _____

    - Key of F major, Chord VI, second inversion: _____ _____ _____

    - Key of D major, Chord IV, root position: _____ _____ _____

    - Key of G harmonic minor, Chord IV, root position: _____ _____ _____

    - Key of G major, Chord vi, first inversion: _____ _____ _____

    - Key of E natural minor, Chord ii, root position: _____ _____ _____

8. Correctly play from memory the following scales: G major, D major, F major, Bb major. The correct fingering for each scale can be found in Appendix A, "Scales."

9. Transpose the following major key three-chord progression (I, IV, V) into the required keys.

C major	C E G	F A C	G B D
Bb major	_____	_____	_____
D major	_____	_____	_____
F major	_____	_____	_____

10. Correctly play from memory the arpeggios of the following scales: G harmonic minor, D melodic minor, E natural minor, B harmonic minor. The fingering is identical, as for the A minor arpeggios. For example:

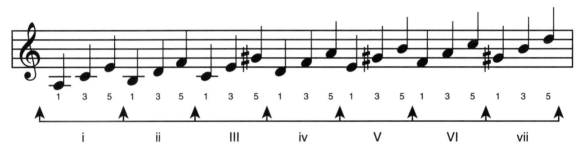

11. Transpose the following minor key three-chord progression (I, IV, V) into the required keys:

A natural minor	A C E	D F A	E G B
G harmonic minor	_____	_____	_____
D melodic minor	_____	_____	_____
E natural minor	_____	_____	_____
B harmonic minor	_____	_____	_____

12. Play correctly from memory the following scales: G and D harmonic minor, E and B melodic minor. The correct fingering for each can be found in Appendix A.

16 The Pentatonic Scale

Y ou have learned that when writing your tracks, you will be operating within a particular key. The key you are using will be identified by the note that is being used as the tonic. For example, if you are writing in the key of Bb major, you will be using the note Bb as the tonic. For the key of F major, you will use the note F as the chosen tonic. These are differences of key, and the more keys you know, the more choice and freedom you will have when writing your music.

Understanding Mode

Within a particular key—for example, D—you will have a choice of the type of scale to use: major or minor. This brings into play a different distinction—one of mode. *Mode* concerns the type of scale used and its characteristic features. A minor mode is generally used for the mellower, moodier, and darker music, while a major mode has a propensity toward cheer and brightness. However, these are only generalizations and should not be taken as a rule.

When it comes to the choice of mode, there are numerous options for modern music writers, in addition to the major and minor modes. The major and minor modes are an inheritance from the classical music traditions of the west. However, musicians from other parts of the world or from differing traditions have also used and developed other equally valid scale systems. Many of these have found their way into general use in modern popular and electronic music. Therefore, for your education to be complete and for you to enjoy the freedom that many other music writers, composers, and producers share, you need to be aware of these scale systems and what they can offer you as a computer musician.

Introducing the Pentatonic Scale

One such scale system is the pentatonic scale. The most distinctive feature of this scale is that, as its name suggests, it has only five notes as opposed to the seven notes of the major/minor scales. You will benefit greatly from learning about this scale. The pentatonic scale is a truly global musical scale that, in one form or another, has been used all over the world in various forms. It has been used in:

- Folk music of Celtic peoples
- Afro-American music, particularly spirituals

181

- Blues, pop, and jazz improvisation

- Modern dance music

- Healing music (new age)

- Modern ambient styles

- Rock and progressive rock music

- Children's nursery rhymes

- Traditional Japanese and Chinese music

- Eastern Asian music

- Modern classical music

- Eastern European music

- Indonesian gamelan music

- Inuit and Native American Indian music

- Appalachian folk music

- Incidental and film music

In fact, the pentatonic scale is the earliest known musical scale, predating the seven-note major or minor scale by thousands of years. Many ancient peoples developed and used the pentatonic scale independently of one another. The seven-note scale only developed with the emergence of high civilizations, such as Egypt, China, Mesopotamia, Greece, and so on. People not involved in this process—in other words, tribal peoples such as the American Indians—tended to stay with the pentatonic scale. For this reason, the pentatonic scale is and always has been a scale for "the people," as opposed to for the pomp and ceremony of the high state.

The pentatonic scale is sometimes known as the *gapped scale* because when a pentatonic scale is built upon note C, it uses only five white keys, missing out the notes F and B. See Figure 16.1.

Because of the gaps in the scale between notes E and G, and between A and C, the sharp minor seconds between E/F and B/C are missing. This means that all five notes played simultaneously will still sound very harmonious. There is no harshness or dissonance in the sound at all. For this reason, the pentatonic scale is popular in children's music and for the purposes of teaching children music. They can play any of the notes in any combination, and it still sounds good.

Musicians often use the pentatonic scale to enrich basic triads and give them a more complex, colorful sound. These chords are called *added note chords*. Of the five notes of the pentatonic

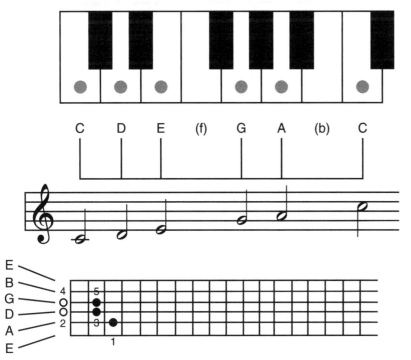

Figure 16.1 The pentatonic scale in keyboard, score edit, and guitar formats.

scale, three of them make up a major triad—C, E, and G. The other two notes of the scale—A and D—offer good opportunities for added note harmony, with the former giving rise to the added sixth chord and the latter to the added ninth chord. When combined, together they produce a chord of the added sixth/ninth (see Figure 16.2).

You can listen to these chords in Track 36 of the audio CD.

Pentatonic influences also inspire the use of suspended chords. A *suspended chord* is when the third is swapped for a note that lies on either side of it. Figure 16.3 shows the most common types of suspended chords.

These chords, readily available in the pentatonic scale, offer a refreshing alternative to ordinary triads. Try them out and see. (The European practice of creating suspended chords through linear suspensions is another application of suspended chords.)

Some of the most beautiful tunes in the world have a pentatonic core. The missing notes—F and B—are touched upon only in passing. The "Londonderry Air" is a good example of this. Another example is Gershwin's "Summertime." Modern dance tunes often use the pentatonic scale, and it is popular in both deep house and trance. A good example you might know is "Sandstorm" by Darude—a pure pentatonic tune.

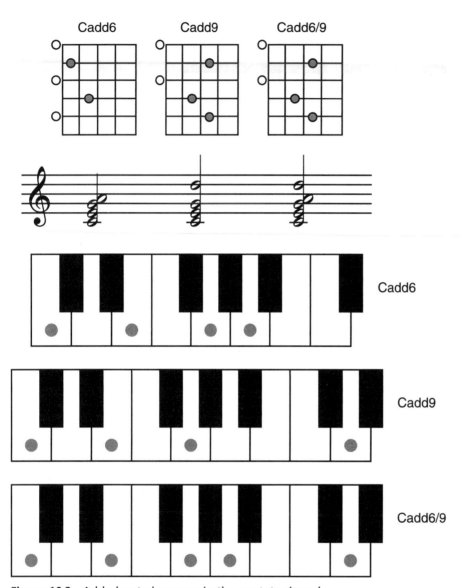

Figure 16.2 Added note harmony in the pentatonic scale.

When improvising, the pentatonic scale offers important neighbor notes to the chord tones (see Table 16.1). These are used to embellish and enhance the melodic interest of the music.

Pentatonic Modes

One of the important features of the pentatonic scale is that, like the seven modes of diatonic music, the tonic note can be moved around. This gives rise to five different pentatonic modes. Because of the asymmetrical pattern of intervals in the scale—tone, tone, minor third, tone,

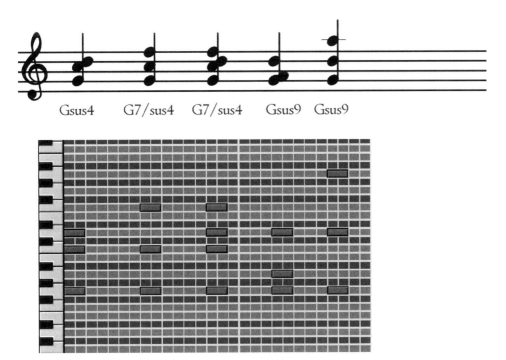

Figure 16.3   Suspended chords.

Table 16.1 Pentatonic Neighbor Notes

			C		E	G		C
C major triad			C		E	G		C
Neighbor notes		A		D			A	
A minor triad		A	C		E			
Neighbor notes	G			D		G		

minor third—five modes are created, each with its own particular character (see Figure 16.4). Track 37 on the audio CD uses a pentatonic mode of this sort to create a nice ethnic-sounding texture.

Like the major and minor modes with their emotional affinities ("mode" comes from the ancient Greek word for "mood"), different modes are suitable for the expression of particular emotions. A parallel to this lies in traditional Chinese music, where music using the pentatonic scale was developed into a high art. Here the five modes were linked to the five elements that, in Taoist

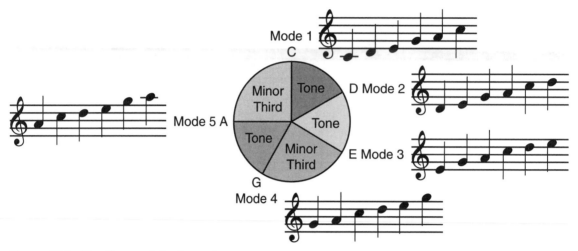

Figure 16.4   The five pentatonic modes.

philosophy, were considered to rule the universe. Associated with each element were characteristic emotions, moods, colors, and so on (see Figure 16.5).

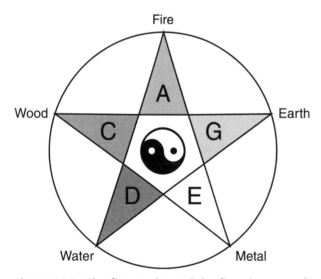

Figure 16.5   The five modes and the five elements of Taoist philosophy.

It is very useful to learn to build all five modes from any keynote. There are 12 keynotes, which means that there are potentially 60 possible pentatonic modes. Figure 16.6 shows the five pentatonic modes built upon note C.

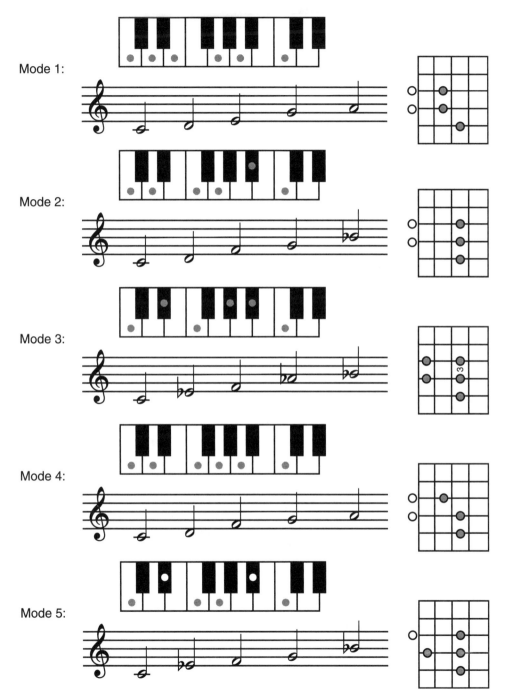

Figure 16.6   The five pentatonic modes built upon note C.

If you want to try to work the five pentatonic modes on any other keynote, you would apply the formula shown in Figure 16.7 for each mode. The numbers refer to the number of semitone steps you need to count up to get the next note of the mode.

Mode 1:	2	2	3	2	3
Mode 2:	2	3	2	3	2
Mode 3:	3	2	3	2	2
Mode 4:	2	3	2	2	3
Mode 5:	3	2	2	3	2

Figure 16.7 Formula for working out pentatonic modes.

Pentatonic Harmony

The pentatonic scale only contains two complete triads—C major and A minor—so the possibilities for pure pentatonic harmony are quite limited. To make up for this, you can harmonize pentatonic tunes using chords from the seven-note diatonic scale. This can be extremely effective, with the other two notes—F and B—being used as harmony notes to complete chords II (Dm), IV (F—the subdominant), III (Em), and V (G—dominant). See Figure 16.8.

The traditional song "Amazing Grace" is a fine example of this type of treatment. Another is the stately horn theme of the slow movement of Dvorak's *New World Symphony*.

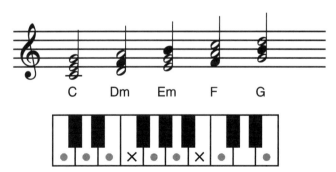

Figure 16.8 Pentatonic harmonies.

You can impart an Oriental flavor to songs by using bare fifths and/or fourths as harmonies, as you'd find in traditional Chinese music. And, you can create some beautiful textures by building up chords by fourths and/or fifths (called *quartal* and *quintal harmony*). A five-note quintal chord uses all notes of the pentatonic scale to give a beautiful, stately harmony (see Figure 16.9). Track 38 of the audio CD sequences this chord on a motion synth patch.

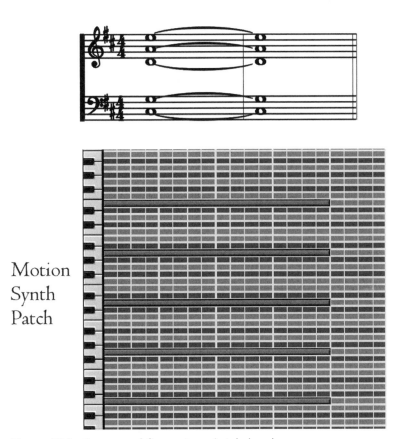

Motion
Synth
Patch

Figure 16.9 Sequenced five-note quintal chord.

It is definitely worthwhile to devote some time to this and experiment with the pentatonic scale on the MIDI keyboard. If you need, refer to Figure 16.7 for the requisite formula for working out any pentatonic mode in any key.

Through studying this chapter, you have learned that there is an important alternative to the major and minor scale in the form of the pentatonic scale and its related modes. In learning this, you have acquired a really valuable additional resource to improve your music-writing capabilities. You can use the pentatonic scale to create beautiful and stunning leads, as well as amazing bass lines. You can also use it to spice up your harmony, a feature which can give your tracks an edge over music that just uses common triads—that is, unadorned major and minor chords.

Exercises

You can download the answers to the chapter exercises from www.courseptr.com/downloads.

1. Name four different types of music in which the pentatonic scale has been used.

2. Label and identify the intervals between each of the notes of this G pentatonic scale.

G	A	B	D	E
▲	▲	▲	▲	▲

3. Build a pentatonic scale on the following keynotes.

   D   _____   _____   _____   _____

   F   _____   _____   _____   _____

   Bb   _____   _____   _____   _____

4. Build all five pentatonic modes on this tonic note C.

   C   _____   _____   _____   _____

   C   _____   _____   _____   _____

   C   _____   _____   _____   _____

   C   _____   _____   _____   _____

   C   _____   _____   _____   _____

5. Identify three added note chords that could be used in the following pentatonic scale.

   F G A C D

   Chord 1: _____

   Chord 2: _____

   Chord 3: _____

6. Compose a lead using the pentatonic scale. When you have done so, add a harmony based on quintal chords—chords composed of superimposed fifths.

17 Major, Minor, Augmented, and Diminished Triads

Most of the chords you use in your music will probably be major and minor—the so-called *common triads*. When you get used to using these, hopefully you will also start to explore and use some more complex chords. This will no doubt include those chords of the seventh, ninth, eleventh, and thirteenth, which you will study in Chapter 21, "Chords of the Seventh," and Chapter 23, "Complex Harmony." As a preliminary foundation for this exploration, it will benefit you greatly to study the complete range of triads available, in addition to the major and minor common triads.

Major and minor triads differ only in respect to their "sweet note"—the third. In the case of the major triad, the third up from the root is major, whereas in the case of the minor triad, it is minor (see Figure 17.1).

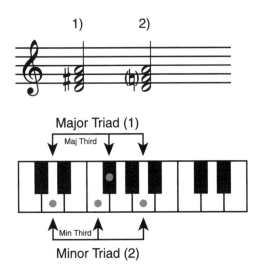

Figure 17.1 D major and minor triads.

Called *common triads*, these account for six of the seven possible triads in the major scale and its corresponding relative minor. These six have a special relationship because there are three major chords and three minor chords in the scale. The seven-toned scale thus offers a balance between major and minor influences. What swings it in favor of the major or minor influence is emphasis.

The three major chords are the primary chords of the major key, while the minor chords are secondary. In the minor key, it reverses. See Figure 17.2.

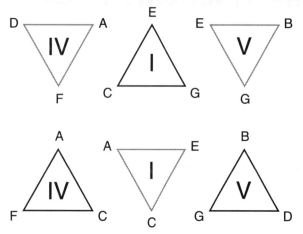

Figure 17.2   Major and minor common triads in the seven-note scale.

The seven-toned scale yields seven triads, though. The missing triad is found on note B—B D F. Traditional theory calls this a *diminished triad* because it occurs when the fifth of the minor triad is flattened (see Figure 17.3).

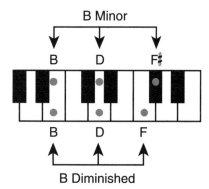

Figure 17.3   The diminished triad.

The Diminished Triad

The diminished triad is built up from two minor thirds. You can see this in the keyboard diagram in Figure 17.3. A minor third has only three semitones. Figure 17.4 shows that from B to D is three semitones, and from D to F is three semitones.

Played on its own, the diminished triad has a mysterious quality due to the interval between root and fifth—B/F—which is a diminished fifth or, when inverted, the infamous "devil's fourth."

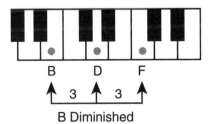

Figure 17.4 Semitone gaps in the diminished triad.

This is a dissonant interval, which makes the diminished triad that uses it an unstable harmony. Indeed, there is something strange and unsettling about the sound of this chord. Play it on your MIDI keyboard and have a good listen. For this reason, perhaps, it is not used much in popular music. But it is used on occasion to good effect, and it is a chord you should certainly be aware of and know about. It is used to good effect right at the opening of Madonna's "Like a Prayer."

Occurring as chord VII in the major mode (B D F in C major), it is called the leading note triad in classical harmony. This is because it occurs on the seventh scale degree—also called the leading note—which performs an important function in tonal music. Rising definitively up to the tonic, it helps the ear to recognize the tonal centre. Have a listen to Track 39 of the audio CD, and you will hear what I mean. In chord progressions, therefore, the diminished triad most often acts as a substitute for the dominant or as an incomplete dominant seventh chord. You will understand this more clearly when you study Chapter 21.

The harmonic minor scale also has some oddities you should be aware of. It has only four common triads (major or minor chords), those on degrees I, IV, V, and VI. These form the staples as far as chord progressions in the harmonic minor scale are concerned. It also has two diminished triads—on degree II and degree VII. Because these are unstable, they contribute a sense of tension and pathos to harmony in this scale. See Figure 17.5.

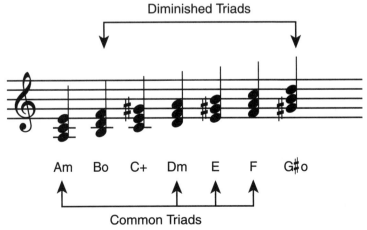

Figure 17.5 Common and diminished triads in the harmonic minor scale.

Using this tension effectively in modern electronic music requires considerable skill. This is because it was over-exploited by classical composers to create dramatic impact. This formula was further worn thin by its overuse in silent-movie music. Suffice it to say, use these chords with extreme caution; otherwise, they can raise a giggle!

The Augmented Triad

Another strange-sounding triad outside of the common chord category is the augmented triad. You'll find augmented triads on degree III of the harmonic minor scale and degrees III and IV of the rising melodic minor scale. The distinctive feature of the augmented triad is that it is built up from two major thirds. Figure 17.6 shows its relationship to the major triad. It is like a major triad except the fifth has been sharpened by a semitone.

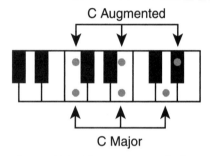

Figure 17.6 The augmented triad.

Like the diminished triad, the augmented triad is unstable, owing to the dissonant augmented fifth. This gives it an almost otherworldly quality. Because of this, it is not used often in popular music, although it does figure prominently in film scores because it can produce some very atmospheric harmonic effects. It is most often used to suggest the ethereal quality of outer space or the mystery of the oceanic worlds. These effects are often enhanced through the use of numerous augmented triads a whole tone apart. This gives a distinct effect of the type of weightlessness that you would encounter in outer space. Harmony of this type has evolved into its own separate scale system called the *whole tone scale* (See Chapter 22, "Exotic Scales," for more information.) To hear an example, listen to Track 40 of the audio CD.

In jazz harmony, which has considerable range in the type and breadth of chords used, the augmented triad is used more often. It is also often used as part of a seventh chord (Cmaj7/5+), where it gives a very atmospheric harmony. You'll find more information on this in Chapter 21.

The Four Types of Triads

Between them, the four kinds of triads mentioned in this chapter—diminished, minor, major, and augmented—account for all triad types available in the major and minor modes. Mathematically, the four types can be explained by the fact that a triad can be composed of two thirds.

Because there are two kinds of third—major and minor—this means there are thus four types of triads (see Figure 17.7).

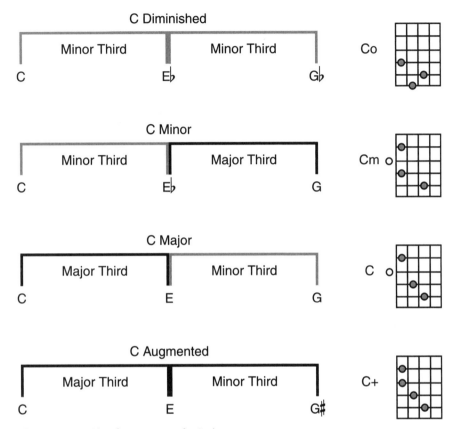

Figure 17.7 The four types of triads.

A useful rule of thumb to work out any of these four triads from a given note is the semitone rule:

- Diminished Triad: 3 plus 3 semitones

- Minor Triad: 3 plus 4 semitones

- Major Triad: 4 plus 3 semitones

- Augmented Triad: 4 plus 4 semitones

Armed with this rule, you can work out all four triads as they occur on any note of the chromatic scale.

In popular music songbooks, each of these triads is represented in a customary way. A major triad is represented by the capital letter of the note that serves as the root. C thus signifies a chord of C major, while F# signifies a chord of F# major. A minor triad is represented in the same capital-letter format except with the addition of a small m to signify minor. Dm thus signifies the chord of D minor, while Ebm signifies the chord of Eb minor. An augmented triad is represented in the same way as a major triad except for the addition of a plus sign to signify the augmentation of the fifth. C+ thus signifies a C augmented triad, while G+ signifies a G augmented triad. Finally, the diminished triad is represented by the capital letter that represents the third, to which a small o has been added. Bo thus signifies a diminished triad whose root note is B, while G#o signifies a diminished triad whose root note is G#. Sometimes, though, you will see the diminished triad represented in a different way. The root note is given, say, B, to which the abbreviation *dim* is added. Ddim thus signifies the D diminished triad.

Having learned about the four types of triads, you should now be capable of identifying any triad in the traditional tonal system. This ability forms an important preparation for the appreciation and use of more complex chords, such as sevenths, ninths, and elevenths, which tend to use the four types of triads as their foundation. You will study these more complex types of harmony in Chapter 21, "Chords of the Seventh," and Chapter 23, "Complex Harmony."

In addition to being able to identify and use the four types of triads, you must study the principles that lead and guide the progression from one chord to another. An appreciation of these principles is vitally important for you to create strong and interesting chord progressions involving a wide variety of different types of chords. Here, the most important principle to grasp is the concept of root movement. Because this is such an important principle, the next chapter will undertake an exploration of its nature and significance for the computer musician.

Exercises

You can download the answers to the chapter exercises from www.courseptr.com/downloads.

1a.   What kind of triads are the following?

1. Example: C E G is a major triad.

2. C Eb G is a _____ triad.

3. C Eb Gb is a _____ triad.

4. C E G# is a _____ triad.

1b.   Which of the above do the following symbols denote?

- Cm denotes chord 2.
- C+ denotes chord _____.
- Co denotes chord _____.
- C denotes chord _____.

2.   The semitone rule: Fill in the number of semitones required for each triad.

   ▪ Diminished Triad: _____ plus _____ semitones.

   ▪ Minor Triad: _____ plus _____ semitones.

   ▪ Major Triad: _____ plus _____ semitones.

   ▪ Augmented Triad: _____ plus _____ semitones.

3.   Identify the following triads. Include the inversion.

A)   B)   C)   D)   E)

   A. _____

   B. _____

   C. _____

   D. _____

   E. _____

4.   What kind of triads are the following?

   A   B   C   D   E   F

   A. _____

   B. _____

   C. _____

   D. _____

   E. _____

   F. _____

5.   Identify:

A. The key of each scale given below.

B. The scale used.

C. Each of the seven triads.

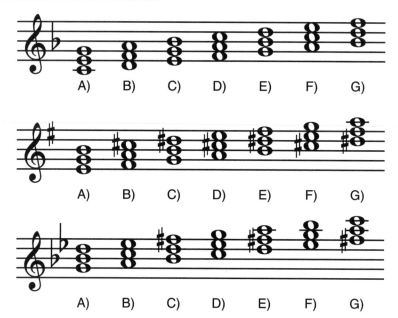

A)   B)   C)   D)   E)   F)   G)

A)   B)   C)   D)   E)   F)   G)

A)   B)   C)   D)   E)   F)   G)

18 Chord Progressions and Root Movement

To write tunes successfully using the resources of a particular key, you must know the notes that belong to the key. If the only instrument you play is a MIDI keyboard, this means being able to at least play the scale through without any difficulty.

This represents an important first stage. Once you have accomplished this, you can work out the seven triads that belong to the key. You can do so by taking each note of the scale as the root of a triad and adding to it the third and the fifth (being careful to remain within the bounds of the chosen scale). This procedure will yield the seven relevant triads.

When you're comfortable with the chords that belong to a particular key, you can then start stringing these chords together into a sequence that makes sense to the ear—a chord progression. As I've made clear already in this book, chord progressions are very important for all styles of popular music, because they allow the listener to make sense of where the music is actually going.

So what is it that actually makes a chord progression? What are the principles upon which logical chord progressions are based?

Root Movement

For the ear, the most important feature of chord progressions is the sense of *root movement*. Recall that every triad has a root, a third, and a fifth. The root is the essential note that gives the chord its identity. Therefore, a chord whose root note is F is always a chord of F—no matter what type of chord it is. It is the presence of the root, therefore, that enables the ear to identify a particular chord.

It makes sense, then, that the essence of good chord progressions lies in root movement—that is the identifiable movement between the roots of different chords. If the root movement is strong, clear, and logical, then so will be the chord progression upon which it is based. According to this logic, the succession of three chords in Figure 18.1 is not a chord progression because in all three cases the root is the same note C.

Because the three chords are simply inversions of the chord of C major, no root movement takes place, and therefore there is no sense of progression for the ear. A sense of progression or forward movement only occurs when there is a change of chordal roots—for example, in Figure 18.2.

199

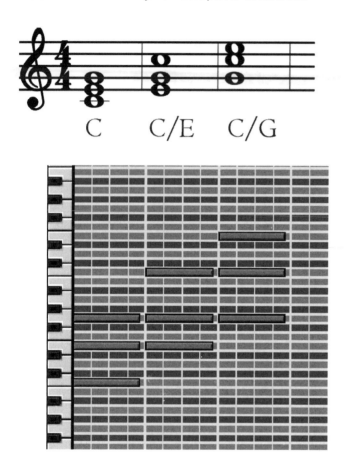

Figure 18.1 Static chord of C major.

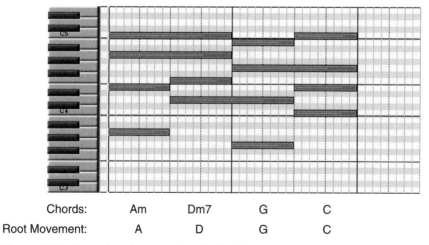

Chords:	Am	Dm7	G	C
Root Movement:	A	D	G	C

Figure 18.2 Four-chord progression in A minor.

Notice that in Figure 18.2, the scheme of root movement follows a pattern—A D G C. All four roots are linked by fourths. This is very important because root movement is subject to definite principles.

There are three kinds of root movement, shown in Figures 18.3 through 18.5.

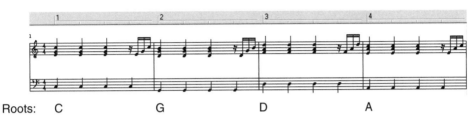

Roots: C   G   D   A

Figure 18.3   Root movement by fourths (rising or falling), for example in C major: C – G – Dm – Am.

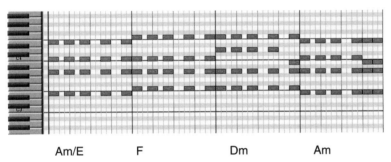

    Am/E   F   Dm   Am

Figure 18.4   Root movement by thirds (rising or falling), for example in A minor: Am – F – Dm.

Figure 18.5   Root movement by seconds (rising or falling), for example in D minor: Dm – C – Bb – A.

All chord progressions involve root movement of these three types, although they can often employ a mixture of movements.

Root Movement by Fourths

When you are developing chord progressions, the principles of root movement reduce the choices from any given chord to three: root movement by fourths, thirds, and seconds. In the case of the first choice—root movement by fourths—the two chords will always have one note in common (see Figure 18.6).

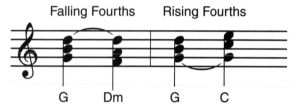

Figure 18.6 Root movement by fourths.

This one note acts as a link between the two, with the other two notes offering contrast by change. Root movement by fourths is the strongest kind of root movement, and it is often used sequentially, such as in a cycle of fourths.

Root Movement by Thirds

In terms of root movement by thirds, the two chords will always have two notes in common. This makes them very similar, although the connection between them is very smooth. This type of root movement does not offer the same kind of contrast as root movement by fourths (see Figure 18.7).

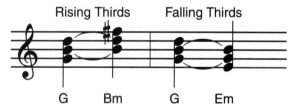

Figure 18.7 Root movement by thirds.

Root Movement by Seconds

Finally, there is root movement by seconds, in which the two triads have no notes in common. This kind of change offers the maximum possible contrast, although because the two chords share no notes, the connection is not so smooth (see Figure 18.8).

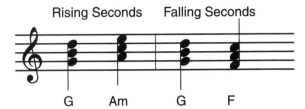

Figure 18.8   Root movement by seconds.

Focusing on these three types of root movement is a good way to expand your knowledge of chord progressions. Take a key and play the seven chords in all three orders—root movement by seconds, thirds, and fourths. This will assist you in getting to know the key, and it will probably give you inspiration for your chord progressions. See Figure 18.9.

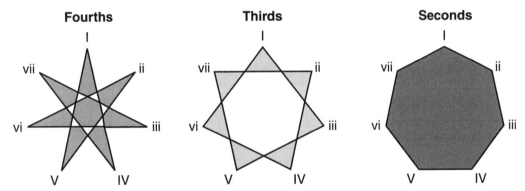

Figure 18.9   The three types of root movement.

In this chapter you learned about the three types of root movement. You can use them individually or in combination. The importance lies in creating a strong and logical sense of root movement over which chords can be built. This becomes especially important when you are using really complex harmony of the type discussed in Chapter 23, "Complex Harmony." When harmony is dense and complex, a strong scheme of root movement gives it anchorage and makes it easier for the ear to interpret.

Exercises

You can download the answers to the chapter exercises from www.courseptr.com/downloads.

1. Fill in the missing words. A sequence of chords is called a _____.
    The most important feature of chord progressions is the sense of _____,
    of which there are three types: _____ by seconds, thirds and fourths.

2a. What key is the chord progression given below in? _____.

2b. Identify each of the chords below (such as Em/G, and so on).

2c.   Circle the roots of each chord.

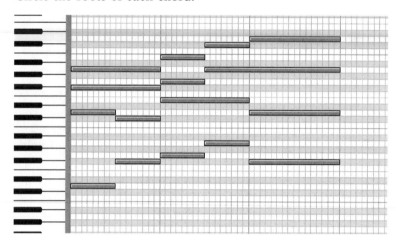

3.   Using your sequencer, complete the harmony by adding three parts above the following chordal roots.

4a.   Compose and sequence a four-chord progression in the key of F major based on root movement by fourths.

4b.   Compose and sequence a four-chord progression in the key of D minor that uses root movement by thirds.

4c.   Compose and sequence a four-chord progression in the key of G minor that uses root movement by seconds.

19 The Cycle of Fifths

In Chapter 15, you looked at some new keys—namely G, D, F and Bb major keys, together with their relative minors. As a result of this, we generalized some important principles. A major scale whose tonic (keynote) lies a perfect fifth above the keynote of C requires the addition of a sharp in the key signature (the key of G major). This gives the requisite whole-tone gap between the sixth and seventh degrees of the scale (TTSTTTS). Similarly, a major scale whose tonic lies a fifth above G (D major) requires two sharps.

Keys on the Bright Side (Sharp Keys)

This is a very important observation because it represents a pattern of key relationships, which can be further extended to include keys that have three sharps, four sharps, five sharps, and so on (see Figure 19.1).

Important Principle: Each key whose tonic is a fifth higher requires a further sharp in the key signature.

Keys with sharps in them are often thought by musicians to be emotionally bright keys. The more sharps a key has, the brighter it is felt to be. Whether or not this is entirely subjective is difficult to say. But it can affect your choice of key for a particular project. You can further appreciate this by considering the converse—that is, keys with flats in them.

Keys on the Dark Side (Flat Keys)

Recall from Chapter 15 that a major scale whose tonic lies a perfect fifth below the keynote of C requires the addition of a flat in the key signature (F major). Go down a further fifth to Bb, and another flat is required. This pattern can also be further extended, as shown in Figure 19.2.

Important Principle: Each key whose tonic is a fifth lower requires a further flat in the key signature.

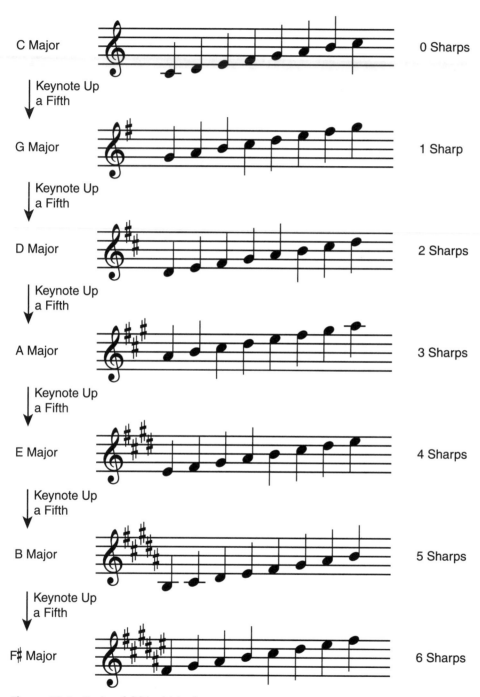

Figure 19.1 Cycle of fifths (rising).

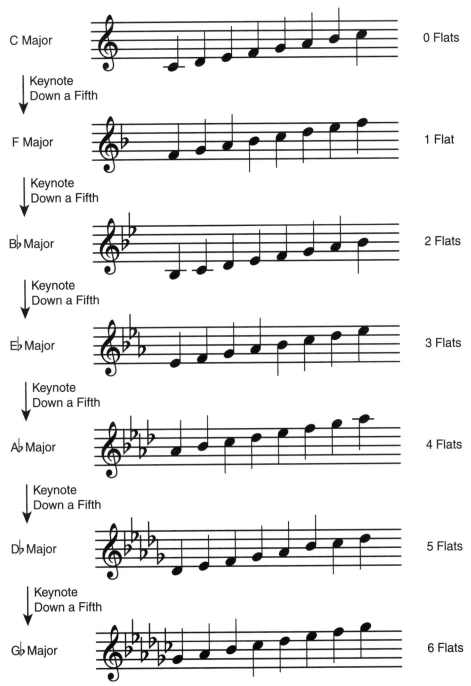

Figure 19.2 Cycle of fifths (falling).

In this way another set of keys are generated—those keys with flats. The further on in the scheme of falling fifths, the more flats the key has. It is interesting to observe that keys with flats are generally felt to be emotionally darker or more somber than the sharp keys. The more flats a key has, the darker it is felt to be. In this respect the key of C—a key with no sharps or flats— represents a pivot or point of balance between the bright sharp keys and the more somber flat keys. Inevitably, as you get to know the different keys, you will develop your own associations and preferences, which will influence your choice of key. The association of bright and dark with particular keys seems to be the most enduring. Yet sometimes musicians develop strong color associations with different keys, and it is the color of the key that influences their choice of which key to use for a particular musical purpose.

Closing the Cycle

Knowing the two important principles generalized earlier in this chapter, you can work out the key signature of any key by knowing where it lies in what is termed the *cycle of fifths*. Why is it called the cycle of fifths? To answer this question, you need to look at an intriguing anomaly. After B major in the cycle, which has five sharps, comes F# major, which has six. Similarly, after Db major in the cycle, which has five flats, comes Gb major, which has six. Notice that the keys with six sharps/flats have the same keynotes—F# and Gb.

Advanced note: With pure tuning (see Chapter 25, "Intonation"), the note F# is slightly higher in pitch than note Gb by a tiny microtonal interval called the *Pythagorean comma* (about 1/5 of a semitone). Because we use an equally tempered system of tuning, the two are struck by the same key/fret. The keys of F# and Gb major are therefore enharmonically equivalent keys—that is, the same key but spelled differently (see Figure 19.3).

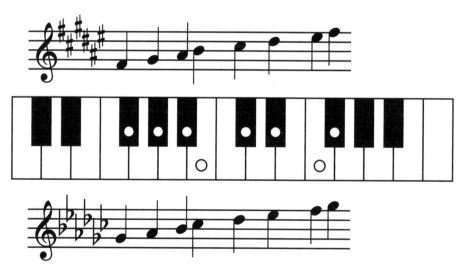

Figure 19.3 F# and Gb Major as enharmonically equivalent keys.

The anomaly is that those keys on the extreme sharp side of the cycle meet those keys on the extreme flat side of the cycle. This meeting point (F#/Gb) is the point of closure of a cycle of 12 keys whose keynotes embrace all 12 notes of the chromatic scale. Hence, the concept of the cycle of fifths. Beginning with C, you can go either way around the circle until you arrive back at C again (see Figure 19.4).

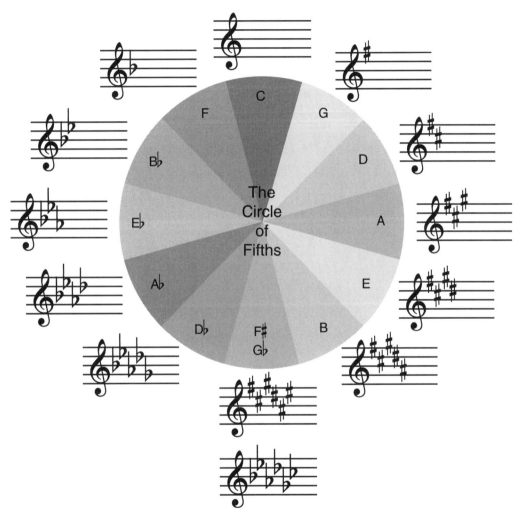

Figure 19.4 The cycle of fifths.

The importance of the cycle of fifths is that it shows how all keys are related within a circular scheme. Keys to the left and right of a particular key are the major keys most closely related to it. This closeness lies in the fact that keys to the right and left of a given key in the circular scheme have the most notes in common. The most closely related keys to D are, therefore, G and A. This is useful to know when you are attempting to modulate (in other words, change key). Key changes to closely related keys are the most common and occur in many types of music.

By contrast, the most distantly related key to C major (for example) is Gb major, simply because the two keys share the fewest notes in common. This distance of relationship is seen in their placement on diametrically opposite points of the circle.

The Cycle of Fifths and Minor Keys

With minor keys the cycle of fifths works according to exactly the same principle, the difference being that the cycle begins with A minor because this is the minor key that has no sharps or flats (see Figure 19.5).

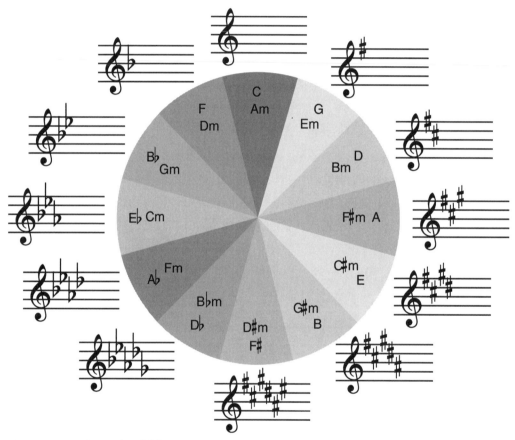

Figure 19.5 The cycle of fifths—minor keys.

The principles of key relationship that apply to the major keys also apply to the minor keys in that the most closely related minor keys are those which lie a fifth above and below the original tonic. In the case of D minor, these are, therefore, A minor (a fifth above) and G minor (a fifth below). Should a modulation (change of key) be needed from a major to a minor key or vice versa, the relative minor key is the closest association. Expanding on this, a scheme of the most closely related keys to any other key (in this case, C/Am) shows itself in Figure 19.6.

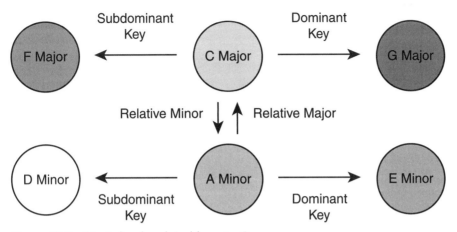

Figure 19.6 Most closely related keys to C.

For more information on modulation, see the Chapter 21, "Chords of the Seventh," where it is discussed in more detail.

Learning of the cycle of fifths as it applies to both major and minor keys puts you in a fortunate position. The scheme of 12 major and 12 minor keys linked by a common cycle of fifths represents the practical summary of the key system of Western music. Learning it gives you access to all of the different keys used in music, together with the complex web of relationships that are generated between them. Musical software manufacturers generally assume such knowledge. Cakewalk SONAR, for example, offers recognition to a full 15 major and minor keys (see Figure 19.7).

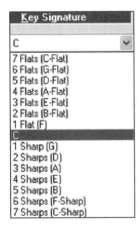

Figure 19.7 Key change/key signature tab in Cakewalk SONAR.

The onus now lies with you:

■ To ensure that you become capable of identifying all of the major and minor keys

■ To know your key signatures

- To be able to effect the correct alterations for the relevant harmonic and melodic minor modes

- To be able to locate all of the relevant chords in each of those keys.

If you can achieve this, you will then have mastery over the key system of Western music. This represents a considerable accomplishment because it means that you have access to the entire key spectrum and all of its resources. At this stage, it is then possible to extend your knowledge and ability even further. The primary direction lies in the use of more advanced, interesting, and intriguing scales within each key. The pentatonic scale is a good example, and each of its five modes can be used in all 12 keys, thus giving you 60 possible options. Another example is the use of the old church modes that preceded our major/minor system. These are a fascinating topic of study, and one which will be covered in the next chapter.

Exercises

You can download the answers to the chapter exercises from www.courseptr.com/downloads.

1. Fill in the missing words. A major scale whose _____ (keynote) is a perfect fifth above the keynote of C requires the addition of a _____ in the key signature (the key of G major). This produces the requisite semitone gap between the _____ and _____ degrees of the scale. Similarly, a major scale whose tonic is a _____ above G (D major) requires _____ sharps in the key signature.

2. Fill in the missing words. A major scale whose tonic lies a _____ below the keynote of C requires the addition of a _____ in the key signature (F major). A major scale whose tonic is a further fifth down (Bb) then requires _____ flats in the key signature.

3a. Fill in the notes required to complete each of these major scales.

3b. When you have done so, circle the note that is the tonic of the relative minor key in each case.

	T	T	S	T	T	T	S
C							
G							
D							
A							
E							
B							
F♯							

4. Play the following major scales correctly from memory in the following order: C – G – D – A – E – B – F#. The correct fingering for these scales can be found in Appendix A, "Scales."

5a. Fill in the notes required to complete the following major scales.

5b. Circle the key that is enharmonically equivalent to the key of F# major.

	T	T	S	T	T	T	S
C							
F							
Bb							
Eb							
Ab							
Db							
Gb							

6. Identify the keys that use the following key signatures. Those in the left-hand column are all major keys; those in the right-hand column are all minor keys.

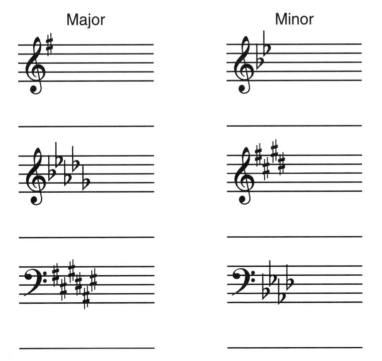

Major

Minor

7. Play the following minor scales correctly from memory in the following order: A – E – B – F# – C# – G# – D#.

8. Put in the accidentals—sharps or flats—required to convert each of these natural minor scales into melodic minor scales.

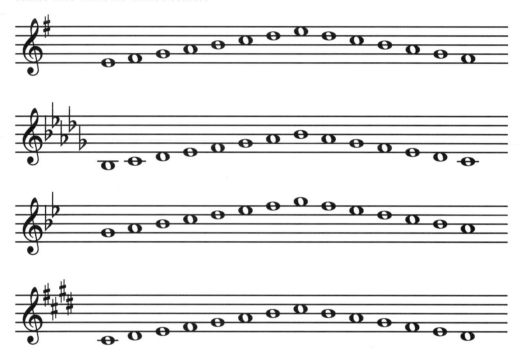

9. Play the following major scales correctly from memory in the following order: C – F – Bb – Eb – Ab – Db – Gb.

20 The Seven Diatonic Modes

Once you have grasped the key system, which includes the major and minor scales, together with the cycle of fifths, which defines all of the keys in which they occur, you are in a really good position to start exploring some fascinating alternatives to that system. The key system, which in the West we have all been musically educated into, is only really pertinent to the classical music period between, say, 1720 and 1870. Its retention in today's popular music is largely due to the strong influence of the music of that period upon both audiences and songwriters. It did, after all, give rise to a music that used elements that still appeal to us as listeners today—a strong, distinctive melody line; a nice, clear bass to give the music foundation; and clear, simple contextual harmonies. For this reason, the key system will probably always be around in popular music. And for the computer musician wishing to write professional-sounding music, it represents essential education.

Modal Music

Toward the end of the 1800s, however, composers started to feel restrained by the key system, and they began to experiment outside of it. One very valuable source of experimentation was looking back to what composers were doing before the key system established itself. At that time, composers were using a more complex set of scales that today we call *modes*. With a different kind of sound to major and minor scales, they enabled composers to write some very fresh, original, and inspiring music.

Seeking alternatives to the major/minor system, composers also looked to the music of their own native traditions—that is, folk music. Through incorporation of folk elements into classical scores, some highly individual and often very national music was created. It is interesting to see that these old modes were still used in the folk music of many countries. So basically, modal music, as approached from both directions, offered composers a nice, refreshing alternative to tonal music—music based on the key system.

Used to great effect in the sphere of so-called "serious music," these old modes also gradually found a way back into popular music. The output of the Beatles, for example, owes a lot to the use of modal scales. The song "Norwegian Wood" is a very good example. Progressive rock also makes good use of these modes, as do jazz and blues. They are also used in film, folk, and all styles of modern dance music.

Although modal scales were originally introduced by the Church into European music in the Middle Ages, they are thought to originate from ancient Greece. Their distinctive names come from here—names such as Mixolydian, Dorian, and so on. I am sure you have heard recordings of Gregorian chant sung by Christian monks. This is ancient modal melody at its very best. The chants of Hildegard von Bingham—recordings of which are sampled in electronic tracks on occasion—are also pure modal music.

"Sumer Is Icumen In," a song that became well-known through the film *The Wicker Man,* is a good example of an early European modal tune. But even before that, there are records of modal scales being used. They were noted for their ability to exert profound emotional effects upon an audience. Similar types of scales are still found in Indian and Middle Eastern music, although this represents a separate branch of study.

With the advent of loop-based music—found, for example, in trance, techno, house, drum and bass, and so on—modal scales have also gained a newfound popularity. They favor the use of repetition and looping techniques as each scale creates its own characteristic atmosphere and mood. In fact, the word "mode" comes from the ancient Greek word for "mood."

An easy way to appreciate the concept of mood as it applies to scales is to the think of the major and minor scales. The major is linked to bright, sunny moods, whereas the minor is much more somber and inclined toward sadness and melancholy. Modal scales evoke similar states or moods, although because there are more of them, there is a greater variety of expression.

The Seven Modal Scales
So what are these modal scales? The major scale itself is one of the old modal scales, except that it had a different name.

The Ionian Mode
As mentioned a moment ago, the major scale is one of the old modal scales, but it was called the *Ionian mode* (see Figure 20.1). This mode had a bad reputation in the Middle Ages, being also called the *Wanton mode.* This is because ancient Greek musicians and philosophers linked it with the planet Venus—the goddess of love and lust. The Church was thus rather afraid of its use in case it inspired carnal feelings amongst the brethren!

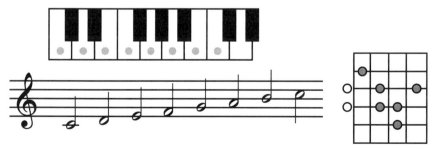

Figure 20.1 The Ionian mode: Key of C.

As in the major and minor modes, the most important note is the tonic, which represents the first degree of the scale. In modal music, this is often heard throughout the tune in the form of a drone or pedal point that provides an anchor for the harmony. In loop-based music, it often represents the most important note in the bass—that is, the note around which the bass revolves.

There are seven diatonic modal scales in all, and to obtain these, the position of the first degree of the scale (that is, the tonic) is changed (see Figure 20.2).

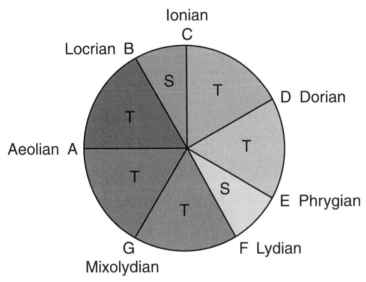

Figure 20.2   The seven diatonic modes (obtained through rotation of the tonic).

The Dorian Mode

If the tonic is placed on note D, you obtain the *Dorian mode* (see Figure 20.3).

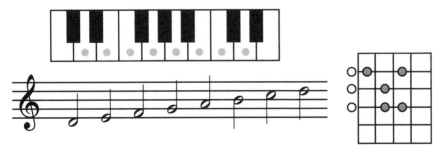

Figure 20.3   The Dorian mode.

The Dorian is a fascinating mode. It was particularly revered in ancient Greece, where it represented an ideal of mood or state of mind. It is similar to the natural minor scale except that in the

Dorian mode, the interval between the tonic and the sixth is major instead of minor. This gives the scale a strange character somewhere between major and minor. A chord progression from Dm to G—as found in the song "House of the Rising Sun"—is characteristically Dorian. In the Dorian mode, good triads to use are Dm (tonic chord), F, G, Am, and C. You can also hear the Dorian mode at work in the songs "Greensleeves," "Scarborough Fair," and "The Age of Aquarius." A more modern example you might be familiar with is Gary Jules's "Mad World," which uses the chords Dm, G, and C. An example of Dorian music is also given on Track 41 of the audio CD.

The Phrygian Mode

When the tonic is placed up to the next note E, you obtain the *Phrygian mode* (see Figure 20.4).

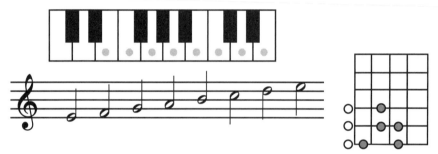

Figure 20.4   The Phrygian mode.

This mode is identical to the E natural minor mode, except that the second degree is flat. It has the mellow character of the minor mode, although the flat second gives it a more stately, exotic quality. This flat second represents one of the main characteristics of early Goa trance. And these days, the psy-trance genre uses this mode almost exclusively. Check this out on Track 42 of the audio CD.

The Phrygian mode was also used to good effect in older songs, such as "So Cold the Night" by Jimmy Somerville and "White Rabbit" by Jefferson Airplane. The English classical composer Vaughan Williams also used this mode in his "Fantasia on a Theme" by Thomas Tallis.

Good chords to use in this mode are Em (tonic), F, G, Am, C, and Dm. Em to F gives the characteristic Phrygian progression, with the chord of F usually being referred to as the *Neapolitan triad*.

When the chord of E major is used as a substitute for the chord of E minor, a mode called the *Spanish Phrygian* results. It is the same as the regular Phrygian except with a sharp third degree (see Table 20.1). It is used all of the time in Spanish Flamenco music.

The major chords of E, F, and G are also often used to give that particular Spanish feel to the progression.

Table 20.1 The Spanish Phrygian Mode						
I	II	III	IV	V	VI	VII
E	F	G#	A	B	C	D

The Lydian Mode

The next mode is obtained when F is taken as the tonic. This is called the *Lydian mode* (see Figure 20.5).

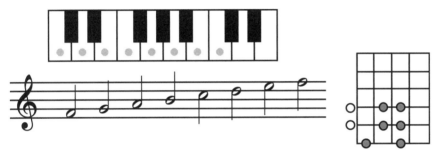

Figure 20.5   The Lydian mode.

The Lydian mode is virtually the same as the F major mode, except that the fourth degree is sharp. This produces an augmented fourth with the tonic, which, when used properly in a modal tune, can produce a euphoric sense. To appreciate this, try experimenting with it—it can produce some really interesting tunes. The theme from *The Simpsons* is probably the most famous recent example of a Lydian-inspired tune.

Sometimes the Lydian mode is used with the flat seventh, where it is called the *harmonic scale* because the first 11 members of the harmonic series naturally suggest this scale (see Table 20.2).

Table 20.2 The Harmonic Scale						
I	II	III	IV	V	VI	VII
F	G	A	B	C	D	Eb

The harmonic scale is very atmospheric and works particularly well with the chords F or F7 and Cm.

The Mixolydian Mode

Raise the tonic up to note G, and you'll obtain the *Mixolydian mode* (see Figure 20.6).

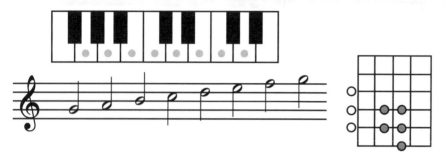

Figure 20.6   The Mixolydian mode.

The Mixolydian mode is similar to the G major mode. The difference is that the seventh degree is flat. This gives tunes written in this mode a distinct folk flavor. Instead of the usual semitone between the leading note F# and the tonic G, there is a whole tone—F to G. This gives the mode its characteristic tonal feeling. The main chords, which give off that Mixolydian feeling, are G to Dm, with F being a good intermediary between the two. Listen to the Beatles' "Norwegian Wood" or ABBA's "The Visitors," and you will get the idea. Interestingly, the themes for both *Star Trek* and *Star Wars* use the Mixolydian mode, as does Holst's "Jupiter" from *The Planets* suite.

The Aeolian Mode

The next mode is called the *Aeolian mode;* you obtain it by placing the tonic on note A (see Figure 20.7).

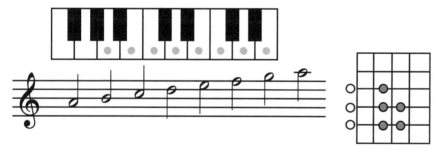

Figure 20.7   The Aeolian mode.

This mode is one of the best known of the group—it is also called the *natural minor mode,* and it is the mode in which most popular music is written. As the mainstay of rock, pop, and all kinds of dance music, it will probably remain so indefinitely. But for something different, experimentation with the other modes is worthwhile.

The Locrian Mode

The final mode of the seven is called the *Locrian mode,* resulting from placing the tonic on note B (see Figure 20.8).

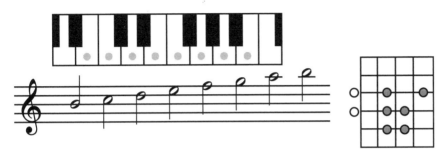

Figure 20.8   The Locrian mode.

This mode is virtually identical to the B natural minor mode, except that the fifth degree is lowered. This gives the mode a diminished fifth with the tonic—its salient characteristics. In terms of chord progressions, the Locrian mode is problematic because it doesn't have a proper tonic triad—B D F. However, it is used to great effect in techno, drum and bass, and some of the harder styles of trance. The diminished fifth (*diabolus in musica*) between the tonic B and F gives a really dark feeling, which suits the character of some of the harder, darker styles of loop-based music. Track 43 of the audio CD features an example of this.

Modes in Other Keys

The seven modes as shown all occur on the white keys of the keyboard. But they can also be used in any other key. This means that there are 84 (12×7) modal possibilities to contend with. Usually these are referred to by name, with the addition of a prefix indicating the key. Consequently, F# Dorian means the Dorian mode in the key of F#. Bb Locrian means the Locrian mode in the key of Bb, and so on. Should you want to work out a particular mode in a particular key, you will find the table in Figure 20.9 helpful. It gives the tone-semitone formula for each of the seven modes from any given starting note.

The modes we considered in this chapter were obtained by rotating the tonic. As such, they did not go beyond the use of the seven-toned white-key scale. To have use of all seven modes in one key, however, represents a totally different situation. You need more notes than the seven white keys. If you choose the tonic to be note C, then for the Phrygian mode, you also need the notes Db, Eb, F, G, Ab, and Bb. For the Lydian mode in the same key, you will also need the notes D, E, F#, G, A, and B. The result is a more complex scale than we have so far encountered (see Figure 20.10).

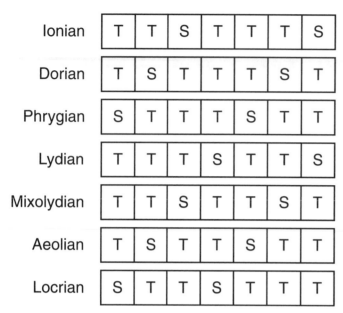

Figure 20.9 Table for working out modes.

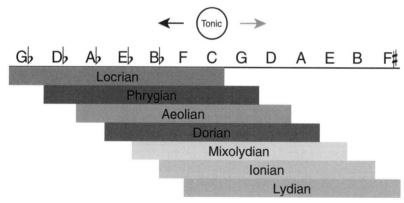

Figure 20.10 The seven diatonic modes sharing common tonic C.

To use all seven modes in the key of C, you need the full spectrum of notes seen in Figure 20.10. This is because only the Ionian mode in the key of C exclusively uses the white keys. All of the other modes require the use of one or more black keys. You can see, for example, that the Locrian mode in the key of C uses five such keys. What this means is very significant for your music writing. To use any of the seven modes in a particular key, you are in effect drawing the notes that you use from a full chromatic scale. The name for this type of scale is the *harmonic form of chromatic scale* (see Table 20.3).

Table 20.3 The Harmonic Form of Chromatic Scale—Key of C

Note	Interval (with Tonic)
C	Prime
Db	Minor second
D	Major second
Eb	Minor third
E	Major third
F	Perfect fourth
F#	Augmented fourth
Gb	Diminished fifth
G	Perfect fifth
Ab	Minor sixth
A	Major sixth
Bb	Minor seventh
B	Major seventh
C	Octave

There is a particular technique for playing the chromatic scale involving the thumb, first, and second fingers of the right hand, which are numbered 1, 2, and 3, respectively, in Figure 20.11.

Fingering: 1   3   1   3   1   2   3   1   3   1   3   1   2

Figure 20.11   The harmonic form of the chromatic scale (key of C).

The importance of the harmonic form of chromatic scale is that it uses all 12 keys on the keyboard, but referenced against a single tonic. Therefore, each note represents a particular relationship to that tonic. From this relationship, the note itself acquires its meaning and significance in the scale. The note Db, for example, is significant as the flat second that may be found in the Phrygian mode. It is this note, you will recall, that gives the Phrygian mode its unique character. The note F# is significant as the augmented fourth used in the

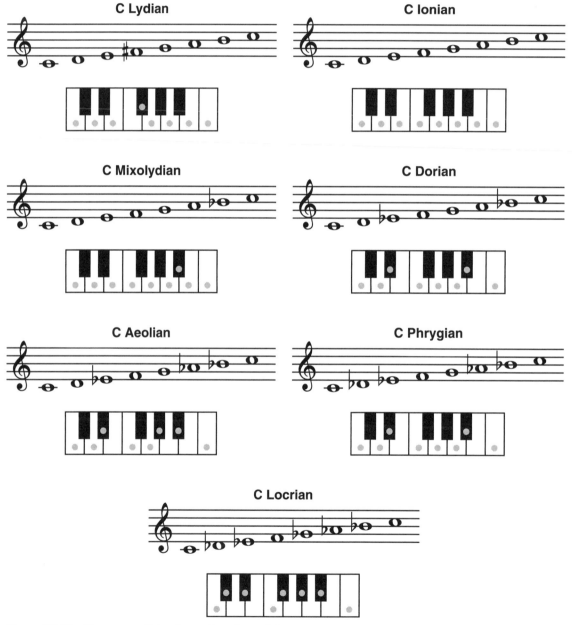

Figure 20.12   The seven diatonic modes—key of C.

Lydian mode. Again, it is this note that gives the Lydian mode its unique character. Viewed in this context, the harmonic form of the chromatic scale is simply a complete summary of modal interval relationships to a fixed tonic note. For composers, therefore, it is very much like an artist's palette of color. Knowing the complete harmonic form of chromatic scale, they are able to select whichever notes they need from it to create a mode—and therefore, by implication, a mood—that suits their expressive purpose: major, minor, pentatonic, modal, or exotic.

When you have learned the harmonic form of the chromatic scale, the process of writing music thus gets that much simpler. There is only one scale of 12 notes to think about—a scale that operates on two levels: as a scale of 12 keynotes from which the tonic is chosen, and as a host scale from which the notes for the modes are selected.

I should point out that there are many such modes in addition to those we've considered so far. We'll make more progress in this direction in Chapter 22, "Exotic Scales," where we'll do further study of more exotic scales. For present purposes, Figure 20.12 shows the seven diatonic modes as they occur in the key of C.

In this chapter you have learned about the seven diatonic modes and various ways in which they can be used. You have also learned that all of these modes are simply a selection of notes from a more wide-ranging scale—the harmonic form of chromatic scale. This scale, as it is represented and written down in different keys, is given in Appendix A, "Scales."

Now that you have advanced your knowledge of modes and scale systems, it is time to advance your knowledge of harmony. In the next chapter, you'll study chords of the seventh. These are of great importance to many types of modern music because they have a greater complexity than common triads. They thus provide a richer and more extensive bank of chordal resources. Learning them will enormously improve your ability to write effective harmonies and chord progressions.

Exercises

You can download the answers to the chapter exercises from www.courseptr.com/downloads.

1.   Choose the note that is the tonic or first degree of the following modal scales:
   - Ionian mode: C D E F G A B C
   - Mixolydian mode: C D E F G A B C
   - Dorian mode: C D E F G A B C
   - Aeolian mode: C D E F G A B C
   - Phrygian mode: C D E F G A B C
   - Locrian mode: C D E F G A B C
   - Lydian mode: C D E F G A B C

2.   Identify the following modes on two levels. First state the keynote, and then state the mode (such as F Phrygian, and so on).

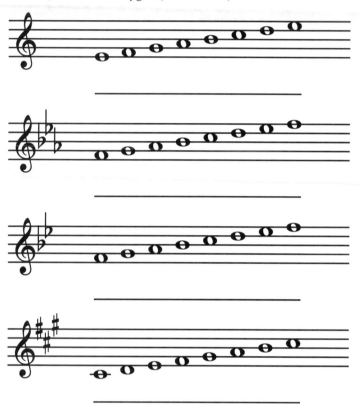

_____

_____

_____

_____

Tip: First, find the major scale indicated by the key signature. Second, find the degree of that scale upon which the above are built. This will tell you what the mode is. In other words, if the mode begins on degree four of a particular major scale, then it is a Lydian mode, and so on.

3. Using your sequencer, complete the following chord progressions in the mode and key indicated. One or two bars per chord would make the task easier and simpler to accomplish. Begin and end upon the chord given.

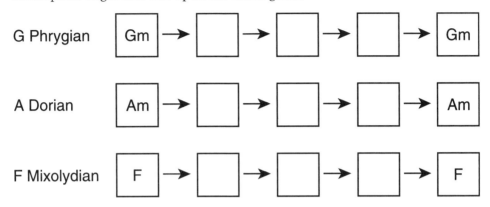

4. Fill in the notes required to complete each mode in the key indicated.

	1	2	3	4	5	6	7
C Dorian							
F# Locrian							
G Aeolian							
Eb Lydian							

21 Chords of the Seventh

The purpose of this chapter is to further your ability to produce effective and awe-inspiring harmonies. So far in this book, we have considered only triadic harmony—which centers mostly around the use of major and minor common chords—in any detail. Once you come to grips with this, it won't be long before you want to start spicing up your harmonies with more complex chords. At this point, the study of harmony starts to get really interesting, involving the use of more sophisticated chords of the seventh, added sixth, ninth, suspended fourth chords, and so on. In this chapter, we'll do an initial study of seventh chords, along with how they are constructed, used, and represented in popular song format.

To do this successfully, it is useful to review the foundation for seventh chord harmony—that is, triadic harmony. You have already seen that there are four types of triad: major, minor, augmented, and diminished. These are represented in popular music format as shown in Figure 21.1.

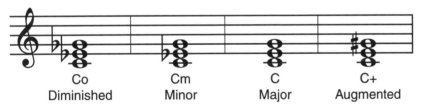

| Co | Cm | C | C+ |
| Diminished | Minor | Major | Augmented |

Figure 21.1 Four types of triads.

Seventh Chords

You obtain a chord of the seventh when you add to the root, third, and fifth of any of the aforementioned triads a fourth note that is a seventh above the root of the chord. This seventh is usually taken from the scale or key in which the triad occurs.

Because you are already familiar with the C major scale, we will study the seventh chords in this key. The chord built upon the first degree, which is called Cmaj7, is obtained as shown in Figure 21.2.

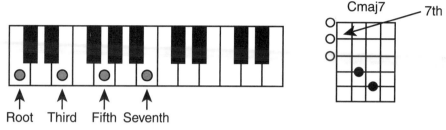

Figure 21.2   Construction of seventh chord: Cmaj7.

The principle is simple, provided you know the scale of the particular key. From the root, count up seven notes within that scale. This locates the seventh, which is then added to the triad to form a four-note sonority or tetrad (see Figure 21.3).

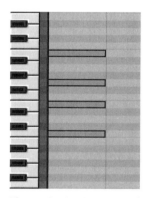

Figure 21.3   Sequenced Cmaj7 chord.

The consequences of the addition of a seventh to a triad lie in the fact that the seventh is a dissonant interval—in other words, it presents a certain degree of tension. Experiment on the keyboard with the chord of Cmaj7. Listen to how the seventh sounds on its own—it gives quite a sharp dissonance.

Generally, there are two ways in which you can deal with this dissonance. The first derives from the most common treatment of this chord in classical music. The seventh is resolved stepwise to the nearest point of concord (see Figure 21.4).

In this case, the seventh resolves downward to a consonant third. John Lennon's "Imagine" uses this type of resolution: Cmaj7–F. Although in this case the seventh resolves, there is no rule that says the next chord cannot be a seventh either. In this case, the same stepwise resolution is embedded within an Fmaj7 chord, which in turn sets up another dissonance (see Figure 21.5).

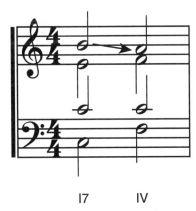

I7   IV

Figure 21.4 Resolution of seventh.

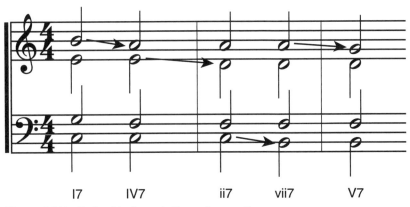

I7   IV7   ii7   vii7   V7

Figure 21.5 Embedded resolution of seventh.

This technique was favored by classical composers—chains of seventh chords would be set up, each one serving to resolve the other.

Another equally valid way of dealing with the seventh is to place it in an environment where sevenths are so abundant that the ear accepts them as being stable sonorities. Track 45 of the audio CD—Eric Satie's "Gymnopedie No. 1"—is a good example of this. This technique is favored in jazz, where all sorts of what were in classical times viewed to be dissonant sonorities are strung together without a second thought. Both methods work equally well, provided that they occur in context.

Because seventh chords have four notes, they offer more opportunities for interesting types of chordal spacing. Figure 21.6 presents some examples of a differently spaced Cmaj7 chord.

In Figure 21.6, the letter A designates the chord in closed position harmony, in which the notes of the chord are crowded together as closely as possible. The letter B shows the chord scored in

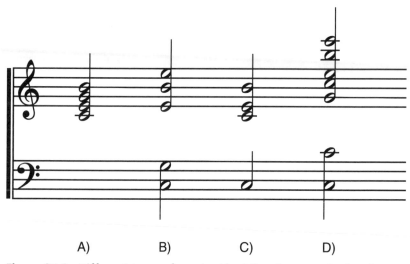

Figure 21.6 Different types of spacing/doubling for seventh chord.

five parts by doubling the third. This wide spread gives a rich, balanced sonority. The letter C shows one of the notes of the seventh omitted. This is generally the fifth—as in this case—for the seventh and the third are the intervals that define the chord in its essential aspect. To make the harmony fuller, the root is doubled in the octave below. Finally, the chord is presented in a very wide-open sonority in seven parts, in which the root has been doubled three times and the third of the chord twice (letter D).

Experiment with a single seventh chord, paying attention to spacing and doubling. Obtain as many different combinations as possible. Through this experimentation, your knowledge of seventh chord harmony will grow significantly. Track 44 of the audio CD gives you some examples of a differently spaced Cmaj7 chord to give you an idea of how it can be varied.

Like triads, you can use seventh chords in different inversions. Because the chord has four notes, this means the chord has four possible positions (see Figure 21.7).

The first is root position, indicated simply by Cmaj7. The first inversion seventh chord has the third in the bass—note E; it is therefore a slash chord, indicated as Cmaj7/E. Both second and third inversions are also slash chords, indicated as Cmaj7/G and Cmaj7/B, respectively. Again, you need to study each of these in a musical context—you need to play and hear them so you acquire knowledge of their particular qualities.

To build a seventh chord upon any degree of the scale, follow this simple two-step procedure:

1.   Establish the triad of root, third, and fifth.

2.   Add the seventh above the root, being careful to stay within the chosen scale.

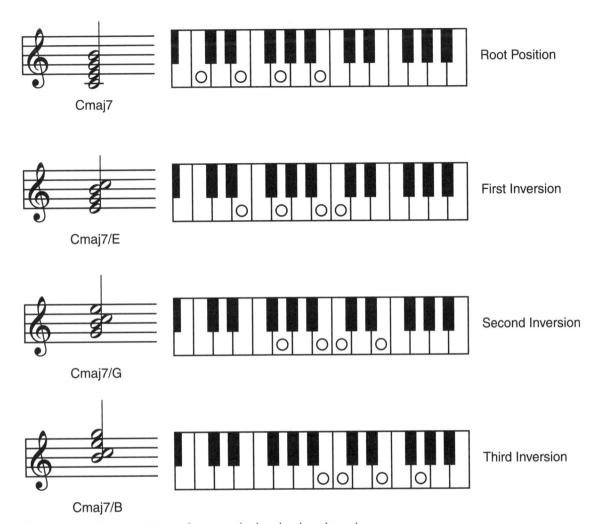

Root Position

Cmaj7

First Inversion

Cmaj7/E

Second Inversion

Cmaj7/G

Third Inversion

Cmaj7/B

Figure 21.7 Four positions of a seventh chord—closed spacing.

Sevenths in the C Major Scale

Applying this procedure to the C major scale, you obtain a series of six other seventh chords (in addition to the chord of Cmaj7 we just considered). See Figure 21.8.

Some of these chords have a major seventh, as in C E G B, while others use a minor seventh, as in D F A C. What is the difference? The major seventh has 11 semitones and is quite a sharp dissonance, whereas the minor seventh has 10 semitones and, although dissonant, is much mellower in its sound.

This means that there are two kinds of seventh chords: chords of the major seventh and chords of the minor seventh. Because the seventh chords in Figure 21.8 are mostly minor sevenths,

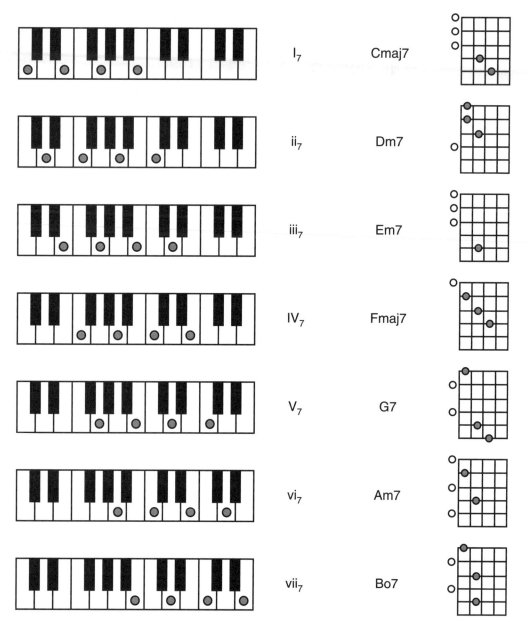

Figure 21.8 Seventh chords in the key of C major.

convention rules that these are simply represented by a 7. In contrast, major seventh chords require "maj7" after the letter—for example, Fmaj7. The abbreviation Cm7 would thus signify a C minor chord with a minor seventh added, while Cm/maj7 would signify a C minor chord with a major seventh added.

The Dominant Seventh Chord

The most popular and frequently used seventh chord is the dominant seventh chord, which occurs on the fifth degree of either the major or the minor scale (chord G7 in Figure 21.8). For this reason, the chords of C and G7 are often the first two chords that guitarists learn to play. These chords play a crucial part in so many songs that this makes sense. The reason for the popularity of the dominant seventh chord lies in the strength of its resolution to the tonic triad. Earlier we talked about the perfect cadence, a progression from chord V to the tonic of either major or minor key. When a seventh is added to the dominant triad, the perfect cadence is even more incisive and final. Primarily, this is because of the tritone present in the chord—the dissonant interval that in C major occurs between notes B and F. This dissonance resolves beautifully to the third of the tonic triad (see Figure 21.9, paying attention to the labeled a, b, and c): The note B (the leading note) passes smoothly up to the tonic, and the note F falls down to the third of the scale (a). Combined with the perfect fifth root movement from dominant to tonic degree (b), a powerful cadence results (c).

Figure 21.9   V7 to I progression.

To appreciate this, try it out on the MIDI keyboard.

Modulation

Because of the strength of resolution to the tonic triad, the dominant seventh chord has always represented the main agent for a change of key in a song—called *modulation*. It is important to remember that when you are trying to change key, the target chord is the dominant seventh of the new key, rather than the tonic. This is because the ear will only accept that a modulation has occurred when it registers a perfect cadence in the new key. Without such a cadence, the ear will register only a transitory shift toward that key.

This is why the minor mode is so vulnerable to alteration. It does not possess the requisite chord for a perfect cadence. So it needs to be chromatically altered in order to have one. This also highlights one of the major problems encountered in modal harmony: To achieve success in modal harmony, you must avoid at all costs any semblance of a perfect cadence because when it *does* occur, the ear will automatically focus upon the implied tonic toward which the cadence occurs. And the Ionian mode is the only mode in which this is desirable.

Using Seventh Chords

Probably the best way to learn to use seventh chords is to insert them between triads so that the seventh resolves in the next triad. A good example of this is to go Dm – Dm7 – G (see Figure 21.10).

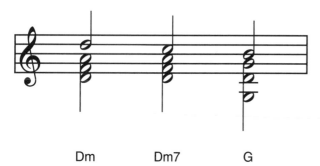

Dm   Dm7   G

Figure 21.10   Chord progression using seventh chord.

In this context, the seventh of the chord ii (note C) appears as a passing note between two triad notes—the D of the Dm triad and the B of the G triad. When you are familiar with this type of progression, you can attempt to create chord progressions in which all of the chords are seventh chords. You should use the principles of root movement to assist this process.

Seventh Chord Harmony in the Minor Scale

Seventh chord harmony in the minor scale involves adding a seventh to each triad present in the minor scale. The sevenths for the natural minor scale are the same as those present in the relative major scale. Experience in dealing with seventh chord harmony in the major scale will be fruitful here because, as I mentioned before, the difference between the two systems is one of emphasis—where the tonic chord is placed.

With regard to the entire minor key system—embracing natural, harmonic, and melodic minor scales—the principles of seventh chord harmony become more complex because there are more triads to be extended through the addition of a seventh. Within the minor scale complex as a whole, the main seventh chords to contend with are shown in Figure 21.11.

So which chord should you use when faced with multiple choices? On the second degree of the scale—note B—for example, you can see in Figure 21.11 that you could choose to use either Bo7 or Bm7. The answer depends entirely on the context. Ultimately, your ear must be the final arbiter. My advice when attempting to deal with such complexities is to learn to handle the dominant seventh of the minor key first. Because this is the same chord found on degree five of the major scale, it should present few problems. Then start to look at and incorporate other

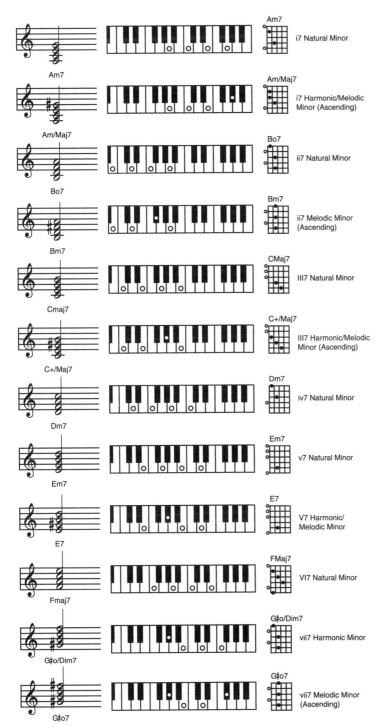

Figure 21.11   Main seventh chords in the minor key (key of A).

seventh chords. With chords more complex than triads, you can learn a lot by playing them at the MIDI keyboard and experimenting with combining different chords.

In this chapter you have studied the construction and makeup of seventh chords, how to name and identify them, and the types of seventh chords that you get in the major and minor modes. This study of seventh chords provides a nice, gradual transition into the world of complex harmony, which includes chords of the ninth, eleventh, and thirteenth. You will study these in Chapter 23, "Complex Harmony." For now, it seems appropriate to take a break from matters of harmony and look at a totally fascinating area of modern electronic music—one of vital significance for the computer musician wishing to generate a fresh, new, or original kind of sound. This is the area of exotic scales, which you will study in the next chapter.

Exercises

You can download the answers to the chapter exercises from www.courseptr.com/downloads.

1. Name three types of complex chords (chords other than triads).

    A. _____

    B. _____

    C. _____

2. Fill in the missing words. A chord of the seventh is obtained when a _____ above the root of the chord is added to the root, third, and fifth of a _____.

3. Sequence a closed position Cmaj7 chord for strings. Then produce as many different types of spacing of the same chord as you can. Listen carefully to each sonority to assess its strengths and merits.

4. Fill in the other three notes required to complete each of the indicated seventh chords.

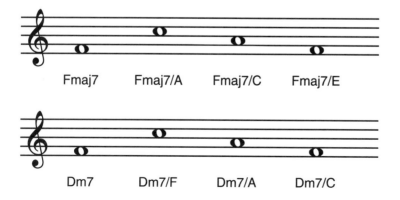

5. Identify and label the following seventh chords in the key of C major in the manner indicated. The first seventh chord has already been identified and labeled for you.

I_7 Cmaj7

6. Below you will see Cmaj7 progressing to three different seventh chords—the first (Fmaj7) involving root movement by fourths, the second (Am7) involving root

movement by thirds, and the third (Dm7) involving root movement by seconds. Complete the harmony as indicated below. Resolve the seventh of each chord stepwise.

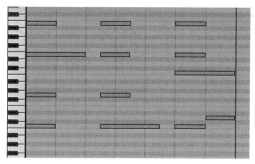

Cmaj7–Fmaj7   Cmaj7–Am7/C   Cmaj7–Dm7

7.   List and identify the seventh chords belonging to the following keys.

D natural minor:	D	E	F	G	A	Bb	C	D

Chord I:

Chord II:

Chord III:

Chord IV:

Chord V:

Chord VI:

Chord VII:

B natural minor:	B	C#	D	E	F#	G	A	B

Chord I:

Chord II:

Chord III:

Chord IV:

Chord V:

Chord VI:

Chord VII:

F# major:		F#	G#	A#	B	C#	D#	E#	F#
Chord I:									
Chord II:									
Chord III:									
Chord IV:									
Chord V:									
Chord VI:									
Chord VII:									

22 Exotic Scales

As really useful alternatives to the major and minor scales, so far we have looked at the pentatonic scale and the five modes that can be derived from it, as well as the seven-note diatonic scale and its group of modes (Ionian, Dorian, and so on). Another really great source of inspiration for new musical ideas can come from the so-called *exotic scales*. These scales often are drawn from music outside of our Western traditions.

Two Kinds of Exotic Scales

Generally, exotic scales can be of two kinds. The first kind derives from music writers' attempts to imitate or emulate the native music of faraway places. Famous examples of this are the Hungarian minor mode, otherwise known as the *Gypsy scale,* often used to suggest an Eastern European atmosphere. (You'll learn more about the nature of this scale later in this chapter.) Another kind includes the various Japanese pentatonic scales. These are different than the pentatonic scale you are accustomed to because they use semitones. These will also be considered later in this chapter.

The second kind of exotic scale includes those simply invented at one time or another by composers for particular musical purposes. A good example of this is the Mystic scale—a scale of six notes based on the harmonic series, originally developed by Alexander Scriabin. Using this exclusively, Scriabin created a totally unique sound unlike anything anybody had ever heard before!

Experimenting with Exotic Scales

Such scales are well worth experimenting with, especially if you want to suggest the atmosphere and influence of faraway and exotic places. To use exotic scales to their full potential, though, you shouldn't always think about harmony in a limited chordal sense. Many exotic scales have the character of musical modes—that is, they suggest certain types of moods and atmospheres. Consequently, they often work best in the melodic dimension, where there is a different kind of harmony at play—the harmony of the interval.

Pure modal music often employs drones and such to fix the pitch of the tonic in the listener's mind. Indian music is a good example. The sitar upon which much of the music is played has a series of resonating strings that continually sound the modal tonic and its fifth. Each note of the mode is then heard as a harmony note with that tonic, and from this harmony, the note gains its modal coloring. From this perspective, a mode is not a collection of notes, but rather a collection of intervals, each of which contributes its own character to the mix. For this purpose, knowledge of and experience with the various intervals in the chromatic scale becomes essential. Each interval, as considered in relation to the modal tonic, has its own character, place, and significance. To remind you, Table 22.1 provides a full chromatic scale that takes note C to be the modal tonic.

Table 22.1 The Harmonic Form of Chromatic Scale (Key of C)

Degree of Scale	Note	Modal Interval
1	C	Modal tonic
2	Db	Minor second
3	D	Major second
4	Eb	Minor third
5	E	Major third
6	F	Perfect fourth
7	F#	Augmented fourth
8	G	Perfect fifth
9	Ab	Minor sixth
10	A	Major sixth
11	Bb	Minor seventh
12	B	Major seventh
1	C	Octave

Neapolitan Modes

The notes for an exotic scale are drawn from this scale. A good example is the so-called *Neapolitan* family of modes. Their name comes from the fact that they all have a flat second degree, like the Phrygian mode. The flat second is a very evocative interval and, when used, it can bring great color and expressiveness to music. You can turn any mode or scale into a Neapolitan simply by flattening the second degree. Figure 22.1 shows four well-known examples of Neapolitan modes taken using the keynote of C.

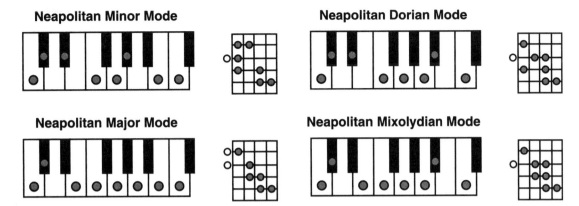

Figure 22.1   Neapolitan modes.

The first example is the harmonic minor mode with a flat second. The presence of the flat second gives the mode a distinct Eastern sense. The second mode offers a compromise between the Dorian and Phrygian modes. And although these modes don't always offer suitable harmonies, if you *do* want to use chords, some of them offer up some really interesting chord combinations. The mix of Bbm, Eb, and F in the Neapolitan Dorian mode is a good example, as is the mix of Bbm and C in the Neapolitan Mixolydian mode.

Note: Although the examples in Figure 22.1 were built in the key of C, they can be used in any key you want—as can any of the scales/modes that follow. In this context, note C is simply a familiar reference point upon which to construct, compare, and view the scales. Should you want to try them out in other keys, work out the number of semitones between each note and build up the scale accordingly.

Middle Eastern Scales

Another important group of exotic scales includes those used by composers to generate a Middle Eastern atmosphere. Among this group, it is well worth your time to experiment with the scales shown in Figure 22.2. The names given to these scales are recognized common property, as are the scales themselves.

To be more authentic, in some cases you would need to use a proper Arabian form of tuning. For an example of how this works, see Chapter 25, "Intonation."

Eastern European Scales

Another form of local scale includes those suggestive of Eastern Europe. Among scales used by composers to suggest such locations are the ones shown in Figure 22.3.

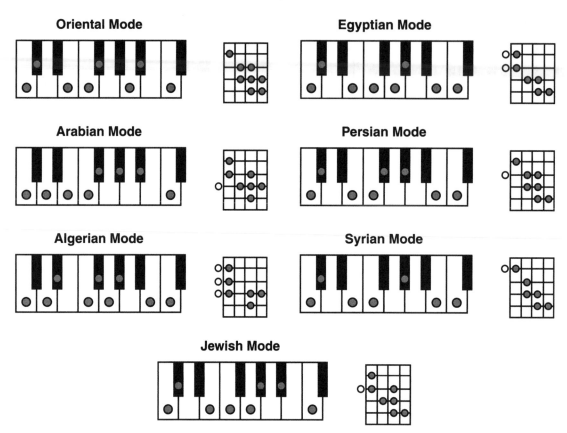

Figure 22.2 Middle Eastern scales.

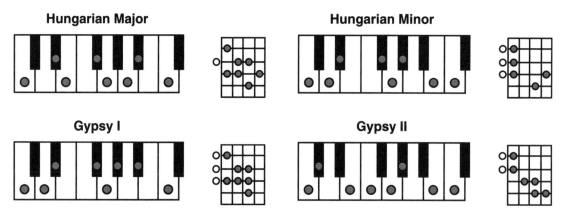

Figure 22.3 Eastern European scales.

What make these scales so interesting are their characteristic inflections—sharps or flat notes that make them different than the regular major and minor scales. The Hungarian Major has a distinctive sharp second and fourth and a flat seventh. The Hungarian Minor is basically the same as the harmonic minor scale except that the fourth has been sharpened. Gypsy I is the same as the natural minor scale, but again with the fourth sharpened. Gypsy II is like a regular major scale except that the second and sixth degrees have been lowered by a semitone. The use of these inflections gives music written within these scales its own unique character.

Hindu Melas

Another rich modal tradition often referenced by composers is that of India. Here the best point of reference for a Western musician would be the Carnatic system of Hindustani music, which uses a set of 72 basic scales called *melas*. These are well worth investigating should you ever have the time.

Although this is clearly a varied and complex tradition that requires specialized study, many of their basic modes have passed into more or less common usage by composers. Figure 22.4 shows some examples.

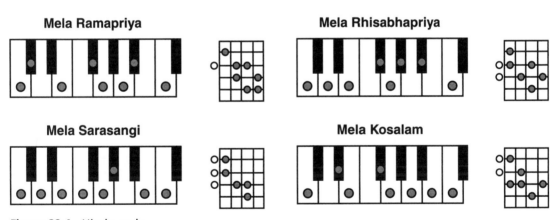

Figure 22.4 Hindu mela.

These are best used melodically over a drone or sustained notes.

Jazz and Blues Scales

Although they started out with our conventional major and minor scales, jazz and blues styles of music have also evolved their own characteristic modal scales. In addition to using other diatonic modes (such as in modal jazz), there are particular modes in which characteristic inflections are implicit. Amongst these are the ones shown in Figure 22.5.

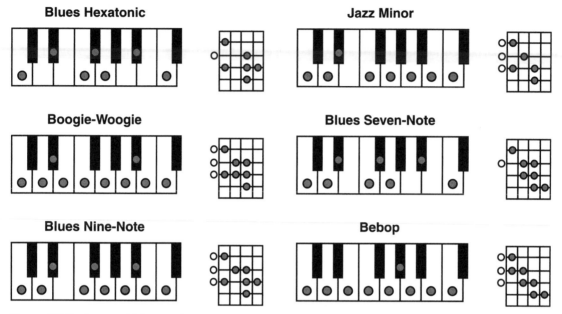

Figure 22.5 Jazz and blues scales.

The characteristic features of these scales are again the various inflections of ordinary scale notes, referred to as *blue notes*. In the blues hexatonic, seven-note, and nine-note scales, these are the notes Eb, F#, and Bb.

Ancient Egyptian Pentatonic Scales

There are some beautiful and exotic variations of the pentatonic scale. The music of ancient Egypt reputedly used a scale that was basically the same as pentatonic mode 4, except that the second and fifth degrees were flattened. This resulted in the so-called *hemitonic* five-note scales—that is, pentatonic scales that use semitones (as opposed to *anhemitonic* scales, which are pentatonic scales without semitones). See Figure 22.6.

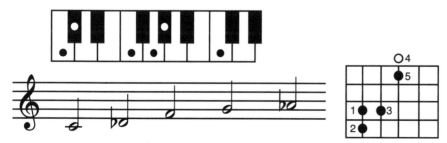

Figure 22.6 Ancient Egyptian pentatonic scale.

Japanese Pentatonic Scales

You'll find similar hemitonic variants in traditional Japanese music (see Figure 22.7).

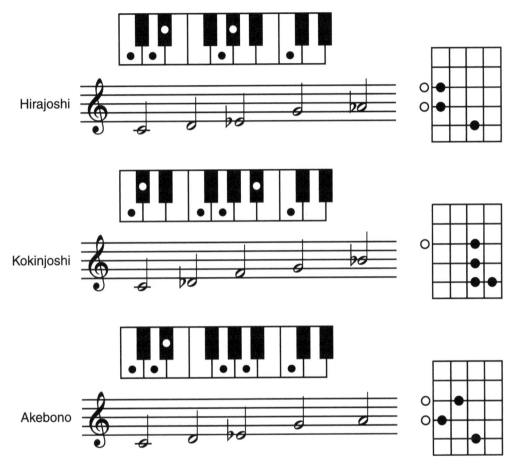

Figure 22.7   Japanese pentatonic scales.

Balinese Pentatonic Scales

One of the most exotic forms of pentatonic scale is used in traditional Balinese music (see Figure 22.8).

Although the Pelog version is similar in profile to the ancient Egyptian scale discussed earlier, it is tuned in a certain way that sounds very strange to our ears. Yet when used on traditional Balinese instruments, it sounds quite beautiful. This tuning often comes as one of the alternative tunings presented on modern-day synths, such as the Korg Triton. Check it out when you can, being careful to use a Balinese metallophone program that will show this tuning at its best. (See also Chapter 25.)

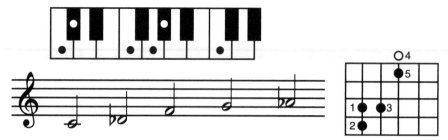

Figure 22.8 Balinese Pelog scale.

Whole Tone Scale

Some types of exotic scales result from the use of certain characteristic types of harmony. A good example is the whole tone scale (see Figure 22.9). As its name suggests, this scale is built up entirely from whole tones. Every chord within that scale is an augmented triad. Originally popular with early 20th-century Impressionist composers Debussy and Ravel, the harmony it produces is quite unique. The lack of semitones gives music written in this scale a wandering, abstract quality. Try to play it on your keyboard, and you will see what I mean.

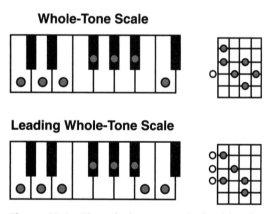

Whole-Tone Scale

Leading Whole-Tone Scale

Figure 22.9 The whole tone scale (and leading whole tone scale).

Because of the lack of semitones, and therefore the absence of a leading note, there is no sense of a tonic in the whole tone scale. To impart at least some sense of a tonic, the leading whole tone scale is sometimes used. The semitone below C suggests a leading note and therefore persuades the listener that the scale does have a tonic.

Artificial Scales

In addition to studying and collecting exotic scales—which itself is interesting—you can try to invent your own. Generally, these invented scales are called *artificial scales*, and some really good ones have been invented. To start you off, Figure 22.10 shows some well-known examples of artificial scales.

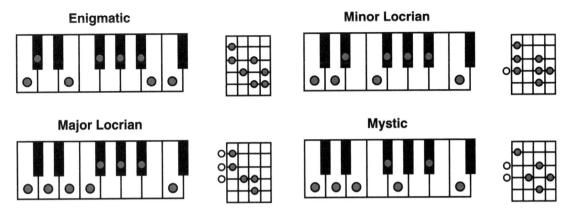

Figure 22.10 Artificial scales.

If you are ever looking for inspiration or for a fresh new sound, exotic scales are a good place to start. If you use exotic scales, you'll never get into a creative rut. Listen to Tracks 46 and 47 on the audio CD—they provide you with a couple examples of exotic and artificial scale textures.

Exercises

You can download the answers to the chapter exercises from www.courseptr.com/downloads.

1. Exotic scales work well in many types of electronic music. They are especially good for creating unusual, exotic atmospheres. To use an exotic scale effectively, you must collect important information beforehand. This exercise will show you how to do that. Simply answer the following questions.

   ■ Name: Syrian

   ■ Keynote: B

   ■ Type: Exotic Hexatonic

   ■ Pitches: B C D# E G A# B

   A. What are the intervals formed by each note of the scale with the keynote (tonic)?

      A. Unison
      B. _____
      C. _____
      D. _____
      E. _____
      F. Octave

   B. What are the salient harmonies of the scale? (Look for conspicuous triads that can be used to help add and create harmonies and list them here.)

   C. What are the salient melodic features that define the scale? These are groups of two or three notes that give the scale its particular character. You can discover these by playing the scale on your keyboard and listening carefully for its strongest and most characteristic features. For example, the strongest feature of the Neapolitan group of modes is the flat second between the first and second degrees. In the Neapolitan major modes, this creates a note group of C Db E, which is a very strong and recognizable feature of those modes. What do you feel is the strongest feature of the Syrian mode? There might be more than one. List these here.

2. Complete the whole tone scale using the keynote given below. Underneath, list the augmented triads that come from it.

Note: Ab   _____   _____   _____   _____   _____

Triad 1:   _____   _____   _____

Triad 2:   _____   _____   _____

3. List two modes that you feel would be useful to create a traditional Japanese atmosphere. List the reasons for your choice.

4. Devise artificial scales using the following criteria.

A. A pentatonic scale that uses two minor chords.

B. A hexatonic scale that has no whole tones.

C. An octatonic scale that uses four major triads.

23 Complex Harmony

Triads and seventh chords very much represent the staple harmonies of most kinds of popular and electronic music. As such, for the aspiring music writer, their use represents essential knowledge and education. When you have acquired this knowledge and learned to apply it effectively in your own music, you will discover that you can improve your ability to produce professional-sounding harmonies even more. To discover how, read on.

By adding a seventh to a triad, you get a more complex harmony. The dissonant seventh gives the chord punch and bite—a bit of extra interest to the harmony. Because of its dissonant quality, the seventh chord also acquires a leaning—a desire for resolution that gives chord progressions that use it great power and momentum.

So why stop there? Once you've added a seventh to a triad, it becomes possible to add a ninth, an eleventh, and even a thirteenth. The logic of this is based on what is called the *chain of thirds*. Figure 23.1 will help you further understand this.

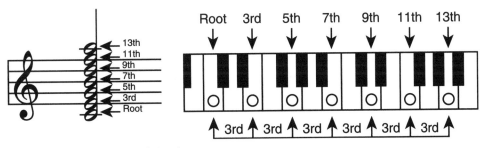

Figure 23.1 The chain of thirds.

As you can see, a triad is composed of two thirds stacked upon each other. In a seventh chord, this is increased to three, with another third added to the triad. You can obtain more complex chords by adding yet more thirds. Principally, these are of three varieties. Add another third to the seventh, and you get what is called a *ninth chord*. Add another third to the ninth, and you get an *eleventh chord*. Add another third to the eleventh, and you get a *thirteenth chord*. The chain of thirds stops with a thirteenth because a fifteenth would bring you back to the starting note. As you can see in Figure 23.1 a third above the thirteenth gives note C, which is the same as the root note.

Chords of the ninth, eleventh, and thirteenth belong to the sphere of what is generally called *complex* or *extended harmony* (see Figure 23.2). Although they have been in use at least since the classical era, their complex sound, together with the large number of notes that they have, makes them quite difficult to handle. I would advise you to play through the three chords in Figure 23.2 on your MIDI keyboard. By the time you get to the thirteenth, you will realize how complex and dissonant this type of harmony can become. A thirteenth, after all, uses all seven notes of the scale at the same time!

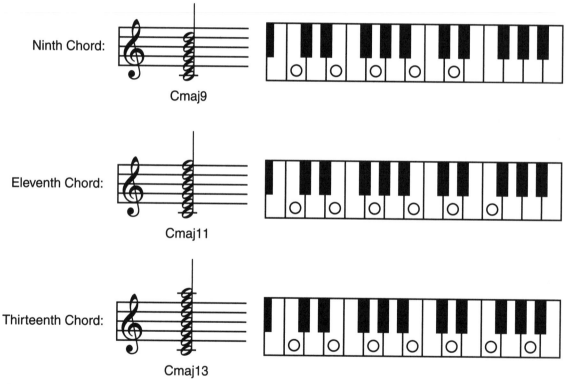

Figure 23.2 Chords of the ninth, eleventh, and thirteenth.

Ninth Chords

A ninth chord contains five notes, and it is derived from adding another third to the chain of three thirds used in a seventh chord (see Figure 23.3). Ordinarily, the extra note involved would originate from the scale/mode that you are using, although, as you will see later, there are always exceptions.

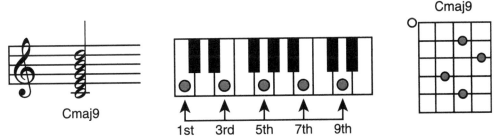

Figure 23.3   Ninth chord (C maj9).

Chords of the ninth originally occurred in classical music, often resulting from the use of passing notes between ordinary triad tones. In Figure 23.4, the chord Cmaj9 appears briefly between the triads of C and F.

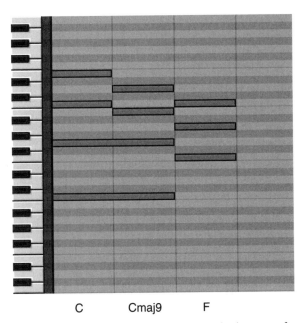

Figure 23.4   Cmaj9 appearing through the use of passing notes.

The discord set up by the ninth chord is only brief, and it is resolved on the fifth of the F major chord that follows. Owing to our classical heritage, we often still use ninth chords in this way, although modern use is not governed by any particular rules. You can use ninths freely to spice up triadic harmony.

Although a ninth chord has five notes, you don't need to include all five of those notes in a sonority. The factors that qualify it to be a ninth chord are the seventh and the ninth. Without the seventh, it would be construed as a simple added ninth chord. When scored for four parts, the fifth is usually omitted because it is the least important chord member (see Figure 23.5).

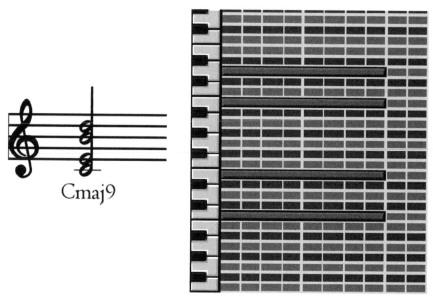

Figure 23.5 Scoring of ninth chord in four parts.

Ninth chords are used in all styles of popular music, and you can use them on any scale degree. One of the most commonly used ninth chords is the dominant ninth chord, which is built on the fifth degree of the scale. As shown in Figure 23.6, built on the root note C, it represents the dominant ninth chord of the key of F major.

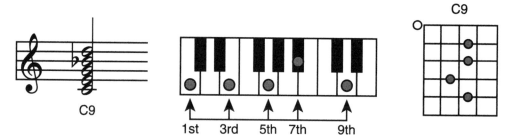

Figure 23.6 Dominant ninth chord (C9).

Generally, the dominant ninth is used to enhance the resolution of dominant seventh chord to the tonic (see Figure 23.7).

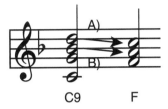

C9   F

A) Ninth resolves to fifth of tonic chord
B) Seventh resolves to third of tonic chord

Figure 23.7 Resolution of dominant ninth to tonic.

This enhancement is even more extreme in the harmonic minor mode, where the dominant ninth chord appears in a different form. The ninth is minor, an interval that has a much sharper bite. To distinguish this chord from the regular dominant ninth, the ninth is indicated as being flat (see Figure 23.8).

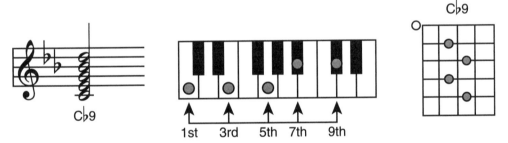

Figure 23.8 Dominant minor ninth chord (Cb9).

The dominant minor ninth chord is not often used in a simple popular music context because it has a particular dramatic quality that made it a favorite of silent-movie piano players! Try playing it on your MIDI keyboard and you will see what I mean.

You can build ninth chords above the roots of any degree of the scale. Figure 23.9 shows the other ninths as they occur in the key of C major.

The addition of a ninth to any of the minor chords in the scale works very well. Minor chords with a ninth have a beautiful mellow quality that is often exploited in deep and funky house, Detroit techno, nu jazz, and ambient textures. The most commonly used chords are the chord of m9 as it occurs on the second degree of the major scale (that is, Dm9 in C major) and the sixth degree of the major scale (that is, Am9). In the relative minor key, these same chords are the tonic ninth and the subdominant ninth. Together, they form a beautiful pair of chords that work very well with one another.

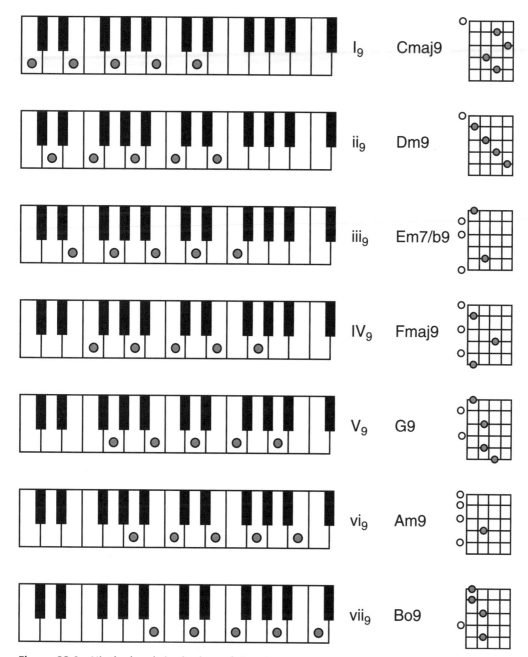

Figure 23.9 Ninth chords in the key of C major.

The ninth on the third degree is not used very often because it has a minor ninth that gives it an unpleasant sound. If used, it tends to be altered so that the ninth is major. (See the information on the Lydian eleventh in the upcoming "Chords of the Eleventh" section of this chapter.)

Figure 23.10 shows the chief ninth chords used in the minor key.

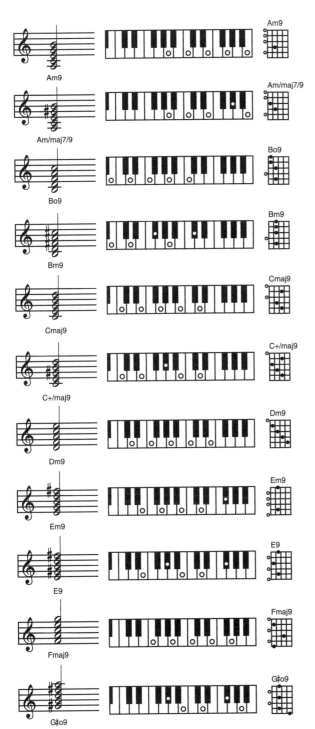

Figure 23.10   Ninth chords commonly used in the minor scale complex (key of A minor).

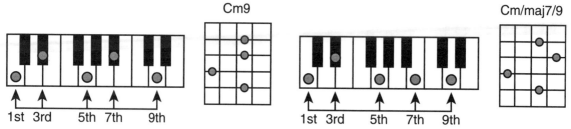

Figure 23.11 Chords of Cm9 and Cm/maj7/9.

If the seventh is major (as in i9 of the harmonic minor scale), then the chord has more punch (see Figure 23.11).

Ninth chords work extremely well in parallel textures. (You saw parallel fifths in Chapter 8—this technique is known as *parallel ninths*.) To achieve this type of harmony, try sampling a single ninth chord and then playing it on different keys of your keyboard (see Figure 23.12).

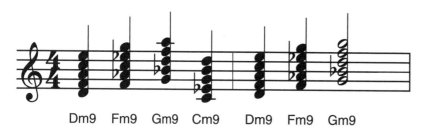

Figure 23.12 Ninth chord in parallel texture.

With complex harmony, there is a great degree of freedom in terms of what you can do, provided that there is a really strong sense of root movement in the chord progression. In Figure 23.12, the roots move from D, up to F, to ~G, and then down to C. This strength of root movement serves as an anchor for the ears' efforts to interpret the complex harmony.

When faced with a whole spectrum of ninth chords, the task of mastering their use can seem daunting. Probably the best way to learn to use ninths is to first spend some time investigating a single ninth chord. Try it out in different inversions and different types of spacing. Then look at the different types of ninth chords upon each degree of the scale. Study their intervallic makeup carefully and get to know their particular sound. Then try composing chord progressions involving successive ninth chords. Doing this will put them on your palette of available chords. Once you have them there, your ear will guide you the rest of the way.

Chords of the Eleventh

Chords of the eleventh are even more complex. These involve adding another third to the chain of thirds to give a sixth chordal note (see Figure 23.13).

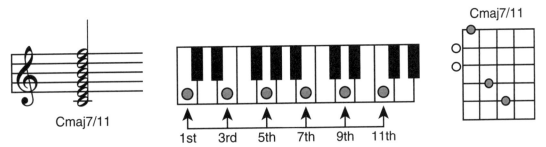

Figure 23.13   Chord of the eleventh.

Here the most important notes are the root, third, seventh, and eleventh. This means that an eleventh chord can be effectively scored in four parts. With the particular chord shown in Figure 23.13, there is a clash between the third of the triad (note E) and the eleventh (note F). Because the core foundations for the harmony have already been laid by the triad and seventh, the offending note—the eleventh—is often sharpened to give an eleventh chord that would normally be found in the Lydian mode: C E G B D F#.

This results in a very beautiful harmony, and, again, the ear will still discern the sense and direction of the chord progression (provided that the harmony is anchored by a strong sense of root movement). The alteration of a chord using a note not in the scale—as described in terms of the Lydian chord here—is called *chromatic alteration,* and it is a common practice in all types of modern music that use complex harmonies.

The chord most vulnerable to chromatic alteration is the dominant. Provided that the third and seventh are present to maintain the chord's dominant pull, you can apply a wide variety of chromatic colorings. Principally, these apply to the fifth, seventh, ninth, and eleventh as shown in Figure 23.14.

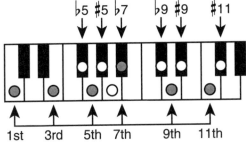

Figure 23.14   Common chromatic alterations of dominant harmony.

This creates a great number of complex sonorities, many of which are the staples of the jazz musician's diet. Figure 23.15 presents a few of the possibilities.

Figure 23.15 Chromatically altered dominant chords.

Another common practice with complex harmony is borrowing from other modes. Here root movement rules the day, which means that there is nothing wrong with borrowing notes and even whole chords from other keys and modes. Provided that the root movement scheme is clear, the harmony's sense of direction will be retained. In Figure 23.16, the root is clearly static, and the sense of change comes from the alternation between the tonic eleventh of the major and parallel minor mode.

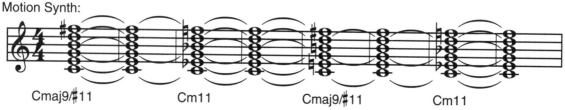

Figure 23.16 Major/minor chromatic alteration.

To advance in the use of eleventh chords, study the intervallic makeup of a single eleventh chord carefully. The chord of the dominant eleventh would be a good place to start. Examine its properties when certain notes are removed. (To qualify as an eleventh chord, it needs at least a root, a seventh, and an eleventh.) Then try to introduce chromatic alterations and see how they color the chord.

Then look at secondary eleventh chords built on degrees of the scale other than the fifth. Doing so will reveal the different types of eleventh chords and their intervallic makeup. And then, when you are ready, incorporate them into chord progressions.

Chords of the Thirteenth

Thirteenth chords represent the most complex harmonies available within a seven-toned format (see Figure 23.17). This is because the introduction of a fifteenth would bring you back to the root. Thirteenth chords theoretically involve all seven notes of the scale.

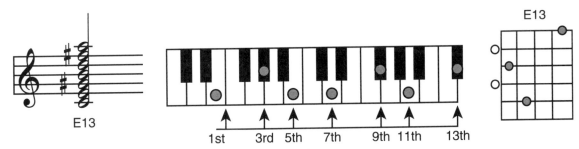

Figure 23.17 Chord of the dominant thirteenth (C13).

The central problem with a thirteenth chord is what to leave in and what to leave out. The most essential elements are the root, the seventh, and the thirteenth. This not only reduces the chord to its most essential format, but it also shows the principal job of the dominant thirteenth chord as an approach to the dominant seventh or ninth chord—the latter only applying if the ninth is included as a fourth chord member. You can see this in Figure 23.18.

Here the discord between the thirteenth—note A—and the seventh—note Bb—is very prominent. The resolution of that discord to the G that follows is a really nice effect.

You can further thicken dominant thirteenth chords by including the eleventh and fifth. The third is generally avoided because it clashes with the eleventh. If it is included, the eleventh tends to be sharpened by way of chromatic alteration.

Thirteenth chords on other degrees of the scale are all useable depending upon the context. Because thirteenth chords can involve all seven notes of the scale, such harmonies can produce dense, complex textures that can be quite beautiful when sequenced correctly. Such harmonies are a strong feature of ambient music, especially when gentle pads, strings, and such are involved. Usually no more than two or three chords are involved.

To use thirteenths, you must study a single chord very closely. Sequence a single chord sustained for, say, eight bars, and then experiment by taking certain notes out, swapping notes around between different registers, and so on. In other words, have fun! When you do this, you will find that the sound will take over and readily suggest how it should be progressed. There are no rules for such complex harmony, simply because the possibilities are so numerous.

In studying this chapter, you have learned the basic foundations for complex or extended harmony. You have learned how to build a ninth, eleventh, and thirteenth chord on any degree of the scale that you choose. You have also learned the important notes to put in and leave out. How you use these chords is very much a matter of your own taste, judgment, and creativity. Complex harmony is very much an open field. As such, it is something that is on the cutting edge of new music. Through use of complex harmony, altogether new types of sounds and textures become possible. To discover these, you must ignore rules and conventions and simply immerse yourself in the wash of complex sounds that they produce. Your ear will do the rest for you. For

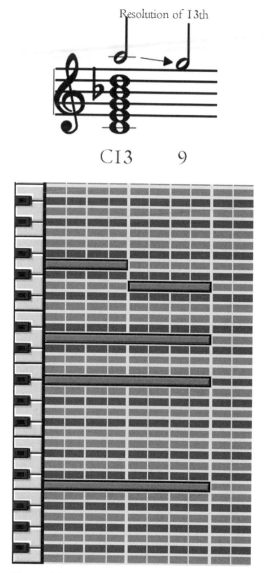

Figure 23.18 Dominant thirteenth chord as an approach to the dominant seventh/ninth.

some examples of the use of complex harmony, listen to Tracks 48–50 on the audio CD. The text in Appendix B will explain what you should be listening for.

When you gain sufficient experience in the use of harmonies in your songs, there is a technique at which you will no doubt start to look closely. Chords produce notes that are to be heard simultaneously. The ear analyzes the relationship between those notes in terms of the intervals they form, and by so doing works out what the chord being used is. But there is another important technique that is crucial for all styles of computer-generated music. This is the technique of *arpeggiation,* otherwise known as *pattern sequencing.*

In an arpeggio, the notes of a chord are presented successively—that is, as a melodic line. This creates a sense of motion, so although the chord itself may be static, there will be a strong sense of movement engendered by the arpeggio. A simple example of arpeggiation is the picking technique of guitar players. By plucking different strings in succession, you produce a sense of motion that affects whatever chord is being used at the time. This vital subject is the subject of the next chapter.

Exercises

You can download the answers to the chapter exercises from www.courseptr.com/downloads.

1.   Ninth chords work well in many styles of modern electronic music. To use ninth chords, you must be able to build them on any degree of the scale that you are using. The purpose of this exercise is to help you do that. List all of the ninth chords that can be built using these scales.

C natural minor: C D Eb F G Ab Bb C

I: _____

II: _____

III: _____

IV: _____

V: _____

VI: _____

VII: _____

Tip: Build the triad first. Then, to each triad, add a seventh and a ninth in that order.

2.   Ninth chords are commonly used in different positions. To use these, you must be able to work out what they are so that you can play them. List the five possible positions of the following ninth chords.

Cmaj9: C E G B D

A. Root position: _____

B. First inversion: _____

C. Second inversion: _____

D. Third inversion: _____

E. Fourth inversion: _____

Fm9: F Ab C Eb G

A. Root position: _____

B. First inversion: _____

C. Second inversion: _____

D. Third inversion: _____

E. Fourth inversion: _____

3.   List the dominant ninth chords of the following keys.

A. G minor: _____

B. D major: _____

C. Bb minor: _____

D. E major: _____

4.   List all of the eleventh chords that can be built in the key of F major.

A. _____

B. _____

C. _____

D. _____

E. _____

F. _____

G. _____

5.   List four chromatically altered variations of the following dominant eleventh chord: G B D F A C.

A. _____

B. _____

C. _____

D. _____

6.   List all of the thirteenth chords that can be built in the key of Bb natural minor.

   A. _____

   B. _____

   C. _____

   D. _____

   E. _____

   F. _____

   G. _____

24 Arpeggiation

A common technique in much modern electronic music is to use arpeggios of various sorts, deriving from the use of automatic arpeggiators and pattern-sequencing devices. Many synthesizers have an abundance of arpeggio patterns preprogrammed and ready for use. In such cases, it is simply a matter of selecting the pattern you require and sequencing. However, dependence upon such preprogrammed patterns can be limiting, and sooner or later you will want to produce your own patterns. This chapter will show you some of the principles behind this concept.

Arpeggios

First of all, what is an arpeggio? An arpeggio in its simplest form occurs when the notes of a chord are played successively. They arose primarily in relation to instruments such as pianos and harps that do not have much sustain. Through use of arpeggios, one could sustain a harmony through any number of bars. Beginning with a simple triad, there are a limited number of ways in which it can be arpeggiated. Figure 24.1 shows some of the principal patterns applied to a C major triad.

However you accomplish this, the goal remains the same—to create a sense of motion within the static field of a given harmony. As such, you can arpeggiate any chord, including entire chord progressions themselves. Track 51 on the audio CD provides an example of arpeggiation that moves through a simple four-chord progression.

Arpeggiation and Non-Chord Tones

The process of arpeggiation becomes more complex when arpeggios make reference to non-chord tones. A *non-chord tone* is any note that does not form part of the chord. The use of these in arpeggio patterns is very effective because they are capable of enhancing the melodic interest of the arpeggio.

Passing Notes

There are a certain number of generic types of non-chord tones that are extremely useful to know when you are writing arpeggio patterns. One of the most important of these is the

Figure 24.1 Some common arpeggio patterns.

passing note. A *passing note* is the note between two chordal tones that are a third apart. Occurring on a rhythmically weak part of the bar and safely nestled between two chordal tones, the passing note's use provides melodic interest but does not in itself affect the harmony. Figure 24.2 shows an example using the triad of A minor, in which both notes B and D are used as passing notes.

Importantly, the use of passing notes does not disturb or affect the implied A minor harmony.

Returning Tones

Another important non-chord tone is the returning tone. The characteristic feature of the returning tone is that the chord tone rises or falls to the non-chord tone and then immediately returns to it. This tone is often a step above or below the chord tone. In Figure 24.3, the note A is used in reference to the chord tone Bb.

Using Non-Chord Tones

The principle behind these generic figures is that they are melody notes that do not disturb the harmony. As long as the harmony is sufficiently referenced, you can exercise freedom in where you place these non-chord tones. In Figure 24.4, the non-chord tone appears on the strong beat like a classical appoggiatura or accented passing note. It references the D minor harmony through its resolution to the chord tone F. There is also another non-chord tone—note E— that acts as a delayed returning tone.

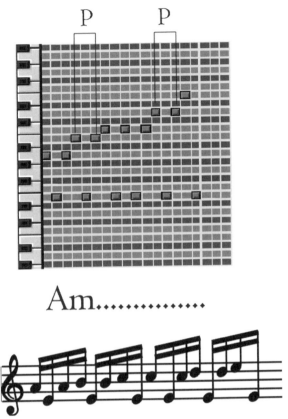

Figure 24.2 A minor arpeggio with passing notes.

For arpeggios with greater range than an octave, using non-chord tones gives them musical interest and variety. The same pattern moving through a chord progression gives a very musical effect (see Figure 24.5).

Steps in an Arpeggio

In addition to non-chord tones, you must think carefully about the number of steps in an arpeggio. Ordinarily, arpeggios are in four, eight, sixteen, or thirty-two steps, which means that the arpeggio is in sync with the bar. However, you can obtain amazing effects with step numbers out of sync with the bar. Here again, there are a number of generic types that have found their primary application in various styles of dance music. These include five-step, seven-step, and eleven-step patterns.

The beauty of these is that because the number of steps is odd, different notes of the arpeggio are highlighted on the strong points of the measure. This is a sort of wheels-within-wheels effect that generates inner melodies in addition to the arpeggio. In Figure 24.6, I've circled the notes that occur on the strong points of the measure. Notice that these are different each time.

R   R

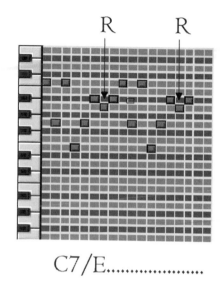

C7/E......................

Figure 24.3   Use of returning tone figure in C7 arpeggio.

A   R   A   R

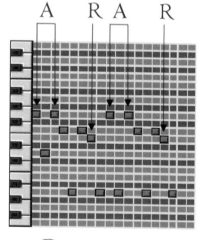

Dm........................

Figure 24.4   D minor arpeggio.

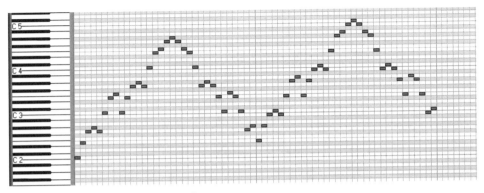

Figure 24.5   Multi-octave arpeggio.

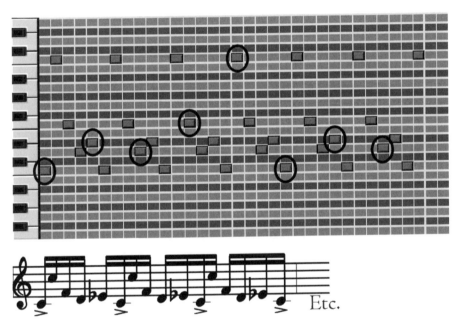

Figure 24.6   Five-step pattern.

Seven-step and eleven-step patterns work by the same principle. Figure 24.7 presents an example of a seven-step pattern.

And, of course, you can omit notes in order to set up a characteristic rhythm. In terms of rhythmic arpeggios, set up the rhythm that you want first on a single note. When you've done so, then introduce the changes of pitch. This is much easier than trying to do both at the same time.

Whatever software or hardware you use for your musical productions, it is likely to have some kind of arpeggiating device. Propellerhead's Reason offers two nice devices specifically for this purpose—the Matrix Pattern Sequencer and the RPG-8 Monophonic Arpeggiator (see Figure 24.8).

Seven-step Cycle

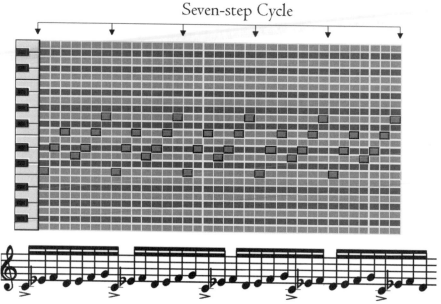

Figure 24.7 Seven-step arpeggio pattern.

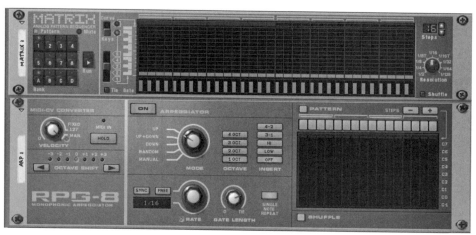

Figure 24.8 Arpeggiating devices in Propellerhead's Reason.

Through the use of such devices, you can generate a virtual infinity of patterns once you understand how to operate the device and you know musically what you are doing. This chapter has shown that, first, the harmonic foundations need to be laid down—that is, the harmony that is going to be arpeggiated. When the harmonic foundations have been laid down, you can introduce other notes—non-chord tones—that enhance the melodic interest of the arpeggio. Don't worry too much about what these non-chord tones are called. Basically, they are notes a step up or down from any given chord tone. As always, let your musical taste guide you.

Exercises

To complete these exercises, you will need to use an arpeggiator or a pencil tool with which to compose and draw the notes of an arpeggio pattern (onto, say, piano roll view of your sequencer).

You can download the answers to the chapter exercises from www.courseptr.com/downloads.

1. Develop and sequence an eight-step arpeggio pattern using a resolution of sixteenth notes that traces the following two-bar chord progression.

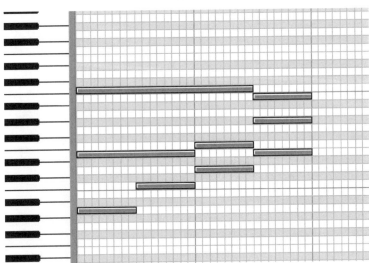

2. Compose and sequence a sixteen-step arpeggio pattern that traces the chord of A minor. Introduce at least two passing notes into the pattern.

3. List three kinds of non-harmonic tones.

    A. _____

    B. _____

    C. _____

4. Compose and sequence a 32-step arpeggio pattern that moves through three octaves and employs two kinds of non-harmonic tones. Build the arpeggio pattern around a Cmaj7 chord.

5. Compose and sequence a five-step arpeggio pattern that uses an exotic scale of your choice.

6. Compose and sequence a seven-step arpeggio pattern that emulates the acid house bass lines popular in the late '80s and early '90s. Build it around note E, making occasional incursions to other notes of your choice. Tip: Once you have sequenced the pattern, experiment with the filter frequency and filter resonance to achieve that characteristic acid sound.

25 Intonation

Intonation concerns the fine points of how a scale is tuned. The 12-tone chromatic scale used in Western music is tuned according to the system of equal temperament. In this system the octave is divided up into 12 mathematically equal semitones. The reality of tuning is that this represents only one option and represents a compromise to what is actually possible. Another kind of tuning is called *just intonation*. This favors pure intervals as defined by their ratios—in other words, perfect fifths of 3/2, major thirds of 5/4, major sixths of 5/3, and so on.

History of Intonation

During the second half of the last century, a lot of experimentation took place, exploring alternative kinds of intonation to our equal temperament. American musicians such as Californian La Monte Young became very interested in the use of pure intervals; his improvisatory 1964 work *The Well Tuned Piano* required that the piano be tuned in pure thirds (5/4), fifths (3/2) and harmonic sevenths (7/4).

Since then, many software programs have looked at this issue and provided means for musicians to use their own favored tunings. This technology has advanced so much that it is even possible to invent and come up with your own tunings. The way this works is that the octave is divided up into 1,200 cents, in which each equal semitone is worth 100. By providing a fine-tune option on a synthesizer or sampler, it is possible to adjust each semitone up or down in increments of a single cent. The principal advantage of this is that it becomes possible to use pure intervals.

Steinberg's Cubase offers a remarkably effective and very straightforward way of tuning your intervals, enabling you to tune each key up or down in increments of a single cent (see Figure 25.1).

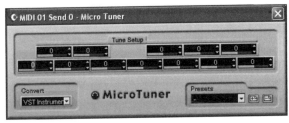

Figure 25.1 Cubase micro-tuning options.

Just Intonation

The equally tempered tuning that is forced upon us by instrument manufacturers is not actually true to pure intervals. Compare, for example, a pure major third with an equally tempered major third. The tempered third is equivalent to 400 cents, while the pure major third is 384 cents—a difference of some 16 cents (or 16 percent). Through use of fine-tuning options, such as those provided by Cubase, you can now employ pure intervals. This is called *just intonation*.

Pythagorean Intonation

Another type of intonation is *Pythagorean intonation,* in which each note of the scale is tuned in pure fifths of ratio 3/2. Also used in traditional Chinese and Arabian music, it generates its own unique interval set, too. The 12-toned chromatic scale as tuned in equal temperament, just intonation, and Pythagorean intonation would appear as you see in Table 25.1.

Table 25.1 Twelve-Toned Chromatic Scale Tuned in Equal Temperament, Just Intonation, and Pythagorean Intonation

Equally Tempered		Just Intonation		Pythagorean Intonation	
Note	Cents	Ratio	Cents	Ratio	Cents
C	0000	1/1	0000	1/1	0000
Db	0100	16/15	0112	256/243	0090
D	0200	9/8	0204	9/8	0204
Eb	0300	6/5	0316	32/27	0294
E	0400	5/4	0386	81/64	0408
F	0500	4/3	0498	4/3	0498
F#	0600	45/32	0590	729/512	0612
G	0700	3/2	0702	3/2	0702
Ab	0800	8/5	0814	128/81	0792
A	0900	5/3	0884	27/16	0906
Bb	1000	9/5	1018	16/9	0996
B	1100	15/8	1088	243/128	1110
C	1200	2/1	1200	2/1	1200

Problems with Alternative Tunings

The central problem with alternative tunings to equal temperament is that it is not possible to construct a pure scale for more than one diatonic key. And, even then, the requirements of producing pure-sounding chords necessitate having more than one type of Bb, for example. To create pure organic music in all keys, you would need a scale of about 60 microtonal notes. It is just not always practical.

With modal music it is more viable because modal music tends to stay in the one key. You can obtain some good results. You can opt for pure tuning or even some of the more exotic types of tuning found in the world.

Tuning Balinese Scales

The music of Bali is a good example that has a seven-tone scale tuned quite unlike any other tuning system in the world. Figure 25.2 shows the cents measurements necessary to fine-tune a Balinese dedicated keyboard.

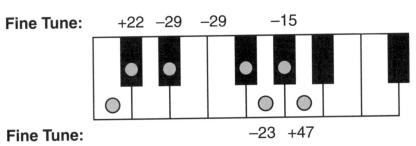

Figure 25.2 Balinese metallophone tuning.

However, you must bear in mind that precise tunings can vary depending upon the locality. Therefore, Figure 25.2 is merely a sample tuning. If you want to hear an example of fine-tuning from this area, listen to Track 52 on the CD. The scale has been tuned to Thai seven-tone equal temperament—a unique tuning in which the gaps between the seven notes of the scale are tuned as equal intervals (that is, 1/7 of an octave).

Tuning Arabian and Hindustani Scales

The tuning of both Arabian and Hindustani scales is also a fine art. The basic scale of Arabian music has 17 notes based on Pythagorean tuning. The how and the why is very much a specialized subject that would demand further study. A sample scale adjusted for fine-tuning would appear as you see in Figure 25.3.

Fine Tune: −10   −6   −2 −12   −8   −4

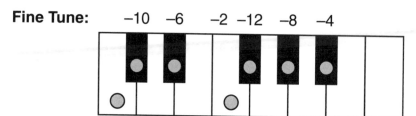

Figure 25.3   Fine-tuned Arabic scale.

Hindustani music also values tunings offset from our equal temperament. In Northern Hindustan, the notes that belong to each raga are selected from a microtonal scale of 22 notes to the octave. Using fine-tune options, you can faithfully reproduce the tuning of such exotic modes. As to usage, this is another matter. In general, ragas are much more than just a mode. Certain conventions exist with regard to each raga in terms of important notes, characteristic melodic turns, the time of day it should be used, the ideal ethos, and so on. To discover what these conventions are, you would need to do extensive research.

Raga Bageshri, which is very similar to our C major scale, would need to be fine-tuned as you see in Figure 25.4.

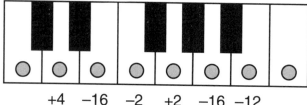

Fine Tune: +4   −16   −2   +2   −16 −12
Figure 25.4   Fine-tuning of Raga Bageshri.

Tuning Overtone Melodies

Fine-tune options are useful for the purposes of overtone melodies. Characterized by instruments such as the didgeridoo and the Jew's harp, overtone melodies use only the overtones or partials of a fundamental. (Refer to Chapter 1 to review an explanation of what these are.) Buddhist monks sing overtone melodies, and they have developed remarkable singing techniques where they can sing two notes at the same time—the fundamental and the harmonics. The effect is quite amazing.

Equal temperament does not give the correct pitches for overtone melodies. To create an overtone melody, you would need to fine-tune the keyboard as you see in Figure 25.5.

This gives every harmonic up to the twenty-first.

Using fine-tune technology, you can also invent original tunings. The Korg Triton synthesizer offers this option in the form of slots for a dozen or so "user scales." This is all worth experimenting with

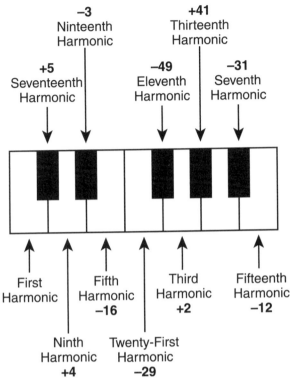

Figure 25.5 Harmonic series fine-tuned keyboard.

if the idea of using pure intervals interests you. Who knows—you could come up with the next big thing to bring music into a higher state of evolution!

Exercises

You can download the answers to the chapter exercises from www.courseptr.com/downloads.

1. Fill in the missing words. Intonation concerns the fine points of how a scale is
    _____. The 12-tone chromatic scale used in Western music is tuned
    according to the system of _____. In this system, the octave is divided
    up into 12 mathematically equal _____.

2. Name three kinds of intonation

    A. _____

    B. _____

    C. _____

3. Fill in the missing words. For the purposes of fine-tuning, the octave is divided up
    into _____ hundred cents, in which each equal semitone is worth

_____ cents. By providing a fine-tune option on a synthesizer or sampler, it is possible to adjust each semitone up or down in increments of a single _____.

4. Name three kinds of music in which alternative tunings might be useful.

   A. _____

   B. _____

   C. _____

5. Fill in the missing words. _____ intonation uses pure intervals as defined by their mathematical ratios in the _____ series—such as perfect fifths of ratio 3:2, major thirds of ratio _____, major sixths of ratio 5:3, and so on.

26 Conclusion

Through your study of the content of the previous chapters, I hope that by now you have developed a much broader understanding of music theory as it applies to and proves relevant to the computer musician. I devised the content of this book with this very purpose in mind. Music theory is nearly always taught through the framework of classical music, and it is a learning process that depends heavily upon the musician being both an instrumental performer and a reader of written music. For somebody more interested in writing drum and bass or hip-hop, classical music theory can prove both daunting and in many ways irrelevant to the needs of the computer musician. By presenting the content of this book mostly through piano roll view and keyboard diagrams, in addition to the usual musical score format, those who don't read music no longer need to feel disadvantaged. You do not have to be a classical musician; you can now learn all of the essential musical theory using nothing but the equipment at your disposal—your computer and MIDI keyboard.

Appendix A: Scales

Major Scales

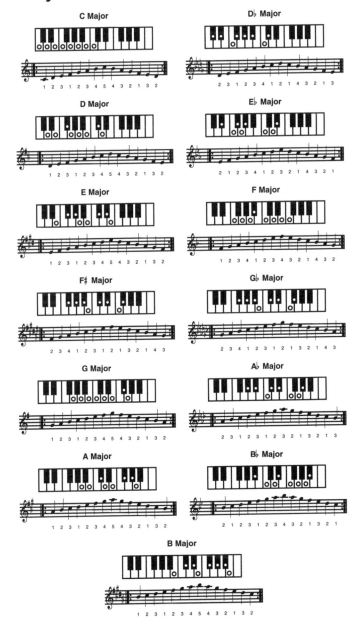

Natural Minor Scales

Harmonic Minor Scales

A Harmonic Minor

B♭ Harmonic Minor

B Harmonic Minor

C Harmonic Minor

C♯ Harmonic Minor

D Harmonic Minor

E♭ Harmonic Minor

E Harmonic Minor

F Harmonic Minor

F♯ Harmonic Minor

G Harmonic Minor

A♭ Harmonic Minor

Melodic Minor Scales

The Chromatic Scale Harmonic Form

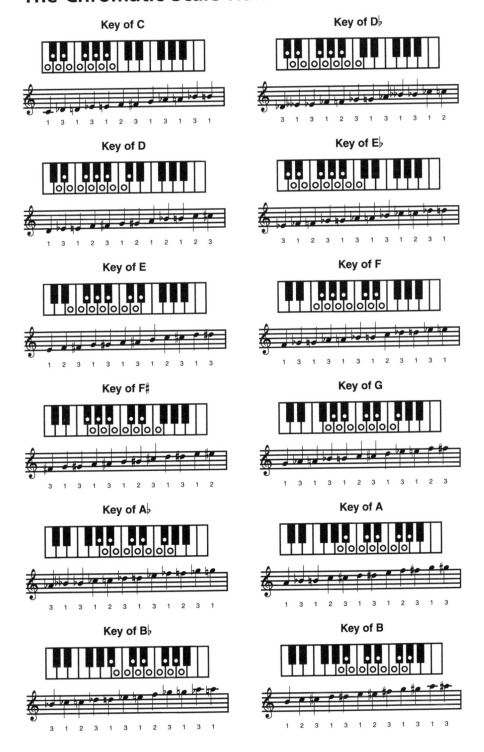

Triads in the Chromatic Scale (Harmonic Form: Key of C)

Seventh Chords in the Chromatic Scale (Harmonic Form: Key of C)

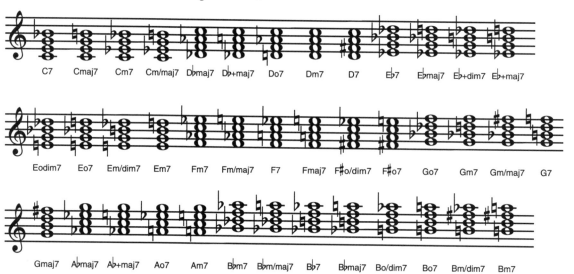

Appendix B: Audio CD and Accompanying Text Sidebars

This appendix contains information about each of the tracks on the audio CD included with this book.

Track 1

This audio file presents three sounds in succession. In the first, you hear an example of white noise, which, because it contains so many random frequencies, represents itself to the ear as a hissing sound of indeterminate pitch. The second example is of a sine wave, a single frequency whose pitch, amplitude, and timbre are readily audible—a true musical sound. The third example uses the white noise sample already given to create a series of percussive sounds, showing that even noises can be used if they are presented in an intelligible musical context.

Track 2

In this audio file, the expressive powers of the three basic parameters of musical tone are demonstrated through use of a string chord sample. In the first excerpt, the chord is subjected to a series of rises in pitch. In the second excerpt that immediately follows, the chord slowly builds in intensity. In the third excerpt, the chord is subjected to qualitative changes—that is, transformations of tone quality accomplished through discrete use of a filter.

Track 3

Uniform levels of velocity lead to dull and uninspired parts for tracks. In the synthesized congas pattern that you can hear on this track, both variations of velocity and subtle changes of panning are used to give a realistic and expressive-sounding drum track.

Track 4

In these four excerpts, the pitch of the note being played is the same. The differences heard are purely ones of tone color as sine, square, triangular, and sawtooth waveforms are heard and presented respectively.

Track 5

The harmonic series is tremendously important in all areas of both acoustic and electronic music. Here the first eight harmonics of note A2 are heard in succession. Collectively to the ear, they sound like a dominant seventh chord—root note A—although to duplicate the harmonic series accurately, those oscillators producing the third harmonic need to be detuned by +2 cents, the fifth harmonic by −14 cents, and the seventh harmonic by −31 cents.

Track 6

When you are practicing playing the C major scale, start off playing it slowly, as in this example. It is a common mistake to rush such exercises. Because this is the foundation of good keyboard playing, it is important to learn it properly.

Track 7

Kick-drum quarters and hi-hat eighths.

Track 8

The bass drum and snare tend to have their own axis that revolves primarily around the quarters—1 and 3 for the bass drum; 2 and 4 for the snare—the latter being called the *backbeat* (see Figure B.1).

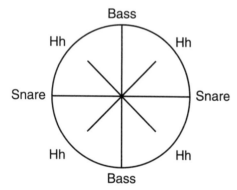

Figure B.1

Although capable of infinite variance, this cycle provides the basic template for most drum patterns.

Track 9

If a faster pace is required, hi-hats are also played on the sixteenths.

Track 10

In this example, the kick starts off on the quarters and then progressively moves through eighths, sixteenths, thirty-seconds, and the machine-gunning sixty-fourths. You have probably heard this technique used in dance music—the exponential increase of pace creates a sense of increasing excitement.

Track 11

In this track, you can hear the simple intervals in immediate succession. The peaks in the wave-form of the audio file correspond to the change of interval, commencing with the first and then proceeding on to the second, third, fourth, and so on up to the octave (see Figure B.2).

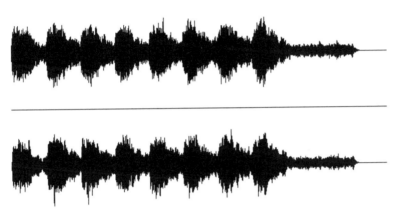

Figure B.2

Track 12

Compound intervals have important uses as well. The file in Figure B.3 shows typical use of the interval of a tenth within the type of material used in the euphoric breakdowns of the late '90s trance style.

Track 13

Here, again, are some simple beats so you can count along to get a good grasp of compound time signatures. This audio file presents a 6/8 beat, immediately followed by a 9/8, and then a 12/8 beat.

Track 14

Syncopated rhythms are popular in all styles of modern music. The off beat stresses give a sense of energy and excitement. In Figure B.4, the bass drum is displaced onto various sixteenths, ordinarily weak points in the bar.

Track 15

Triplet sixteenths on the tambourines add a sense of pace to the drums.

Track 16

Here is a demonstration of shuffle on the hi-hats of a basic drum track. Shuffle is also extremely popular in most styles of dance music, even the faster styles.

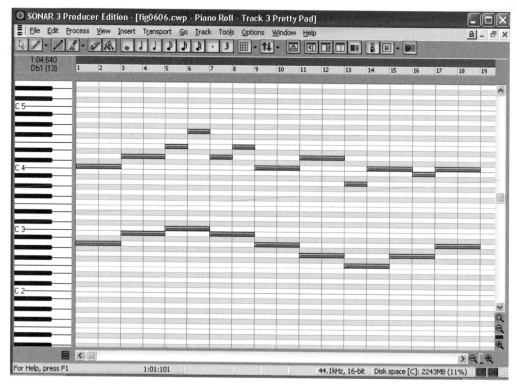

Figure B.3

Figure B.4

Track 17

Hemiola rhythm is demonstrated on two tambourines. It is also well worth experimenting with cross-rhythms, such as three against four, four against five, three against five, and so on.

Track 18

In this track, you hear the clichéd sound of harmony by fourths and fifths.

Track 19

This track features the characteristic sound when the second oscillator of a synth patch is tuned up by a perfect fifth.

Track 20

This is a contrast to the sweet thirds and sixths. This string texture uses nothing but the dissonant intervals of major and minor seconds and sevenths. Such is the power of intervals to create atmosphere.

Track 21

Major and minor triads are the staples of all musical harmony and still provide the basis for the chord progressions of most popular songs. It is no coincidence that they are collectively called *common triads*. In this track, you can hear a major chord triad followed by a minor triad.

Track 22

The V to I chord progression is the most basic of all, and it is used in all types of songs. In this track, you can hear the chords I progressing to V and back to I. Notice the sense of finality as chord V progresses back to the home chord—the tonic—chord I.

Track 23

In this example, the previous audio file has been extended to bring chord IV into the picture (see Figure B.5). Between them, chords I, IV, and V provide the basis for all of the most fundamental chord progressions. They certainly are not subtle, but they do represent a good place to start learning about chord progressions.

Figure B.5

Track 24

In this track, you can hear the four-chord progressions respectively illustrated at the end of Chapter 8.

Track 25

The three primary triads of A natural minor are all minor chords. The result is primary chord progressions that are extremely mellow, as you can hear in this example, which goes from chord I, to v, to iv, and back to I again.

Track 26

This is a simple chordal motive.

Track 27

Here you have an ambient texture created by repeating the same motive at different pitches and on different parts in various tracks.

Track 28

In loop-based music, the motives drive the music and give it a sense of coherence and forward progression. This track uses a simple wah guitar motive of the type that can be imported into a loop-based composition.

Track 29

Once a motive has been developed, it can be treated in various ways. Augmentation is where the motive is expanded through the use of longer note values. Diminuition is the exact opposite—the motive is compressed through a shortening of the time values. There is also inversion, where the motive is placed upside down; retrograde, where it is played backwards; and, of course, retrograde inversion. In this audio file, you will hear a string motive that is played forward. Immediately following, you will hear exactly the same motive played backward. To achieve this, the whole audio file was simply reversed using a proprietary WAV editor.

Track 30

This is a comparison of v to I (minor dominant triad) and V to i (major dominant triad).

Track 31

The melodic minor scale offers a really interesting major triad on degree four, as opposed to the minor triad on degree four of the harmonic and natural minor scales. Harmonically, it gives rise to some interesting atmospheres, as in this example sequenced for strings, in which you can hear a progression involving chords i – IV – I – V.

Track 32

This track has the chord of A minor heard first in closed position and second with numerous doublings. Here the root has been quadrupled, the fifth has been tripled, and the third has been doubled. The result is a much stronger, more incisive sonority (see Figure B.6).

Track 33

Here you have various ways of sequencing an A minor triad for strings using variations of spacing, doubling, and register. Notice that although they are all the same chord, each different method of scoring the chord has its own atmospheric connotations.

Figure B.6

Track 34

Here you have the example of voice leading given at the end of Chapter 13 and sequenced for a choral patch. While the first example sounds disjointed, the second sounds much more like a real choir singing. This is all due to the smooth and vocal voice leading.

Track 35

This is a simple sine wave lead in 15/8 time signature. Here 15/8 is broken down into 3+3+3+2+2+2=15 beats.

Track 36

Listen to the way pentatonic notes enrich a basic triad. The first chord is C add 6, the second is C add 9, and the third is C add 6/9—a chord that includes all five notes of the pentatonic scale. See Figure B.7.

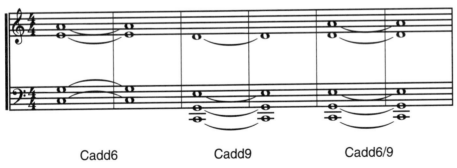

Cadd6   Cadd9   Cadd6/9

Figure B.7

Track 37

The pentatonic scale is very good for creating exotic, ethnic-sounding textures, as in this example for blocks, which uses the third pentatonic mode, sometimes known as the minor pentatonic —A C D E G.

Track 38

Here you have a quintal harmony that uses all five notes of the pentatonic scale. The chord is here sequenced with strings.

Track 39

In this track, you can hear the progression from chord vii—the leading tone triad. It has a final sense, which makes it a useful chord at cadences. Second, you will hear the leading tone triad resolving onto chord vi. This also has a final sense, which makes the leading tone triad useful when shifting from the major to the relative minor key.

Track 40

Here mysterious string harmonies are created by using parallel augmented triads.

Track 41

Music written in the Dorian mode tends to have a natural grace and beauty about it.

Track 42

Psy-trance makes much use of the Phrygian mode, as you can hear in this example, which uses the Phrygian mode built on note E.

Track 43

The Locrian mode is particularly suited for hard, dark textures. This bass line exploits the tritone axis between the notes B and F—the first and fifth degrees of the Locrian mode.

Track 44

Here you have four typical positions in which the chord of Cmaj7 might be used (see Figure B.8).

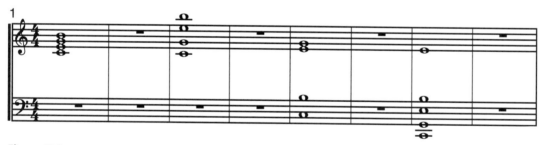

Figure B.8

Track 45

Eric Satie's "Gymnopedie No. 1" is a particularly beautiful example of Lydian-inspired music. The harmony of the music is based essentially on seventh chords. The opening phrases played here gently rock between Gmaj7 and Dmaj7.

Track 46

This is a representative exotic scale texture.

Track 47

Equal hexatonic harmonies are often used by composers to represent the mysteries of deep and outer space.

Track 48

Complex harmony figures in all types of electronic music. Here is a drum and bass combinator patch involving five Malstrom synths and a Dr. Rex loop player. The Dr. Rex is triggered to play the Drb08 – Giant Step loop, while all five of the Malstrom synths are set to the "In Memoriam" string patch. The semitone settings on the oscillators of each respective synth are set to 0, +3, +7, +10, +14, which means that when a single key is pressed, it will trigger a complex ninth chord.

Track 49

Eleventh chords produce a complex modern-sounding texture, as you can hear in this progression.

Track 50

Here are typical chromatically altered complex dominant chords (see Figure B.9).

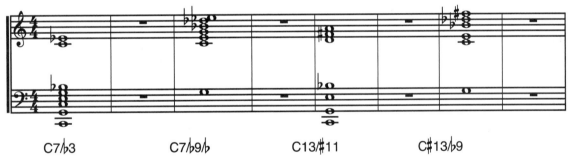

Figure B.9

Track 51

This is a typical arpeggiated trance riff moving through a simple four-chord progression in the minor mode.

Track 52

This is an exotic bell patch in which the scale has been tuned to Thai seven-tone equal temperament in which the octave is divided into seven equal steps, unlike the twelve equal steps of Western tuning.

Index

License Agreement/Notice of Limited Warranty

By opening the sealed disc container in this book, you agree to the following terms and conditions. If, upon reading the following license agreement and notice of limited warranty, you cannot agree to the terms and conditions set forth, return the unused book with unopened disc to the place where you purchased it for a refund.

License

The enclosed software is copyrighted by the copyright holder(s) indicated on the software disc. You are licensed to copy the software onto a single computer for use by a single user and to a backup disc. You may not reproduce, make copies, or distribute copies or rent or lease the software in whole or in part, except with written permission of the copyright holder(s). You may transfer the enclosed disc only together with this license, and only if you destroy all other copies of the software and the transferee agrees to the terms of the license. You may not decompile, reverse assemble, or reverse engineer the software.

Notice of Limited Warranty

The enclosed disc is warranted by Course Technology to be free of physical defects in materials and workmanship for a period of sixty (60) days from end user's purchase of the book/disc combination. During the sixty-day term of the limited warranty, Course Technology will provide a replacement disc upon the return of a defective disc.

Limited Liability

THE SOLE REMEDY FOR BREACH OF THIS LIMITED WARRANTY SHALL CONSIST ENTIRELY OF REPLACEMENT OF THE DEFECTIVE DISC. IN NO EVENT SHALL COURSE TECHNOLOGY OR THE AUTHOR BE LIABLE FOR ANY OTHER DAMAGES, INCLUDING LOSS OR CORRUPTION OF DATA, CHANGES IN THE FUNCTIONAL CHARACTERISTICS OF THE HARDWARE OR OPERATING SYSTEM, DELETERIOUS INTERACTION WITH OTHER SOFTWARE, OR ANY OTHER SPECIAL, INCIDENTAL, OR CONSEQUENTIAL DAMAGES THAT MAY ARISE, EVEN IF COURSE TECHNOLOGY AND/OR THE AUTHOR HAS PREVIOUSLY BEEN NOTIFIED THAT THE POSSIBILITY OF SUCH DAMAGES EXISTS.

Disclaimer of Warranties

COURSE TECHNOLOGY AND THE AUTHOR SPECIFICALLY DISCLAIM ANY AND ALL OTHER WARRANTIES, EITHER EXPRESS OR IMPLIED, INCLUDING WARRANTIES OF MERCHANTABILITY, SUITABILITY TO A PARTICULAR TASK OR PURPOSE, OR FREEDOM FROM ERRORS. SOME STATES DO NOT ALLOW FOR EXCLUSION OF IMPLIED WARRANTIES OR LIMITATION OF INCIDENTAL OR CONSEQUENTIAL DAMAGES, SO THESE LIMITATIONS MIGHT NOT APPLY TO YOU.

Other

This Agreement is governed by the laws of the State of Massachusetts without regard to choice of law principles. The United Convention of Contracts for the International Sale of Goods is specifically disclaimed. This Agreement constitutes the entire agreement between you and Course Technology regarding use of the software.

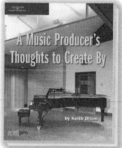